GROWING UP GREAT

LIFE LESSONS AND COACHING

BUTCH PIERRE

Growing Up Great:
Life Lessons and Coaching
by Butch Pierre

Copyright © 2018 Butch Pierre
ALL RIGHTS RESERVED

First Printing – September 2018
Paperback ISBN: 978-1-68111-253-4
Hardback ISBN: 978-1-68111-254-1

Printed in the U.S.A.

0   1   2   3   4   5   6   7   8

DEDICATION

First, to my parents, Joan Gloria Pierre and Joseph U. Pierre Sr.: Words cannot adequately express my deep admiration for you both. Your love, support, and dedication made me the man I am today. You taught me in both word and deed to be kind, loving, and diligent in every endeavor. Everything I am, I owe to you. I thank the Lord you're my parents every single day.

To my wife Clemmie and our beautiful children: Thank you for supporting me all these years, through good times and bad. You raised our kids into the truly impressive adults they have become. Langley, Joe, and Josh, you make me more proud than you will ever know.

To my coaches, who helped me grow both on and off the court, from grade school to high school: You made me a better player, a better coach, and a better man.

To my friends back home: Those of you I knew back in Ascension Parish and St. Amant, thank you for supporting me in my formative years. The friends you make growing up are unlike any others, and I really had some great ones.

To people who always gave me words of greatness: My sister Marcia Pierre Tureaud, Robert and Linnea Ramsey Sr., Glen Soule, Edgar Irvin, Mike and Judy Giorlando, Sydney Crawford, Doug Longman, Drs. Darryl and Lydia Peterson, Ray Wall, Mark Fulton, Carl Mack, Kenny Lloyd, Brian Jolivette, and Tony Clayton.

To the players I recruited and coached: Each of you was a source of great pride to me. I know I was tough and made mistakes from time to time, but my goal was always to do right by you, both in basketball and in life. Whatever you learned from me, I also learned from you.

To the parents of players I recruited and coached: Thank you for trusting me with your children. By doing so, you inspired me to be a better father to my own. I have a special reverence for the single mothers. Your sacrifice is an awesome thing. It is the definition of greatness.

To my mentors: There have been many, but I want to single out a few. I worked for Melvin Watkins for only a year, but we've been friends for thirty. You're like a brother to me, Coach. Tubby Smith, you went out of your way to help a young coach just starting out. Besides my father, you're the man whose respect meant the most. Thanks, Coach. Travis Ford, you put your faith in me at a critical point in my career, and I will never forget that. Thank you, Coach. And last but not least, John Brady, who coached me as a player and hired me as a coach. We were together a very long time, and we both know how much you mean to me. Thank you, Coach.

To all who hired me: Thank you to all the head coaches and athletic directors who believed in me. Your confidence made a difference, and together we accomplished great things.

To the LSU and Oklahoma State University Basketball Programs: Those two organizations meant the world to my family and me. I grew tremendously at both schools, both as a person and a coach. Thank you for bringing so much happiness to my family and me. Glen "Big Baby" Davis sophomore, Tyrus Thomas freshman, Tasmin Mitchell freshman, Garrett Temple freshman and Darryl Mitchell senior. Supporting cast were Magnum Rolle freshman, Ben Voogd Freshmen, and Darnell Lazare junior, the unsung hero.

To my alma mater, Mississippi State University: You molded me into a *true* student athlete, and I appreciate the advantages I received there, both on and off of the court. Thank you for providing the tools I needed to strive for greatness.

To Generation Z: In a world dominated by technology, never forget your humanity. Don't succumb to negative thoughts and false expectations. You are the future. Do great things.

INTRODUCTION

"If you want to be successful, you must learn
to work and perform at a high level under all
circumstances. Learn from failure, stay focused, and
embrace pressure."
Coach Butch Pierre

C OACHING CAN BE A VOLATILE PROFESSION. As hard as you work, as smart as you work, as much as you work, and as dedicated as you are, there are always factors outside your control that can mess up your game. I've coached five teams during my tenure, and I truly believed each time, we could have won a national championship. However, for various reasons, we fell short of that goal. As they say, stuff happens. But I'm still writing my story.

Through it all, those were still great teams. Those were still great players. If I've learned anything from a life in coaching, it's that anyone can achieve greatness, in any occupation, and from any walk of life. You don't have to be an elite athlete or coach at an elite level to be great. Everyone has the capability of finding greatness in whatever they do. For example, from a teacher to a custodian, if you love your work and have passion for it, you can excel, too.

Greatness is using what you have and finding what you need. Greatness is character. Greatness is never giving up on yourself. I have been an assistant coach, an associate head coach, and an interim head coach, but I've never been *the* head coach. At least not yet. And I'm not giving up on that goal.

What has held me in good stead throughout my entire career has been my faith, my family, and my values. To be completely honest, I am blessed. Whenever I have achieved any measure of greatness in my own life or career, I must recognize that some factors were out of my control. And I thank God for every one of them.

Believe in yourself. Never give up. Stay focused. Strive for greatness.

Butch Pierre
May 2018

CHAPTER ONE

"Words spoken at the right time are like
gold apples in silver settings."
Proverbs 25:11

"**G**ET OFF THE COURT."

I said it nice and quiet-like so the other team wouldn't hear, but I was pretty sure my guys could feel the intensity of those words, regardless. I can joke around as much as the next man, and be downright charming when I want to be, but trust me on this: When I'm serious, you know it. And at that moment, I was stone-cold, dead-eyed, heart-attack serious. When I give somebody a certain look, everybody from my wife to my kids to my players knows better than to mess with me.

Well, maybe my wife can mess with me, but that's another story. You know what I'm talking about there.

Still, the players all just stood there for a second, maybe not sure of what I was asking, maybe not sure if they heard me right, maybe just plain not sure. Which was exactly the problem.

I waved them in closer and the team huddled around me. They'd mostly finished their drills, and I'd worked them pretty hard, too, so they could get a good sweat on. After all, this was preparation for the biggest game they'd ever played in their young lives, and if we won, the next game would take its place, and so it would be until we lost.

In other words, it wasn't time to play, it was time to *play*.

I took a second to look each one of them in the eye. The truth was that I'd never been more proud of them. They'd come a long way that season, accomplished more than a lot of people thought they could, and they weren't done yet.

I saw in each one a little of myself, although in different ways. They were young, one of the youngest teams I'd coached at such a high level, with freshmen and sophomores four out of five starters. And they were right on the cusp of greatness. The kind of greatness that makes careers. Highlight *reel* greatness, which was why I had blown the whistle.

"I said drag your ass back to the locker room. NOW."

I saw their wide, innocent eyes get a little wider, but nobody said a thing. They all just moved like I had told them to move. Which is what I want in a basketball player, because I've been there, and I know what I'm talking about. As a coach, I prize initiative and independence, but what I need is for them to do what I say when I say it. So they did.

I stopped them in the tunnel, though. I didn't really want them back in the locker room. I needed them off that basketball court for a quick minute, because I'd just caught 'em looking. After they had warmed up, *which was not for show, I was about to remind them*, the other team walked out onto the court, and I saw my guys looking at them. Not directly, like a challenging, defiant look but out of the corner of their eyes. Looking at them like they were special.

I guess it just hit them that they were in the Sweet Sixteen, about to play the number one seed Duke Blue Devils and Mike Krzyzewski in the NCAA Tournament in front of thirty thousand screaming fans in what was, as I said, the biggest game of their lives.

But as someone who'd been living and breathing basketball for over forty years, *Louisiana* basketball that is, which is hard, fast, and intimidating, I recognized that look. That look said weakness, and I knew those boys were not weak. That look said lack of focus, and I knew those boys were focused.

So, it had to be nerves. Jitters. A few butterflies before they took the big stage. I understood that. I'd been there. I knew how it was. But what I also knew was that I had to stomp the shit out of those butterflies, pardon my French.

So, I stopped them in the tunnel. "You scared of those guys?"

"Huh?"

"I said, are you scared of playing Duke?"

"Hell, no!"

"They're number one. Big dog."

"We ain't scared, Coach!"

I smiled. Now they were mad, which is a lot better than nervous. I knew they'd get focused on the task at hand as soon as I saw their anger. Like I said, there were a lot of people who hadn't thought this team would go this far, so they had a little bit of a chip on their shoulders. As superior athletes playing at a high level, there's nothing more motivating than a lack of proper respect for your game. And as a coach, it's my job to motivate my players to be the very best they can be and sometimes to be even better.

I will use whatever it takes to get that job done, whether it's fear, pride, anger, flattery, or any combination of those or any other emotions or methods that come to mind.

Because that's what champions do. Whatever it takes to win. But even champions need motivation from time to time.

When my twin boys Joseph and Josh were about eight years old, they started having a little trouble getting up in the morning for school, a problem their older sister Langley never had had. My daughter was always up on time and ready to take on the world, but the boys were a different story. Maybe it's a guy thing.

Regardless, as an assistant coach for one of the most elite college basketball programs in the country, I traveled a lot, and, as a result, I wanted the time I spent at home with my children to mean something.

As a parent, you come to understand that it's the quality of the time you spend with your kids that matters most, not necessarily the quantity.

My wife Clemmie did an amazing job with our children when I had to be away, but when I was home, I made them breakfast and took them to school every day, because that was my opportunity to spend some quality time.

Instead, my boys wanted an extra few minutes of sleep. Now, you might think that I would drag them out of bed or yell at them to get up, but that wouldn't really accomplish my goal. I wanted them to *want* to get up. I wanted them to make the decision themselves to forego that little extra sleep, because that would mean they understood the value of spending time with their father. In short, I wanted to instill discipline in my boys.

My own father was away a lot when I was growing up, so I was keenly aware of how important this was. On top of working two jobs, he also held an elected office as a police juror, which is what most folks would call a city councilman unless they live in Louisiana, where politics is unique, to say the least. The point being, Joseph U. Pierre Sr. always had lots of responsibilities, and he took them all very seriously. He's one of the hardest-working men I've ever known, and I inherited that attitude and work ethic.

My dad was also a strict disciplinarian, and I guess I inherited a little bit of that, too. My kids might say a lot! But being a disciplinarian has served me well as both a coach and a father, so when I saw a hint of laziness in my own sons, I made it a personal point of pride to rectify the situation.

Another factor in my thinking was that no matter what city or time zone I found myself in, or how late I was up the night before, for the last thirty years, I've gotten up early enough for at least a one-hour workout, so sleeping in when you could be doing something productive is not something familiar to me.

I gave them a few chances to learn this important lesson on their own, but every morning it was the same old story:

"Just ten more minutes, Daddy," followed by collapsing back into the pillow.

"I'm getting up, Daddy," followed by the sound of light snoring.

And if it wasn't that, they would forget a book or something else they needed for school, which meant we had to rush around to make sure they weren't late, and rushing around wasn't my idea of spending quality time with my sons.

So, one day, I just let them sleep. I told them once to get up but didn't indulge them by continually acting as their own personal snooze alarm.

Instead, I walked across the street where a neighbor boy, about the same age as my sons, was shooting baskets in his driveway. I'd seen him doing that a few days before and instantly had an idea of how to help my sons learn a little self-discipline.

"What's your name, son?"

"Trent."

"Can I shoot a few with you?" I asked.

"Sure!" he answered excitedly and tossed me the basketball.

Now, I was pretty well known around town as assistant basketball coach at LSU, which, while a big-time school, still maintained a small-town feel. Everybody knew me or knew who I was, and on campus, everybody knew my kids, as well, because all three attended LSU's (U High) K-12 Laboratory schools.

So, the neighbor boy was very excited to be in a shoot-around with a big-time college basketball coach.

After a few minutes, I asked Trent if he'd like some breakfast.

"Yeah!"

"C'mon over."

The smell of Creole eggs, grits, and bacon was always guaranteed (eventually) to get my sleepy sons out of bed; only this time, they walked into the kitchen to see their father with a new friend and in no rush at all to get them to school.

Their sleepy eyes were instantly alert. "What are you doing?" Josh asked.

"What does it look like I'm doing?"

"Eating breakfast?" Joseph sounded a little unsure.

"That's right," I said. "Trent and I worked up an appetite, shooting baskets this morning, so I thought I'd fix him some breakfast."

I could see by the look on my sons' faces that they didn't like that *at all.*

But the next morning, it was the same thing. They wanted to sleep in, so I shot baskets with Trent and then made him breakfast, which led to what was basically the same conversation as before with my boys. As the great Yogi Berra once said, it was déjà vu all over again.

But by the third day, both Josh and Joseph were up early, fully dressed and ready to go, hovering over my bed before I woke up. From that day forward, I never had to wake them up again. Not only that, but my boys are early risers to this day. *Young men*, I should say. If they're not ten minutes early, they think they're running late, and my sons never run late.

That was one of the ways I taught them self-discipline. Once they knew I wasn't going to wake them up every day, they took it upon themselves to do so. It was a lesson learned and a good thing, too.

Since I traveled so much, I needed both my sons and my daughter to learn and practice self-discipline. Otherwise, I might have found myself having to be the bad guy every time I came home, and that wasn't the kind of relationship I wanted to have. I would never have wanted my children to feel like I was punishing them for something every time I saw them. There was a lesson in that for me, too: The better I taught my kids self-discipline, the more likely the time I spent with them would be quality time.

Don't get me wrong. I was still a strict father. But I've been blessed with the support of Clemmie, who has been the perfect partner and the best coach's wife I could have ever hoped for, and children who understood the value of self-discipline from an early age.

They all have enabled me to become a better father, a better man, and a better coach. As a result, my players perform at a high level, and I coach at a high level, and it all boils down to motivation.

What makes you do your best?

I ask myself a version of that question every morning when I wake up. How can I do my very best today? What will it require of me? And that's exactly what I do, good Lord willing. I do the best I can do every single day. I give each day's work my all, with the help of faith, family, and fortitude.

"So, you wanna go out there and whoop Duke's ass?"

"Hell, yeah!"

"Then I want you to jog back out there like you're the best team in America, which you very well may be. I want you to jog back out there like you're the SEC champions, which you damn sure are."

I looked at them, one of the best teams I'd ever been associated with. "Understood?"

They all nodded.

"And if I catch even one of you lookin' their way, *I'm* gonna be mad as hell."

Now, you may be wondering why I could do something like that without checking with the head coach beforehand. All I can tell you is that Coach John Brady was and still is one of the finest coaches I've ever assisted.

But even more than that, he's a fine man. And we just had that kind of relationship, built on trust and mutual respect. John Brady knew that if I made a decision, it was always for the good of the team.

We had each other's back every single day, which is one reason we worked together for so long and so well. He trusted my recruiting ability implicitly and never once overruled me in the eleven years we worked together.

John once told me I was the best head coach that never was, though I would later go on to become interim head coach during a very difficult time at LSU. Since then, I've had stops as associate head coach at other universities. I also would like to think he was right, and I'd like to think that one day, I'll prove him wrong when I move up to the top spot.

"Are you ready to whoop some ass?"

They were, and so was I.

We won the game.

CHAPTER TWO

"Love makes your soul crawl out of its hiding place."
Zora Neal Hurston

D ARROW, LOUISIANA, was a town of about five hundred people without a stoplight when I grew up there back in the 1960s and 70s. While we were only twenty-five miles south of Baton Rouge in Ascension Parish, in some ways we were just about as far from the Louisiana state capital as we could be. We had gravel roads, stifling humidity, a single grocery store, and neighbors we could trust with our lives if it came right down to it, and every now and then, it did.

There might be two or three times that number of people there now, but there's still no stoplight, and the nearest grocery store is about four or five miles away.

The tumultuous 60s was something I heard about more than experienced in a vague sort of way. What was happening in other parts of the country back then was pretty far removed from my life in Darrow, at least for a while.

My world was occupied with family, sports, and friends, with fishing in the summer and hunting in the fall. Crawfish and fireworks, football and basketball. I knew some kids who took their shoes off the last day of school and didn't put them back on until school started up again, except for church on Sundays. Things were simple for me back then.

We weren't poor, but my older sister and I thought we were because my parents were savers, frugal folks who grew up during the Great Depression and lived through WWII in the Jim Crow South. They understood hard times were always just around the corner if you weren't careful, and sometimes if you were, so the best way to stave off hard times as best you could was to work hard and keep focused on God and family.

My father, as I've already mentioned, was a strict disciplinarian, but back then, I just thought he was mean. I had a child's understanding of what he was trying to teach me with his uncompromising ways, which is to say I didn't really understand at all. I didn't get what he was doing until much later, which was forcing me to develop self-discipline, the very trait I would work so hard to instill in my own kids and players many years later.

I credit all three of my children with learning those lessons earlier than I did, which is the essence of what it means to be a parent. You want your kids to have a better life than you did in every way, and while that sometimes means the comforts of life, it also means the hard lessons that make us who we are. The experiences that build character. As a husband, a father, and a coach, I understand those things do not come easily, nor should they. They are the fire that forges the steel.

My father raised us with an iron fist, expecting much, with no tolerance for excuses. He was not abusive, but he was tough. He was hard. As a result, I developed a close bond with my mother early on that exists to this day.

I could tell her anything, and she would always listen patiently. No question was out of bounds, no topic taboo. If my father was the hammer, my mother was its velvet sleeve.

That's not to say she was a pushover. Far from it. My mother was an extremely sharp lady, and she could smell bullshit a mile away. She loved her kids and always listened to what we had to say, but if she needed to get her point across, she was not shy about it. As tough as my father could be, I did not want to make my mother mad!

Looking back, it's pretty clear they were a great team in every way. Two people whose strengths and weaknesses complemented each other perfectly. I thank God every day for my parents and how they raised me. In spite of the discipline, you could almost say I led a sheltered existence, at least up until the day my father died six times.

It was my seventh birthday, and I was standing out in our front yard, waiting for my daddy to pick me up and carry me to the Louisiana State Fair. You know kids and carnivals. I was too excited to wait in the house or even sit on the porch. As soon as his car pulled into the driveway, I would jump in. He didn't even have to stop, he could just roll by, and I would dive in the window. Except he never came home that day at all.

My mother had had some health problems and was forced to retire early, so my father worked even harder to support our family. He worked long hours, doing maintenance at two chemical plants along the Mississippi River, so at first I figured he was running late. Until a stranger pulled up to the house in a car I didn't recognize and told me to go get my mama.

I said, "Yes, sir," just like my parents had taught me and went inside. I could tell something was wrong, but I didn't know how wrong until I saw the look on my mother's face when I told her some man was outside, and he wanted to talk to her about daddy.

I will never forget that look in her eyes, the look I imagine war widows have when a uniformed chaplain comes to the door during wartime. My mother just *knew*, somehow.

On his way home to pick me up after working all night long, to take me out for my seventh birthday, my father had been in a terrible car accident. He was driving alone on a two-lane road when an eighteen-wheeler crossed over the imaginary center line and hit him head-on, completely crushing the smaller vehicle. He'd broken nearly every bone on the left side of his body and was not expected to live.

We found out later that my father actually died several times on the operating table during multiple surgeries, six times to be exact, but the doctors had been able to restart his heart each time, and he managed to pull through and survive.

But all we knew then was that my mother had to go to the hospital *right now*. Probably because no one thought he was going to live. As vivid as the memory of my mother's eyes when she heard the news—eyes that told me all I needed to know about the seriousness of the situation—I also remember how she acted afterward.

She called her mother, who was the head of our family, our matriarch, and told her what had happened. She told her to expect me there directly. Then she quickly got dressed, but before she climbed into the man's car to go to the hospital, she knelt down and gave me a hug. When she pulled away, her eyes were dry. She was not crying, and that's my other memory of her eyes on the day my father died more than once.

"You walk straight over to your grandma's house," she said, kissing my cheek. "I'm going for your father."

Now, my mother was not a physically strong person. As I said, she had some health problems that left her unable to work, although after my father's accident, she had a full-time job taking care of him for many months. She was a delicate, sensitive woman, known by all as someone who would dissolve into tears if anything happened to a member of our family. She was kind-hearted, quick to help anyone who needed it, and she would cry at the drop of a hat if a member of her family was in trouble.

But not that day. Not in front of her son. *I'm going for your father,* she told me, and that's exactly what she did. On that day, she was the strongest person I ever knew.

As much as my father had taught me about self-discipline and self-reliance, my mother taught me about strength. She did not panic, she did not cry, she just went for my father. She showed me by her actions that in times of adversity, I needed to be strong for my family and myself, a lesson I've never forgotten.

Whenever I face a problem that seems insurmountable, I remember my mother and the look in her eyes that day. The first look that told me how truly frightened she was, and the second that told me she would find the strength to get through it.

I did like she said and walked to my grandma's. It was only six blocks away, but I swear I walked for hours on those gravel roads to my grandmother's house. I don't remember crying, although I may have been. I don't remember thinking about anything except that I knew something had happened to my father and that I wanted more than anything to see him again. Death was not a concept I had ever thought too much about at that age, and I'm not sure that such a possibility even registered. Like my mother, I just wanted to go for my father.

When I finally arrived at my grandmother's house, I walked in the door and didn't leave again for another two years. That's how long my father was in the hospital.

Of course when I say I didn't leave, I just mean that my sister and I lived there during the time he was recovering. We didn't go back home because our mother wasn't there. She wasn't there because she stayed in the hospital with my father for two years. And when I say she stayed, I mean she literally never left that building until she could take my father home with her. She lived in that hospital, just as he did.

My mother was there for every surgery and every changed bandage and all the rest of the things you endure when you're stuck in a hospital bed and cannot do for yourself. She was there when they turned him to prevent bedsores, and she was there when they emptied his bladder, and she was there when he could finally reach up and scratch his own nose, and she was there for every last excruciating minute of his physical rehabilitation.

I went to visit him with my sister. The first time was a shock, of course. My father had been such a strong man, both physically and mentally, almost like a mythical figure to me as a child, an indestructible man of iron and steel who could do anything, like some kind of superhero.

And my father *was* my hero, even though I thought he was too tough on me. If I'm completely honest, even after nearly losing him, we still didn't see eye-to-eye until I was in my early twenties. We were just too much alike, I guess. Stubborn and prideful.

But seeing him completely helpless like that filled me with emotion as a child, in spite of what I'd been told to expect. I cried when I saw him, and my mother, still strong, took my hand and squeezed it tightly before walking me around the bed to my father's right hand, one of the few places with exposed skin that wasn't bruised and broken.

I felt my father's flesh against my own, with my mother's hand around both of ours, and I was comforted. I didn't know why exactly, but I knew things were going to be all right. Looking back on it now, it seems like that moment was a metaphor for our family. My mother held us together, and through her, we became stronger.

Years later, when I first shook my father's hand as a mature man, a man on his level, so I could look him in the eye, I remembered that day in the hospital and all the days that came afterward. I think it was then that I was finally able to start seeing him for what he truly was, a human being with flaws who did the best he could for his children.

Any man who can say that is a success, in my estimation.

Today, my father is not only my hero; he's my best friend. And I try to be the same type of role model for my own children. I work every day to be the example for them that he was for me, and I try to be that kind of example for my players, as well.

Being a father and being a coach have a lot in common. You take responsibility for a young person, someone you have to both discipline and encourage. Someone who needs the benefit of your wisdom and experience. Someone who puts their trust in you to show them what to do in the best way you know how. Someone who might not always appreciate what you do, but you do it anyway. My father did what he had to do to make me the man I am today.

Joseph and Gloria Pierre have now been married sixty-one years, and Clemmie and I have passed the halfway mark. If we love as completely and share as deeply as those two, through good times and bad, I'd say that's about the best life I could have ever desired.

CHAPTER THREE

"Beautiful is the man who leaves a legacy
of shared love and life."
Stella Payton

"I think the reason why I'm the person I am
today is because I went through those tough
times when I was younger."
LeBron James

MY RELATIONSHIP WITH MY FATHER changed when I got my first job. For one thing, he helped me get it, and if my father vouched for you, especially if you were his son, you did not want to disappoint him.

The day I went to work was an important milestone in our relationship. Almost like I had become a man in his eyes. It was a rite of passage. It felt like he had been waiting for that day, like he had been grooming me to go out into the world and show responsibility.

Since my father was one of the first *black* elected officials in Louisiana East Ascension Parish, a seat which he held for seven terms or twenty-eight years, everybody in the community knew him and his story, who his son was, and what I was doing. There was no point in goofing off or not giving my best effort.

In a small town, everybody knows your business, anyway, but particularly if you're the son of Joseph U. Pierre Sr.

My father was constantly working to make things better in the community. He knew everybody and they knew him. He probably had direct dealings with just about every person in town, and most of the time, it was in their service. He both commanded and expected respect, and he got it. My father was known as a man you could go to in order to get things done, and he delivered.

So, when he told the maintenance supervisor at the local elementary school that I needed a summer job and would be a dependable worker, I wasn't expected just to work hard but to live up to the standards of my father. That was really the crux of the thing, and why it was a milestone in our relationship. I was not only striking out on my own just a little bit at the age of fourteen; I was also carrying on his name, *our* name, and that was a pretty important thing in my family.

My father valued hard work, and he believed that job would do me good, and he was right. But as I mentioned, we didn't always see eye to eye. My father was a hard man who was hard to please.

I always loved my father, but *liking* him was another story. There were times when I flat out didn't come close to that. There were plenty of times when we not only weren't on the same page, we weren't even in the same book. Or in the same library.

It boiled down to the fact that I thought he expected too much of me, combined with the fact that he pretty much didn't give a damn what I thought about his expectations.

I have to laugh about that now because it's one of those things we all go through as parents, and I get a good bit of it as a coach, too. That kid who somehow gets it in his head that his vast life experience, all seventeen or eighteen years of it, somehow trumps the hard-won wisdom of someone two or three or four times his age.

My father didn't give a damn what I thought because he *did* give a damn about *me*. He cared enough to be hard on me. It just took a while before we got in the same library, in the same book, and finally on the same page. I'm in my fifties now, and I'd say we're practically in the same sentence.

Everything I taught my kids came from my parents. They knew how to raise their children, but the discipline came from my father. Every time I talk to my kids, I sound a little more like him. I guess they probably laugh about how much alike we are. It makes me proud that they see it, though. My own kids turned out pretty great, which means I did something right. Which means my father did something right, too.

So, that first job was big. It was big for me and big for him, too. He didn't have to say a word when I went off to that job because he'd already done all the hard work preparing me for that day when I started to take responsibility for myself and make decisions in my life.

As we say down in Louisiana, *every dog has to carry its own hide,* and it was time for me to get started. So, as tough as my father had been on me, I knew he wasn't worried about how I'd conduct myself.

I instinctively knew what to do and how to act because of how my parents raised me, and that was that.

It's like when I coach the fundamentals of basketball. I may drill those players until they drop, and sometimes they might not like me very much. But when the game's on the line, they know how to come through for themselves and their teammates. Instinct, muscle memory, and pure heart have all been ingrained in their game.

The fundamentals of basketball become second nature to my players. With this being said, being responsible and working hard in my first job became second nature for me. I knew better than to give anything less than 110 percent every single day. I would've done that even if my dad hadn't recommended me for the job, but it was a special responsibility because he had.

So, I got up early every day, and when my boss told me what to do, that's exactly what I did. Most of that summer, I spent cleaning fifteen classrooms from top to bottom, and I do mean top to bottom, in the summer heat of Louisiana, with no air conditioning, as hot and sticky as you can imagine. The minute I walked into that building, I couldn't tell if my hair was still wet from the shower or if I was already sweating. And you'd be surprised, or maybe you wouldn't if you have kids, how dirty an elementary school classroom gets by the end of a school year.

Years later when I got my first coaching job at the collegiate level, I swept the entire gym floor, policed the parking lot, taught classes, recruited players, and did just about every other job you can think of in addition to my assistant coaching duties, and I was glad to do so. I took pride in it. Once you learn the fundamentals, they stay with you for life.

That's not to say that at the age of fourteen I was mature. Not by a long shot. I was looking at my watch every two minutes for eight hours a day. Sometimes I'd swear that thing ran backward.

I liked making my own money, but all my friends were running around having fun all day, and I was stuck inside that hot elementary school, working my butt off. Talk about discipline!

But as soon as 3:00 hit, I'd run down to the park and play football or basketball and basically wear myself out until suppertime at 6:00, when my mother always had a hot meal waiting.

Then it was more playing around until dark and back inside to sleep and do it all again the next day. Looking back on those days now, it actually sounds pretty peaceful. It was a simpler time, a time I surely do miss every now and then. A time when everybody looked out for everyone else.

When school got out the next summer, I decided I didn't want to work down at the elementary school again because it was just too hot. But, to be honest, I also wanted to get a job on my own, without depending on my father. I was rebelling just a little bit by doing that, showing him I could get my own job and all, but that was what he wanted, anyway. He wanted me to be independent.

By 'showing him' I didn't need his job, I was really just showing him I'd gotten the message, even if I didn't realize it at the time. That's how it is when you're a kid sometimes. You may think you're big and bad and some kind of rebel, but when you turn your back, parents just nod and smile and remember their own youth.

I went down to the chemical plant and got a maintenance job there, and of course it was just as hot and sticky as the elementary school. In Louisiana in the summer, you're not going to find a tolerable place to work outside of an office or something. But the pay was better, so it all worked out.

The summer after that, my father decided it was time I learned something useful besides general cleaning and maintenance, so he got me a job with a contractor, and, let me tell you, if you ever want to learn how to do a whole lot of different things you'll find useful later, work for a builder.

All summer long, I made forty or fifty bucks a day, which was a king's ransom for a sixteen-year-old kid. I learned how to pour a foundation, hang sheetrock, install flooring and insulation—you name it and I did it. We built a church that summer, and my boss was every bit as tough as my old man. If I thought cleaning classrooms was hard, construction work was a real eye opener. I've rarely been as tired at the end of a day's work unless it was triple overtime. It was a great experience, though, and it definitely kept me out of trouble.

I think my father wanted me to do hard labor on that church, so I would never do hard labor someplace else, if you know what I mean. I'm of the same mind. The best way to keep kids out of trouble is giving them responsibility.

That summer I became a very well-rounded individual with what I could accomplish with my own two hands and a good set of tools, which I think is important for young men, even today. *Especially* today. I know everything now is computers, cell phones, and video games, and most people just call a plumber instead of changing a washer to repair a leaky faucet. But as far as I'm concerned, there's still value in knowing how to fix things yourself.

I was once one of the highest paid assistant basketball coaches in the country, and while I'm usually extremely busy nowadays and will pay an expert to make a repair, there's satisfaction in knowing I could do it myself, if I had to do it.

Just like there's no better tasting crawfish than the ones you boil yourself (and I can boil a mean crawfish), there's no better feeling than fixing something yourself and saving the money you would have spent on the repair.

It doesn't matter how much or how little money I have, every dollar that passes through my wallet is earned by hard work, and I see no reason to be wasteful.

In spite of that and all those skills I acquired building that church, I have to admit that the life of a college coach has mostly kept me too busy to do it myself. I built my reputation as a recruiter, which means I travel *a lot* on top of the long hours required of college basketball coaches, particularly those coaching Division 1(Power 5) teams. But since being a coach also means being a problem solver, I found a way to take care of business even while I was on the road. I married a contractor's daughter!

There's nothing sexier to a busy man than a woman who knows how to handle power tools, and my Clemmie can repair just about anything that breaks, leaks, or just plain wears out. I'm not saying that's why I fell in love with her, but it didn't hurt. That's why my wife has handled all the repairs for most of our marriage, and another reason she's been the perfect partner and coach's wife.

My mother once told me, "Once you get married, and you do something around the house, your wife is going to make sure you continue that chore for the rest of your life."

The rest of my life? I'm a coach, I don't have time for that stuff! So I married well. Which has been all right with Clemmie. She definitely believes that if you want it done right, you do it yourself, and nobody does it better than Clemmie. And after thirty years of marriage, she's shocked when I make a repair.

I worked only one more summer job the following year because I was about to get very serious with sports, and that meant spending summers on basketball and football, but my next and last summer job was kind of unique in that it afforded me the opportunity to observe something I hadn't been around too much in my young life: white people.

My father also got me that job, which was at a skating rink. I basically kept the kids in line, which was kind of funny because most of them were my age. In spite of that, I functioned almost like a chaperone. I made sure everybody was skating in the right direction and no one was getting hurt or anything like that. Maybe a better description would be a bouncer on wheels.

Almost all of the kids were white because everyone had to pay to get in, and the sad fact was that most of the black kids in the area didn't have much money, and even if they did, they didn't spend it going skating with a bunch of white kids.

So, it was an eye-opener, and the expansion of my people skills, which of course comes in handy in my current line of work.

I got along well with everyone at the skating rink, for the most part since I knew a lot of the kids from playing basketball, and I learned quite a bit just from being around kids different than me. Mostly, I realized that they weren't that different when it came right down to it.

Sure, there's always cultural differences, but kids are mostly just kids. They want to play and have fun; some of them are nice, and some of them are mean. There's always at least one troublemaker and at least one peacemaker.

I was hired as a peacemaker, so I used the charisma I had inherited from my mother, who never met a stranger. If I needed to break up a fight or ease my way between two kids who looked like they might get into one, I could usually calm things down with only my personality, although I guess my size and muscular frame might have helped, too.

The fact is that there have always been problems between races, and there probably always will be. But it's good to put yourself out there and see how the other half lives if you get the chance. Most of the time, there's just as much common ground as there is separation if you take a minute and look for it.

And of course, one of the great equalizers has always been sports. There's a beauty and grace to physical competition that transcends color. In my business, if a guy can shoot, he can shoot, and he'll be admired for that skill no matter what color his skin happens to be. The same goes for the girls.

As they say, if you got game, you got game. If you can play, you can play.

I enjoyed that summer quite a bit, and, as I mentioned, I began to develop the people skills that I use to this day in recruiting, coaching, and almost everything else I do.

On my job, I meet all kinds of people from all backgrounds, from the rich and famous to the poor and anonymous, and I've found that I can usually find a way to talk to just about anybody, no matter where they come from. As long as they skate in the right direction, they're all right with me.

RELATIONSHIPS

"I never ever had a platform that I did not share with other people."
"I never walked through a door that I did not bring somebody
else through behind me."

T. D. Jakes

Nobody does it alone. As a basketball coach, that's a no-brainer. There's never been a player in any team sport who ever succeeded singlehandedly. Oh, sure, there are plenty of examples of how a guy "carried the team on his back" or "won the game on his own." But we all know that's not really true. While exceptional individuals can do amazing things, true greatness is a team effort.

Michael had Scotty. Magic had Kareem. LeBron had Dwayne. Not to mention Phil Jackson, Pat Riley, and Erik Spoelstra. Those players didn't coach themselves, pass to themselves, train themselves, or hire themselves.

As it is on the court, so it is in life. To play a great game, surround yourself with great teammates. To live your best life, cultivate great relationships—family, friends, co-workers, superiors, and subordinates. These people are your support group, your teammates in life. Use what they have to offer and respond in kind. Loyalty is key. Treat your relationships with care, and your diligence will be rewarded.

It's really as simple as treating your team like you want to be treated. It's about the choices you make in your relationships.

Of course, you cannot choose your family, but you *can* choose how you relate to your family. You can choose how and when you draw on them for strength and sustenance. You decide how you treat them, so treat them well. It will pay off in greatness.

CHAPTER FOUR

"Character, not circumstances, makes the man."
Booker T. Washington

VINCE LOMBARDI, THE GREAT FOOTBALL COACH, once said, "Winning isn't everything, it's the only thing." Everybody's heard that quote.

The great basketball coach John Wooden said, "Be more concerned with your character than your reputation, because your character is what you really are while your reputation is merely what other people *think* you are."

As a coach, I can definitely relate to both men. They were very different from what I can tell, but they were both great coaches dedicated to bringing out the best in their players.

As an extremely competitive individual, I know what Coach Lombardi meant when he said that. When I was a player, I wanted nothing more than a victory. As a coach, I watch my guys on the court, and I feel every shot as if I was out there. The thrill of competition is something I've never lost, and I hope I never do.

I can also relate to what Coach Wooden said, especially as a coach myself. I'm known as a hard-charging recruiter, and I am. I take no prisoners. I'm just as intense going after a player as when I was on the court going after a loose ball. I see an opportunity and I go after it. Just like my playing days, I want to win more than anything when I'm going after a player that can help my team. And that means my reputation can cause a little resentment at times. Especially from people who wanted to sign the player that I got.

So, I know what Coach Wooden meant. You can't always worry about what other people think when you know you came correct. You have to focus on your job and the task at hand.

Which brings me to what I might add to the philosophies embodied by those two quotes. From my way of thinking, I would add family in there somewhere. As far as I'm concerned, *family* is everything. And if character is what you really are, then family shows who you want to be. Family is aspirational as well as inspirational.

You can tell a lot about a person's character by how they treat their parents, their children, their spouse. And how they're treated in return. A person's reputation is nothing compared to family, because your family knows who you are better than anyone else.

A lot of the kids I recruit come from broken homes, single parent households, and economically depressed environments. Every time I recruit a young man who grew up without two great parents and a hot meal on the table every day, I remember to thank the good Lord for how I've been blessed, and I vow to bring that kid into the family of our team. I sit with that young man and his mother or father or whomever he trusts, and I promise them that I will look after him.

I sit in their living room, and, most of the time, they welcome me like I was a member of their family. I take that very seriously because I know these young men are being entrusted to my care. A seventeen- or eighteen-year-old kid going off to school is in a very vulnerable position sometimes. He may be 6'9" with a million-dollar jump shot, but he's still his mother's child. His father's boy.

I treat these kids like I treat my own. With discipline and guidance, and tough love if they need it. I'm not their father, but I look after them as if I were because that's what I'd want for my own kids if they needed someone, and Clemmie and I weren't around. They're always your children, no matter how old they get.

I guess it all goes back to how I grew up, with everybody looking out for everybody else. If you did wrong back in Darrow, you might catch two or three whippings before you even got home for the main event.

So, I try to set an example of faith and family for my players to go along with the discipline and fundamentals of basketball. Kids learn a lot by example, whether they realize it or not.

My father went to see his mother every Sunday after church to spend an hour or so with her. She lived about twenty minutes away, but he never missed a visit, rain or shine.

His mother was French Creole, 6'3" in her stocking feet, which were size thirteen. She was very wise and very strict, and nobody messed with her. Born a Catholic, raised a Catholic, and died a Catholic. As you can imagine, she was quite an intimidating figure. She and my grandfather were married over sixty years, and they lived to the ripe old age of ninety-two after raising twelve children together.

My mom's mother was one of five kids who raised five of her own, on her own, and she lived to ninety-three. She was a devout

Baptist, well respected by all who knew her, and very family-oriented, as well.

I was steeped in faith and family, raised Catholic, and rarely missed a Catechism class or Sunday Mass.

So you can see that family is something that's very important to me because from the time I was born, I was surrounded by so many people who cared for me. As I mentioned, not all the players I recruit are so fortunate, so I make it my business to go the extra mile for them if needed. Basketball, to me, is just another kind of family.

During the two years I stayed with my grandmother, one of the nuns from church would come to the house once a week for Catechism class at the request of my mom, who was at the hospital with my father. Every now and then, my grandmother would talk to the nun, and I'd get to skip the class. I'm not sure what she told her, but it was nice to skip once in a while, even though I enjoyed the class. My grandmother, who knew the business of everyone in town, seemed to sense the days when I could use a break. Like I said, she was a wise woman.

She cut sugar cane in the fields when she was younger, using a knife she still kept jammed between the wall and the baseboard behind her bedroom door. Then they got machines to do the work, and she went to work for the school district as a cook at the elementary school.

Every Saturday, she would bake all day, and every Sunday, she'd sell her sweet potato pies for a quarter apiece. I learned a lot at the age of twelve, as I handed them their sweet potato pies. The folks that came by would talk to her when they picked up their pies and ask advice, and she'd draw them out and tell them what she'd do if she were in their shoes.

Just the way she spoke to people made them trust her and feel comfortable confiding in her. Sometimes when I'm sitting with a potential recruit and his parents or counseling a player with a problem, I can hear my grandmother's words coming out of my mouth, saying some of the same things to put them at ease that she used to tell those folks way back then.

She was truly a fearless woman and a pillar of the community, one of those older women of respect that no one would dare cross. If she heard of a man who had hit his wife, she'd get right up in his face and ask him why he did it. There was, of course, never a reason that satisfied her. If he wouldn't repent his sin right then and there, she'd warn him about the cane knife jammed between the wall and the baseboard, and the fella would come to Jesus pretty quickly after that.

I'm not sure if there were any repeat offenders who'd encountered my grandmother, but if there were, they at least stopped to think beforehand.

She walked into church every Sunday, wearing her best hat and matching dress. If that woman had a fault, it was pride because she could really strut down that aisle. Everybody watched her walk in, and she loved every minute of it.

I bought her a boxed set of her favorite Estée Lauder perfume every Christmas till the day she died, and the one time I sent it without the fancy box, I got a phone call that very day. She had a box before New Year's.

I played sports from an early age. From elementary school on, I was a natural athlete, and I developed my competitive nature. There wasn't a game played with a ball that I didn't excel at if I put my mind to it, and it was pretty clear early on that athletics would be a big part of my life.

As for basketball, I played on dirt at home and at my friends' houses. Not a one of us had a cement court. Just some old hoop without a net half the time and all kinds of rocks and gravel and things down below, so you never knew where that ball was going to go. Luckily, there was a cement court out back of the elementary school two miles away.

Speaking of which, one of my earliest athletic influences was one of the first white teachers at my elementary school, Mr. Witek. I liked him right away and still remember his quiet, friendly nature. He took a real interest in all of the students, leading a physical fitness program for the boys and girls with tests at the end of the year. Of course, that was motivation for me to work hard and maintain my fitness, something I still do to this day. He introduced us to scouting and other activities that took us outside the community, which was the first time some kids had ever traveled more than a mile or two from their family home.

Witek had actually played in the Negro Baseball League even though he was white, which we all thought was pretty cool. After Jackie Robinson integrated Major League Baseball, I guess some of the Negro league owners decided to sign some white guys. Mr. Witek organized a Little League team and brought in a friend of his to help out, a coach of the Negro league, Mr. Jenkins, who probably could have played professionally. We traveled to other towns after school and in the summer to play games, all of us piling in the back of Mr.

Jenkins's old pickup truck and driving the ten or twenty miles each way, always stopping for sno-cones on the way back.

My father had a relationship with these men. He knew and trusted them with me, kind of like how I form a relationship with the parents of the players I recruit. I remember how my father was with Mr. Witek and Mr. Jenkins, and the principal Mr. Bartley. He knew them and knew he could trust me in their care.

As a matter of fact, Mr. Bartley was the only man other than my father who ever made me cry. He was the only man other than my father to whip me, and he even had special permission from my father to do so with abandon, which was something I didn't know about until it was too late.

Of course it was nothing unusual to spank a kid back then, especially in the South. It was as natural as patting a child on the back or telling him to quiet down. And Mr. Bartley had a mean paddle, if you could even call it that. It was more like a plank of wood wrapped in duct tape. And let me tell you, that tape had met up with quite a few young behinds before it met mine, and I'm sure there were plenty more after that.

When Bartley got hold of me, I took the position as instructed, hands on his desk, and he whacked me hard enough to bring tears to my eyes. I almost forgot what I'd done! It was probably something like coming in late to Mr. Witek's class. He hated kids coming in tardy.

Witek and Bartley were both pretty hard on me at times, in spite of being friends with my father. As a matter of fact, it was probably because they were friends. Both men expected a lot of me for two reasons: because I was a good athlete with real potential, and because I was the son of Joseph U. Pierre Sr.

I didn't understand that, of course. All I knew was that I was getting whupped at school for nothing and it hurt like hell.

There was no sympathy from my father, of course. When I told him what had happened, he just nodded as if he'd whupped me himself, and there was nothing at all to discuss. I learned my lesson and got to class on time from then on.

The only other time Bartley whupped me was when a kid stole my bike. We never liked each other and fought nine times, to be exact, in which I never won a fight. But stealing that bike was the last straw for me. His bullying days were over. When I saw him on the bus the next day, I told him I was gonna whip his ass. As soon as the bus pulled up to the school, we went around back, and I did exactly what I said I was going to do.

The only problem was that we'd been followed by every last kid on the bus and a whole lot more who were arriving at school at the same time by car or on foot, so there was plenty of yellin' and plenty of witnesses. I won that fight for the first time, and that was the last fight he and I ever had. It was worth every blow from Mr. Bartley's plank.

Looking back on those days, I can see that I had a lot of strong male influences, beginning with my father and continuing with teachers and coaches. They were tough on me, and while it wasn't what I wanted, it was definitely what I needed.

The people I knew then, from the teachers to my school friends, were a kind of extended family in a way. One of my best friends back then was best man at my wedding, and those men my father knew and trusted to look out for me when he wasn't around to fulfill the same basic function and responsibility I take with the players I recruit. I try to provide structure, guidance, and the benefit of my experience. I act as mentor, teacher, coach, and friend.

I like to think that the teams I coach are extended families, too, and, like families, we play hard and fight hard. We work together. If we win, we win together. If we lose, we lose together. Through good times and bad, your family is what sustains you.

A team is like a family, and family is everything. Family builds character, it reveals character, it *is* character.

CHAPTER FIVE

"I love what I do, and when you love what
you do, you want to be the best at it."

Jay Z

IN SPITE OF HAVING THE BENEFIT OF THOSE COACHES and teachers in my life to help keep me in line when I was at school, I never forgot who was putting bread on the table at home. That was my father, and he took that role very seriously. He made sure I looked up to those men and respected them and did what they told me to do. But he wouldn't even think of letting me call them role models, because *he* was my role model. He saw that as his job, a job every bit as important as working in a factory or carrying out his duties for the city. In fact, it was *more* important.

To my father, a man who didn't take care of his family was no man at all, and he instilled those values in me every day of my life, both in word and deed.

When I meet players nowadays who haven't had a strong male influence in their lives, I make sure I set that same example and teach those same values to them in every way I can, just like my father taught me.

I feel like it's my job not only to coach them as best I can, but also to be a positive influence in their lives, both on and off the court. I teach them about the game of basketball, but I also help prepare them for life off the court. Any decent coach will tell you the same thing. If I can steer even one player to make the right decision when things are tough, or to avoid a bad decision that could adversely affect his life in some way, then I've done my job. I've had a positive influence on the life of that young man. I've made a difference.

A good coach, like a good parent, teaches as much by example as he does any other way. If you want your players to keep their house in order, you have to make sure your own house is in top shape because young people can sense hypocrisy.

It's funny because when you're young, you think you know everything. Then you grow up some, and you laugh at how little you actually knew. Then you get a little older, and you realize how right you were about some things and how much you still have to learn about others.

And one day you just might find out how much more the kids today know than what *you* knew back in *your* day. And that's when you finally figure out that it never ends. You have to work hard constantly, so you can keep one step ahead of the game. You can never be satisfied. You can never allow yourself to get complacent. Not as a player, and not as a coach. The minute you rest on your laurels, you lose your edge. There's always another game to play, another season to come. There's always another challenge.

To be truly excellent at anything and maintain that excellence over time, you have to work hard every single day. There's no shortcut. It is what it is.

The key to excellence is discipline. In spite of coaches and teachers and parents and mentors, all of whom are important, discipline ultimately has to come from within you.

Some have it naturally, although it can be learned. It can be developed. I've seen players with all the natural talent in the world who got beat by a player who wanted it more. A player with heart. A player with true self-discipline. A player with mental and physical toughness.

A big part of my job is to instill in my players the importance of discipline as a requirement of success. No matter who your parents are or how they raised you, or how many role models you have, nobody can live your life for you. Nobody can step into your shoes and go where you need to go and do what you need to do.

Nobody can play your game but you. And for that, you need discipline.

As I've mentioned, my father was not the only source of discipline in my life growing up. In Darrow, Louisiana, there was never a shortage of folks around to make sure I did what I was supposed to do. To make sure I learned discipline.

Church was a big part of that.

We went every Sunday as a family, always sitting together on the right side of the church, something we still do to this day. It's just one of those things families seem to do, especially in the South. You always sit in about the same place in church, in the same row if it's available. It's always a comfort to be back in the Lord's house so you make yourself comfortable.

Everybody seems to find their place in church. There's back row people who always come in late, but that wasn't my family. Not with my parents. No Pierre comes late to church.

There are front row people who seem kind of showy. People who like to be seen when they walk in and when they leave. I've seen a lot of folks like that, and I admit that I have a certain style, and I like to be appreciated for it at the proper time. As a college coach, you have to be conscious of the image you project because you're representing a university, whether it's during a TV interview or in a timeout with thousands of fans watching you talk to your players.

And then there's balcony people. Whether or not there's a balcony, those are the ones who like to sneak out early and go home to watch the ball game.

My family was none of those. We were steadfast people, who arrived on time, never left early, and formed the backbone of the church.

Our family was steadfast because that's the kind of people my parents were. Reliable. We arrived on time and sat on the right side of the aisle. And because we sat on the right side of the church, that's where all the other black folks sat, too.

The church was located in a mostly black community, but probably 90 percent of the members were white. Most black folks in the area were Baptist, I guess.

This wasn't by design, really, and it didn't feel like segregation to me. It was just what we did. My family came in and sat in their usual place, and since our friends and relatives constituted the bulk of the black membership, that's just the way things worked out.

But separation was there, and it was inevitable that the distance between us would have to be addressed somehow. We go to church to be close to God, to remove whatever separation exists so that we can be nearer to Him. Why wouldn't He want us to commune with each other in Christian fellowship?

Not that I knew any of that at the time. I was kind of a balcony kid in a steadfast family, to be honest. I liked church, but I must admit, I was always in a hurry to get home and see the Cowboys on TV.

I remember there was an older black lady who was very influential in our community who also went to that church. We all knew her and respected her because she'd been around a long time, one of those women you'd call a pillar of the community.

One Sunday, she leaned over just before the service started and asked my mother why we always had to sit on the right side when the white folks sat *over there*, and without waiting for an answer, she got up and went to sit on the left side of the sanctuary.

My mother wasn't about to let her friend make that journey alone, so she got up, crossed the aisle, and sat down next to her friend on the white side of the church. Or the "wrong" side for us.

At first, I didn't know if my mother was just being supportive of her friend or if they had both planned to make some sort of statement, but now the two of them were the only black faces in a sea of white people sitting on the other side of the church. There was no more separation between black and white, which was a pretty big deal.

I was only about twelve years old at the time, and while I knew my mother had done something unusual, I didn't think too much more about it until the next morning when someone left a burning cross on our front lawn.

Up to that point in my life, I was certainly aware of racial issues because we talked about those things in my family very openly, but that was my first encounter with real and personal racism. The kind of racism every black child will experience and which every black parent tries to prepare them for. But nothing can prepare you for a burning cross outside your window.

Even though both my parents were outspoken about civil rights and told me and my sister that we needed to be proud of our heritage and stand up for ourselves, it was still a shock to see my father knocking down that burning cross and my mother helping him put out the fire while still in her bathrobe. It made them seem both vulnerable and heroic at the same time, and so I was proud and scared at the same time. I was afraid for them, mostly.

It was a school day, and I was just getting out of bed when I heard my father shout my mother's name from outside the house. I could immediately smell something burning and thought maybe the house was on fire. But when I ran to the window, I saw my father swinging a shovel at a burning cross while my mother dragged the hose toward him, trying her best to spray water on the flames.

I can't begin to describe the sight and do it justice, but it is a sight I will never forget: My father chopping away at that burning wood and my mother pulling that garden hose around behind him, trying to make sure he didn't get burned.

Once the cross was on the ground, he took the hose from her and finished dousing the fire. The neighbors were all outside by that time and rushing around to help, but by then it was mostly over. One of the neighbor ladies was crying, and my mother was consoling her as if she had been the victim, which she was, if you think about it. Our entire community was victimized. As Martin Luther King Jr. said, "Injustice anywhere is a threat to justice everywhere."

In our neighborhood and our community, we all felt the heat of that cross. Just like countless African-Americans felt the heat of those times. Word spread fast, and we got a lot of calls and visits over the next few days to make sure we were all right.

Just like when I did something wrong at school and would hear about it from lots of folks before I even got home, we heard from almost everybody in town before that wood was done smoldering. That's community. That's togetherness. That's family.

But the very first thing we did after the flames had been put out was pray. We sat down at the kitchen table and joined hands and prayed as a family. I could feel the strength in my mother's hand even as I felt her shaking. There was power in her, and I could feel it in me.

When we opened our eyes, my mother put one hand under my chin and the other beneath my sister's. She raised our faces up and held our gaze in her own, almost as if forcing us to hold our heads high in the face of such ugliness, ugliness she knew we'd have to face again.

There was pain in her, the pain of a mother who understood she would not always be there to protect her children. The pain every parent feels for their child when you want to bear such things for them but you know you can't.

Then she spoke in a clear, steady voice: "This is what happens when you stand up for what's right."

I heard my father's "mmm-hmm," and then he stood up to go back outside and carry off the remains of that cross. As a child, it seemed like blasphemy to me. The worst thing someone could ever do is to use a cross in that way.

My parents showed great discipline during that time. They didn't scream or cry or fall apart because that would have scared their children. They didn't go looking for revenge. They just took care of things and showed us, by example, how to deal with adversity.

They talked more about it with us later on, of course, but that morning sums up my parents' life in a nutshell: Stand up for what's right, deal with what comes, and move on, because there's always more coming. And don't forget to pray.

CHAPTER SIX

"Healing begins where the wound was made."
Alice Walker

I WAS DRIVING by the time I was eight or nine years old. My mother would tell me to jump in the car and go over to my grandmother's house to borrow some sugar or other things that she needed, and I was always eager to do it. It was only a few blocks away, but it seemed like an adventure every time she asked me.

By the time I was thirteen, I was driving clear over to the next town and back to pick up groceries or go to the hardware store or some other such place. My mother always told me not to tell my daddy because she'd be in trouble if he ever found out. Of course, I would never let that happen, but that was really more her way of making sure I was extra careful since I figured out later that my father knew all about it.

Nothing much got past either of my parents, to be honest. I think neither one of them could have kept a secret from the other, even if they tried.

It was just one of those things that evolve in a marriage, especially if your kids are concerned. Your mother says, "Don't tell your father," and your father says, "Don't tell your mother," but everybody kind of figures out what's going on.

The reason it works? Trust. My mother trusted that I wouldn't wreck that car. She trusted that I knew what I was doing. And my father trusted that my mother knew what *she* was doing. And also that I wouldn't wreck the car!

Now, I'm not sure that *I* would have trusted myself as much as they did, but they believed in me, and, over time, their confidence in me gave me confidence in myself.

If you want to teach a kid responsibility, you have to give them something to be responsible *for*. You want them to be trustworthy; you have to trust them.

And to a certain extent, I had earned that trust from an early age. I could be a rowdy kid, but I was always respectful to my parents. I never lied to them. One reason was because I would never have gotten away with it. I could almost believe my mother when she told me she had eyes in the back of her head. No one was getting away with anything if she was around. Same with my father. Like I said, neither one of them missed much.

Another reason I never lied to my parents was because I didn't want to disappoint them. That's something else that comes with trust. When you have the trust of another person, you don't want to let them down. That's how you learn responsibility.

My father used to make me wash his car once a week, and if there were even a single smudge on the chrome bumper, he'd make me wash the entire car again. That may sound harsh, but it also taught me to pay attention to detail. After one or two do-overs, he never had to make me repeat that task again.

One of the things I didn't like was having to do chores when my friends were out playing. It didn't seem fair at the time, but I ended up being the same way with my own kids. Some people repeat the mistakes of their parents. I repeated their lessons.

Even though my father's punishments rarely showed mercy, he did reward me from time to time for a job well done. Once, he took me to the Lincoln Theatre in Baton Rouge to see James Brown, which was an experience I'll always remember. Anyone who ever saw the hardest working man in show business perform live—cape routine and all—likely won't forget it.

That was also where we heard Betty Wright sing "Tonight is the Night," which my mother wasn't too thrilled about since that is a very sexual song. She also hadn't been too pleased a few years before when one of my older friends told me about sex. I was around nine or ten years old, and being so young and innocent, I decided to verify some of that new information with my mother, who had to explain a few things to me a little sooner than she'd planned. She gave my friend a talking-to, as well.

That same friend got in trouble with her again when we were playing with one of those Nerf footballs in his bedroom, two houses down, and when it rolled under the bed, he lit a match under it so he could see where it was.

That mattress went up like a Christmas tree in July, and it probably would have burned the whole house down if we hadn't run outside and found a couple of men on the corner who rushed in and dragged the whole bed out onto the lawn.

My mother was at a neighbor's house and heard all the commotion, and when she saw that smoking mattress and found out what had happened, she whipped my friend's tail like you wouldn't believe, right there on his front lawn.

Whether or not there was any added payback for that lesson on the birds and the bees, I couldn't tell you. But it's certainly possible.

Unlike my father, however, she could temper her punishment with a little mercy every now and then.

The first time I drank alcohol was one of those times. I was about thirteen, and a friend and I went to a party around the corner from my house and downed an entire bottle of Boone's Farm Country Kwencher, which is maybe a half step above Thunderbird. I snuck into the house, crawled into bed and tried to sleep, but that liquor was talking to me. I puked it all up. My mother came in and asked me what happened, and I told her.

"Well," she said, "don't do that again."

So I didn't. She was mad, but I guess she figured the hangover I was going to have the next morning was punishment enough. And believe me, it was.

I didn't take another drink until I was a sophomore in college! I got in my share of serious trouble, of course. I was no angel. But that trust my parents gave me helped keep me on the right path most of the time.

That's another thing I learned from my parents that made me the man I am today and the coach I've become. When I look in a player's eyes and tell him that I trust him to do right, that I *expect* him to do right, I understand the importance of those words. I give respect and demand it in return, just like my parents did.

Of course, back in those days, things were different than they are today. Simpler in a lot of ways. I guess as we get older, most people look back on their youth and think of it like that. Growing up in Darrow in the 60s and 70s, the kind of trouble kids got into was maybe a little drug use and some stealing here and there. But because our community was made up of families, that made a big difference. There was good and bad, like there is anywhere, but mostly we all looked out for each other in the community and in our families.

My sister was first born, a couple of years older than I, and the apple of my father's eye. As hard as he was on me, my dad was even stricter with her because she was a girl. That's just the way things are done down South. She didn't like that very much, but there was no way my father was going to let his baby girl get into any trouble, spending the night at her friend's house or running around town without close supervision like "some Methodist or something" he would say.

My sister was pretty headstrong as a result of butting heads with my father, but that made her only a strong, independent woman. She's been married a long time now and has two great kids, so my parents did something right.

My sister and I got along great. She was very supportive of me, and I was very protective of her. We had our moments, of course, but for the most part, we did just fine. Just like with my parents, I trusted my sister and she felt the same about me.

I also learned about trust from my friends, like anybody does, I guess. And my father was a big influence there, too. Both my parents were. They could assess a person's character pretty accurately, and their advice was always really simple: If someone wasn't a good person, then you shouldn't be messing with them. If they didn't have good habits, steer clear. My father's opinion was that if you stayed away from people who got in trouble, it would be a lot easier to stay out of trouble yourself.

I know that sounds simple, but I'm sure most people have had friends from time to time who just seem to be bad news. The kind of person who brings trouble with them wherever they go. It can be easy to fall under the influence of someone like that.

My advice to my players today is the same as my father's was to me: Stay away from people who can bring you down. I cannot stress that enough.

I've seen big-time college players with all the talent in the world brought down by a friend or hanger-on who didn't care about them at all. They bring trouble into their life and then disappear when things go badly.

Look for a positive influence and *be* a positive influence. That's what makes a leader.

One of the reasons I'm a successful recruiter is that I have my father's ability to read people. I'm exceptional at recognizing and gauging talent, but I'm also great at evaluating character. On the court as in life, if you have both, you're unstoppable.

Both of my parents were really good about explaining how things were with whites and blacks, too. I was always able to develop good relationships with all kinds of people because I looked past skin color to the person underneath. After that cross was burned on our lawn, my parents could have taught me something very different. But they were wise enough to understand I would be going out into the world and dealing with all kinds of people, and they prepared me for that.

My father knew how to look past the superficial qualities that can define a person and get to the heart of things very quickly. I like to think I can do the same thing.

Another thing that kept me out of trouble was sports. I was a natural athlete and very competitive, so I was always looking for a game. I never had a basketball court at my house, which was probably a little unusual for athletes who go on to excel at a high level in high school and beyond, but my friend Leo Graves Jr. had a court at his house, so I spent a lot of time over there. His father was the kind of man my father respected as sharing the same values, so I never had any problem spending time there. My dad didn't have to worry I'd get in trouble if I was shooting hoops at Leo's.

Leo Graves Sr. was one of the men, along with my father and a few others, who took charge of things if there was a hurricane, flood or tornado or some other event that required the community to pull together or get organized. They were the leaders of the community, family men who stepped up to do whatever needed to be done, and I had a unique relationship with each of them. They were all different but real solid. Good men. Old school, I guess you'd call them. Since I'm older now than they were then, I guess that makes me *older* school!

Roy Smith was a tough, mechanically minded guy who probably could have taken a diesel engine apart and rebuilt it blindfolded. He loved sports, but he had three daughters who couldn't have cared less about such things, so he really enjoyed talking to me about football or basketball. He was very tough with my father after his accident, pushing him harder than anyone else so that he could walk again. My dad loved him for that. Roy was all fight and no flight, as my father would say.

Mack Graves was laid back and kind of a ladies' man, soft-spoken, patient and calm, which was probably what made him a good fisherman. Sometimes he'd take me hunting or fishing, along with one of his sons. He worked down at the chemical plant and built his house with his own two hands, which I found pretty impressive.

Ronnie Vallery started working at the chemical plant, like almost everybody else in town, but eventually, he opened his own trucking business. He could build just about anything and usually had a couple of hot rods at any given time. He liked street racing in the summertime, and we'd all go out to watch. Once I got a little older, he'd talk to me about life, and we developed a real friendship.

In spite of all those good influences, I was not immune to the bad. I learned from experience how even the best intentions can turn on a dime and maybe even cost you your life if you're not careful.

I remember one instance that really stood out to me. I was riding around with my friend Snake and his uncle. I was eleven or twelve at the time, and this particular friend was one of those guys who always seemed to get accused of doing things he shouldn't do. His uncle was even worse. They called him Forty, and he was definitely not anyone my parents would have wanted me to hang around.

We stopped at a red light, and old Forty got into a heated conversation with someone in the next lane, and before I knew it, I was in an actual street race.

It was one thing to watch a family friend who built hot rods and who knew what he was doing, but to actually be in the back seat of street racer without a seat belt was something else entirely.

Forty lost the race, and he wasn't too happy about it, but what had the second most dramatic effect on me from that night was when we fishtailed near the makeshift finish line, and I felt the back of the car lift off the pavement below me. For an instant, I thought we were going to fly off the road and into a ditch.

The night's *most* dramatic effect was when I got home and found out my cousin Clay had seen the whole thing and told my mother all about it. I have never before or since seen such fury in my mother's eyes, and this time there would be no mercy. She beat me so badly, I tried to crawl under the bed to get away from her, and my father finally had to step in and physically restrain her. I think she wouldn't have stopped, otherwise. When I managed to look up into her eyes, they were filled with tears, and I realized how terrified she was at the thought of losing her only son.

When she eventually pulled me to her breast and hugged me, I wept. I don't think I've ever cried as hard as I did that night. I felt ashamed that I'd scared her so badly that I never wanted her to feel that way again.

I thought it had been a harmless decision to get into that car with someone I should have avoided. One of those people can get you into trouble. I could have lost my life, but what bothered me the most was that my mother had trusted me, and I had betrayed that trust. She believed in me, and I made one stupid choice that made her question that belief.

I told myself right then and there that I would never disappoint her again, and I hope that's true. I know I've done my best to make it true, anyway. The effort was made.

As a coach, I show my players respect, and I demand respect in return. I put my trust in them so they will trust me, as well.

I know my players won't always respond the way I want them to, but if I've taught them anything, it's that the effort must be made.

CORE BELIEFS

It all starts here. I began with relationships because of family and all, but after being born, the most important thing we will ever do in life is *believe*. Think about that for a second. Everything in life that's important depends on believing. Love is big, but only if we believe in its power. Family is who we are, but we have to believe in family to render it a motivator in our lives.

If you don't believe in something, you're not really living, and you're definitely not succeeding.

When I was thrust into the position of interim head coach of the LSU Tigers men's basketball team, we had a losing record, and our next game was against a team predicted to beat us by 24 points. My boss, the school's athletic director, told me we would lose.

My response? We'll see.

We took Tennessee down to the wire and lost by 2 points. We shattered expectations and played a great game because we *believed* in ourselves and in each other. We chose to *define* ourselves as a team that could win.

In life, your core beliefs are what define you. Typically, we discover our core beliefs through faith. I did, anyway. And it's a continuing process. But whether you look to the Bible or the Torah, the Quran or *Sports Illustrated*, seek out what you believe in. Develop your core principles and stick to them.

Define yourself or the world will do it for you. Greatness comes from within.

CHAPTER SEVEN

"Every man got a right to his mistakes.
Ain't no man that ain't made any."
Joe Louis

I DID A LOT OF FISHING with my friend Leo Jr. and his father, who I always respectfully addressed as Mr. Leo. Just like my daddy gave me his name and expected me to live up to it, Mr. Leo had very high standards for both his sons. The entire Graves family were trusted friends and neighbors, and no one worried about me when I was with them.

Sometimes we'd go way out in the Gulf of Mexico and bring back some grouper or red snapper, and sometimes we'd just cast off the banks of the Mississippi River and hook us a mess of catfish. As far as I'm concerned, Louisiana has just about the best seafood in the world, and after a long day on the water, there's nothing better than a good old fish fry.

After one such deep sea fishing trip, when I was about eleven years old, I remember sitting around the Graves's family table after dinner, just talking, and I heard something that really blew my mind. Another friend of Leo Jr.'s was there, and he told us that a couple of boys, who were our classmates, had apparently gotten into a physical altercation with their father.

I nearly fell over in my chair. "With their daddy?" I asked, incredulous.

"Sure did," the kid answered, almost as if he was proud to tell such a story.

I just shook my head. The very thought of something like that was unbelievable to me. "I'd never do nothing like that," I said. "I don't care what happened, I'd never hit my daddy. Or my mom."

Mr. Leo nodded.

"Or my sister," I added. "That's family, man!"

"You're a good boy, Joseph," Mrs. Graves said. I called her Ma Phene, and she always called me by my Christian name, even though most everybody else called me Butch by that time.

My grandma came up with Butch when I was little. She said from the time I was born, I was restless. Couldn't sit still, always wanted to get up and go somewhere or do something, and for some reason that made me Butch to her, and it stuck. My father never called me Butch or anything except Son, which has always suited me just fine. My mom, on the other hand, just called me Man, as in "Come over here, Man," or "Hand me my purse, Man."

But to Ma Phene, I was Joseph. I think it was because of the respect she had for my father.

"Joseph?" the kid telling the story said. "You Joseph?"

"That's right," I said, suddenly a little pissed off. I think my anger was a combination of the way he repeated my father's name and the story he seemed so happy to tell. It was not only disrespectful to my father but to *all* fathers.

What kind of a person gets into a physical altercation with his own parent?

I think Mr. Leo changed the subject about that time, because I don't remember much conversation with that kid after that. But I found out the next day, he'd been flapping his jaw about my reaction to his story.

The two brothers who'd fought with their father rode their bikes up on either side of mine and forced me to stop.

"What you doin'?" I asked.

"Why you talking about us?" they demanded.

"I'm not talkin' about you."

"You was last night."

They were both a little bigger than I was. I was tall but skinny back then. "Hey, man, all I said was that I wouldn't hit my father. I don't know what's goin' on with you."

One of the brothers stepped up in my face. "You got that right."

I could see in his eyes that he wasn't interested in talking things out. I was steeling myself for a fight when I saw movement out of the corner of my eye and instinctively jumped back, just as the other brother slashed at me with a knife, catching me on the leg. Luckily, I was wearing blue jeans and had quick reflexes, because while he drew blood, there wasn't much damage besides those jeans.

I wasn't worried about the jeans. I saw my opening and took it. I had always been a fast runner, but on that day, my feet didn't touch the ground until I was sitting at my kitchen table, explaining to my parents why I'd come home bloody.

My mom was scared and my dad was angry, and it took a long time before things calmed down. My father wanted to go to the police and press charges, but I was dead set against doing that, and it took a lot of convincing before my parents agreed to let me handle things.

Looking back on it now, I'm even more impressed by their faith in me. I'm not sure I'd be able to let something like that go unreported with my kids, but, in the end, my folks trusted that I could stay out of trouble.

To be honest, that brief conversation with those boys was a real lesson for me. I kept thinking about what one of them told me when I said I didn't know what was going on at their house. *"You got that right."*

The thing is, I *did* get that right. I had no idea what had gone on in their family to cause those boys to fight with their father like they did. Maybe they were getting beat up, or maybe they were protecting their mother. I couldn't possibly know what their lives were like or what they should do without understanding their situation. To understand another person's situation, you need to stand in their shoes.

As the good book says, "Judge not, lest ye be judged." I didn't really think I was judging them, but that's what they thought, and so that was their situation as it related to me. I knew I had to set them straight or I'd be looking over my shoulder for the rest of the school year.

Naturally, I didn't tell my parents I was going to confront those boys because they would have told me not to do it. I just had a gut feeling about what I needed to do, and the sooner I did it, the better.

The next day when they got on the school bus, they gave me the evil eye, walked all the way down the aisle, and sat in the very last row. If looks were knives, they'd have cut me again.

I was sitting in the front row like I always did, shifting gears for my uncle when he hit the clutch. My uncle lived next door and drove the school bus, which he parked between our house and his. He taught me how to drive a stick shift on that bus. I'd get up early every morning and put the windows down, since it didn't have air conditioning. At the end of the day, I'd clean the bus and put the windows back up again.

For doing all that, my uncle paid me a quarter at the end of the day, which was actually a lot of money for a kid my age in those days. I could buy a bottle of soda pop and a candy bar and get a nickel back in change.

I guess I must have seemed a little nervous because my uncle kept looking over at me like he wanted to ask what was bothering me. But he let me be, and when he pulled up in front of the school, I grabbed the handle and opened the door to jump out before he'd completely stopped the bus.

When the two brothers stepped off last, they looked pretty surprised to see me standing there waiting for them. Impressed, even. For a moment, no one spoke. I had plenty to say, but I was also ready to run if they pulled out another knife. They didn't.

"Look, I wasn't telling anybody what you did or didn't do," I said, "because I don't know what you did or didn't do. Somebody just mentioned that thing with your father, and I said I would've done something different, that's all. But you didn't have no business pulling a knife."

They looked at each other and then back to me. "You tell anybody about that?"

"The knife?"

"Yeah."

"Just my parents."

One of them looked mad, and the other looked nervous. It was the nervous brother who spoke. "What'd they say?"

I shrugged. "Said I could handle it." Which wasn't exactly true, but it was true enough, I guess.

They seemed to relax when I said that. I think they were impressed again, this time by the thought of parents who would allow their child to 'handle' something like being attacked with a knife.

I knew then that I'd done the right thing by seeking them out to talk. I could tell that they didn't have the same kind of family environment that I had, which I guess should have been obvious all along.

It was another learning experience for me: In the future, it would be a good idea to get all the facts before I opened my mouth, and I was actually pretty good at conflict resolution. I was a good talker. I was beginning to understand the benefits of de-escalation. It sure beat getting stabbed, anyway.

A couple of years before all that happened, I'd accidentally shot my friend Glen with a BB gun and hit him right above his eye. It scared him more than anything, but he told his mother, and she told my mother, and then my mother and I had a very serious talk.

"You know how folks say you could put someone's eye out with that stick or that rock or that gun?"

I nodded. "Yes, ma'am."

"You almost did it, Man."

"I know, Mama."

She looked at me intently. "Do you?" she asked. "Do you really know?"

I didn't, of course. I had no idea how it would have felt to blind my friend, or be blinded myself, but I took a minute to really think about it, like my mother asked, and I knew afterward that it would have been terrible. Life changing, even. One careless moment could have changed both of us forever.

It's not always enough to put yourself in another man's shoes. Sometimes you have to consider what *you'd* be like if you were wearing a different pair.

If I hadn't been blessed with the parents I had, maybe I would have been the one pulling knives on classmates.

"Do you remember those chips, Man?"

I grinned a little sheepishly. "Yes, ma'am."

"All your friends went in that store and stole a bag, didn't they?"

"Yes, ma'am."

"And that included you."

I nodded.

"But what'd you do after?"

I thought back to that day. There were only two stores in town, so it was pretty stupid to steal from either one of them, but peer pressure being what it is, I went along with my friends and ran out with a bag of Fritos without paying.

The stupid thing was that I had money in my pocket. I could have paid.

I nearly got in a fight over it, but I felt so bad, I ran back to the store and told the owner what I'd done, and I returned the unopened bag of chips.

He looked down at me, scowling. "Get out of here."

"I never stole anything before in my life, sir," I said.

"Get out of my store!"

I thought I'd feel better after returning the chips, but somehow I felt even worse. I knew I needed to confess to a higher authority.

That night at supper, I told my family what I'd done. My sister looked surprised but not my parents. I expected punishment, but instead they both told me they were proud of what I'd done.

"*But I stole, Mama!*"

"*And you went back, Man,*" *my mother said.* "*You made it right.*"

My daddy nodded. "*You did good, Son.*"

I can still remember how good it felt to hear those words.

I went back to the store the next day to properly apologize to the owner, but he shook his head 'no.' He'd calmed down since the day before and told me pretty much the same thing my parents had told me. "*You did the right thing.*"

Then he shook my hand and even thanked me for stopping by, and he never watched me when I was in the store like I saw him do with some of the other kids. He didn't need to because he trusted me.

After that, I couldn't have stolen a loaf of bread from the man if I was starving. *Because he trusted me.*

That changes a person. It changes a child, it changes a player, it changes everything.

There are consequences to everything we do and everything we say. Sometimes the consequences will be positive, and sometimes they'll be negative. A single decision we make in haste, a single moment in time, can change our entire lives. It's important for us to be prepared for those moments, whichever way they go.

And when we make a mistake or take a wrong turn, it's important for us, as much as we can, to go back and make things right.

CHAPTER EIGHT

"The world is before you... you need not take it or
leave it as it was before you came in."
James Baldwin

I REMEMBER WATCHING FOOTBALL GAMES on TV with my
family after church on Sundays. Whenever there was a really
great touchdown, I mean some kind of circus catch or long,
broken field run, I'd turn to my mama and say, "One day you're
gonna be watching *me* do that."

"Mm-hmm."

"On the TV," I repeated. "*I'll* be scoring touchdowns."

"I know, Man."

"I mean it, Mama."

"I know you do, Man," she'd say. "I mean it, too. You think I'd
say it if I didn't?"

"No, ma'am."

"Well, all right then. I can't wait to see you on TV, scoring all
those touchdowns. I'm looking forward to it, Man."

And I believed her.

Of course my mother was required to say that because she was my mother, but I was very serious about it at the time, and I know she was, too. My parents believed in me and my abilities 100 percent from the moment I first stepped onto the field, and that made a big difference in my life. A difference I carried into adulthood. I always had plenty of natural athletic ability, but a kid needs that kind of emotional support, as well. Because no matter how good you are, there will be disappointments. You will win and you will lose, and losing can be awful tough. Hey, even winning can be tough.

All the natural ability in the world won't take you where you need to be unless you're willing to put in the work. The discipline you need to do that work is almost always going to begin with how you've been raised. To play at an elite level means getting your mind and body right and in sync, and that takes a lot of work. It takes a lot of practice. Discipline. Dedication. Emotion. Control. All the things that are easy to say and difficult to achieve.

As hard as you think success will be, you'll only wish it was that easy. Getting to the mountaintop is *hard*.

Athletic excellence is difficult to attain and even harder to *main*tain. A young athlete starting out needs all the support he or she can get if they want to reach an elite status, if they want to score touchdowns on TV. Most people never come close, but everybody dreams about it. It may not be touchdowns, but it's something. Everybody dreams, and they start when they're kids. So parents are a big part of that. A parent can shape the dreams of their child or smother them.

I have been recruiting and coaching elite athletes for most of my life. Hey, I *was* an elite athlete, and I can always tell the ones who have the necessary kind of support at home. Of course I go into the homes on recruiting trips and see the environment for myself, but the support I'm talking about doesn't show up in a fancy swimming pool or an expensive set of weights. It comes from the heart. I can feel that emotional support flowing out of the best parents in waves as soon as I walk in that door. Most of them are single-parent households, too. *Some of the poorest families in wealth raise the richest children in spirit.*

Now, every parent loves their child, no matter what their abilities. But the parents of an elite athlete always show me a little something more. A little bit of extra shine. Because they *know* their child is special. They *know* their child has a gift.

I'm sure the parents of piano prodigies or computer geniuses have that same quality. To know your child has been blessed with a talent that surpasses the average human being is an awesome thing, and it carries an awesome responsibility. God's gifts are not to be wasted.

But there are no guarantees. We're all born with certain tools, and it's up to us to decide how we use them. I planned to use mine to score touchdowns for my mother. On TV. Never hurts to think big, right?

When I was at Marchand Elementary in Darrow, if I wanted to play, I played. No one was left out; the team was whoever wanted to be on the team. And I excelled there.

The first time I actually had to try out to play was at East Ascension Junior High, which was about ten or eleven miles away in Gonzales. All the Marchand kids went there, along with other area feeder schools. I was pretty excited to move up in the world. Besides being good at sports, I had also done very well academically. I even got thirty bucks for being the second smartest kid at the seventh grade graduation.

I can't remember who they said the smartest was, but I guarantee I thought I was just as smart. I've never been accused of having low self-esteem! So, I was eager to show those folks in the big city (five or six thousand at least) what I could do.

I loved basketball, but I *really* loved football, and I made the eighth grade team at tailback and cornerback because I was really, really fast and had really good hands.

The school was kind of elite as junior high schools go because I think the ninth grade football team hadn't lost a game in eight or nine years, so I was really looking forward to being a part of that team the following year. It was my first taste of organized athletics, and I went out for basketball, too.

It was a formative time in my life, as it is for any kid. The school was probably 90 percent white, but I was one of only three black kids in the advanced classes, so I was learning all kinds of new things both on and off the field. Like how people can be very different, but still be pretty much the same.

The school was about thirteen miles from my house, and sometimes my friends and I would walk a couple of miles after practice to the nearby grocery store and then hitchhike home from there. Or maybe walk a little farther and thumb it out on the highway. Seemed like there was usually someone going the way we needed to go, like it is in rural communities. All roads lead home, as they say, and my home was Darrow. I always found a way back.

Sometimes we'd help someone carry in their groceries in exchange for carrying us back to town. Our mothers were supposed to rotate picking us up, but it seemed like mine was the only one who came regularly. My father was deep into politics back then, and he was usually working at that time of day, helping somebody with this or that or attending parish meetings. Small town politicians work hard, at least the ones who care about their people. As a result, my mother became very involved in my sports at that time, and she came to every single game. My father had to miss a few here and there, but he was just as enthusiastic.

When I went out for basketball, I could see right away that there were some very good players competing for a place on the team. The school was pretty big, with maybe fifteen hundred students who came in from the local towns, so there was a lot of competition. Louisianans are very physical people, and we love our sports.

After each practice that first week, Coach Richard Brown made cuts and posted them on the board outside the gym. The list of names went from forty to thirty to twenty pretty fast. It seemed *too* fast to me then, but I can laugh about it now. I'll bet the coach knew pretty much who his starting five would be after watching the first day of calisthenics. It's called coach's instinct.

But I was worried. My name stayed on that list, but the list was getting a whole lot tougher. I saw some really good players on that list, and I wasn't sure I'd make it.

I went home that night and told my mother, "I don't know if I'm gonna make the team."

She looked me in the eye and said, "Is it important to you, Man?"

"Yeah, Mama. It is."

"Then you're going to make it," she said. "Don't you even worry."

I started at point guard that year.

The basketball team turned out to be every bit as competitive as the football team. My old friend Snake was the leading scorer that year, and, man, did we think it was great to play on that wooden floor. Neither one of us had ever done that before. We felt like kings of the court. I'm still friends with most of the guys on that team. A couple of them were in my wedding. I think you don't make friends quite like the ones you make when you're thirteen or fourteen years old.

I worked my tail off that year because there were several guys on the team that I knew were better than I, and I wanted to be the best. I might not end up *being* the best, but I was sure going to make that my goal. That year kind of set the standard for the rest of my athletic career, both as a player and as a coach. I have always wanted to be the best at whatever I do, and it all goes back to that time.

One thing that suffered was my grades. I was so focused on sports that I neglected my studies, which of course was a mistake. But it was one of those mistakes I learned from and became stronger as a result. The consequences of that attitude caused me trouble later on, but I was able to turn that negative into a positive force in my coaching.

I recruit athletes to play basketball, but I stress the importance of an education. As someone who played college sports at an elite level who also has a master's degree, I try and give my players the benefits of the entire experience.

At the end of the school year back in junior high, the coaches gave out awards. Most athletic, most valuable player, most improved, that kind of thing. I got best dressed.

Now you may think that sounds funny, and I guess maybe it does, but I was proud of that award. I have always had a good sense of style, and even back then, I wanted to look good. How you present yourself matters. Looking your best shows pride and confidence.

Besides, I just know I came in second for some of those trophies. After the awards were given out, I was determined to come back the next year and win Most Valuable Player. As a matter of fact, I thought I was going to come back and win *all* the awards. Like I said, it never hurts to think big.

I played pickup games all over the parish that summer, usually with guys older than I. Big, strong, experienced players. A couple of them probably could have played in the NBA. That was food for my game. If you want to improve at anything, hang around people better than you. I wanted to be better than all those guys. And I wanted to dunk the basketball. Not too many guys did that back then.

I was still pretty skinny, but I got into weights and started to fill out. By the end of the summer, I was holding my own against those bigger guys, and my whole perspective on athletics changed. It was one thing to tell my mother that she would see me on TV one day, and it was another thing when I began to actually believe it myself.

I started running. I did a lap around the whole town every day, which was almost exactly a mile. The guy that mowed the Mississippi River levee saw me a few times, and eventually, he cut a path up that hill for my run. I was benching 200 pounds and squatting 220, and I could really see the difference in my body. I went out for football the next year, and by the end of the season, I was starting tailback, and we set the state record for most consecutive wins.

I wasn't worried about making the basketball team anymore. In our first game, I scored 27 points by halftime, which was the school record for most points by a ninth grader for an *entire game*. I was a beast. I couldn't wait to get out there and tear it up in the second half, but Coach Bourgeois made me sit out. He told me the record would be too hard to break. Which made me mad as hell.

Even now, I think he should have let me back in, record or not, but that's the way it was. Records are made to be broken, and I would have destroyed that one. They announced it to the entire school the next day over the loudspeaker that I'd broken the record, but they didn't mention I played only in the first half, which also bothered me.

As you can tell, I was developing a little bit of an attitude.

My father could always keep me humble, though, with tough love and high standards. Just the look on his face when I brought home a C on my report card, which I had been doing more and more lately, was a painful thing to experience. As I've said before, I love my father, but I didn't always like him. He was tougher on me than any coach I've ever had, and I've had some tough ones. *I'm* a tough one. But no one is tougher than my father.

So, I had a great year, but there was a bump in the road every now and then. That's life. You win and you lose, but you keep on playing the game. At the end of the year was when the fireworks really started.

When it came time to give out those awards, I figured that I was a lock for the school's Most Valuable Player. I played both offense and defense in football, even playing quarterback for a while in addition to cornerback and tailback. And as I've already mentioned, I did a lot of scoring at point guard. My name was in the papers all the time, and I had become one of the most popular kids in school. That award isn't a popularity contest, of course, but I had worked hard, played well, and really thought that I had earned the award. A lot of people felt the same way.

I didn't get it. I won't lie. It bothered me a little bit at first. But, to be honest, the player that got it was a very good athlete, so even after all that had happened that year with the scoring record and all, I took it pretty well. I had wanted that award so bad, and now that I didn't get it, it didn't mean all that much, anymore. The difference was that the year before, I really didn't have the confidence I had now. True confidence comes with true ability. Add preparation to the mix, and that eliminates fear and doubt.

The year before was all false bravado. I was an outstanding athlete and I knew it, and that was good enough for me.

So, where did the fireworks come from? My father.

As I mentioned, my name was in the papers a lot for my sports achievements, and so I was well known around the area, not just in school. And the fact was, I probably really did deserve the award that year, and there was talk around town that maybe it was a racial thing.

The school was mostly white, and the boy who got the award was also white. The coach was white.

I didn't necessarily buy it myself, and there was no way I was going to bring it up, but my father wasn't so shy about it. Without my knowing what he was going to do, he went down to the school and raised a little hell.

Now, understand that my father was a politician in the best sense of the word. He was used to dealing with all kinds of people and all kinds of problems. And he never once shied away from a problem. That's not his way. He faced everything head on and did whatever needed to be done. And sometimes, there were problems with racial elements.

He had heard the talk like everyone else, and while he didn't demand anyone change the outcome, he wanted to hear an explanation. My father is a hard man, who's earned everything he has in life. He would be the last person to ask that his son get preferential treatment. *Equal* treatment was a different story.

I walked into the outer office and heard a little of the discussion, and at first I was upset with my father for doing that. I didn't want anyone to treat me any differently than anyone else, and I thought he should have at least told me what he was going to do. When I asked him about it, all he told me was that he'd looked into it and thought something needed to be said.

After that, I saw my father with new eyes. I began to understand how he was outside the family. He was different, but in a good way. He was standing up for what was right. I began to notice more and more how he would help people as part of his job but also understand that it wasn't just a job to him. He was helping people.

Now, when I think of my father walking into that office and speaking to those white men like he did, in a school that was 90 percent white, and telling them he wanted to make sure that not only his son was treated fairly, but every other player as well, I'm filled with pride. Not every man in his position would have done that. It would have been easy for him to just let it go and not make any waves, and I would not have blamed him for that at all. No one would. But that was never his way. My father has never been a man to let something go if he could make it better. He does not pass a problem by. Fairness matters to him in all things, large and small.

Joseph U. Pierre Sr. advocated not just for his son that day but for all the players. And those men treated him with respect because he commanded it. He gave them respect even as he challenged them, which is not always an easy thing to do.

Now, it may seem silly to some people to get all worked up over a sports award at a junior high school, but it was about a lot more than that. For my father, it was about principle, and respect, and fair play.

I keep that story in mind when dealing with my players. When I look at those young men, I remember my father standing up for me the way he did, and that's the way I try to stand up for them. I'm proud to be their coach.

And I'm proud to be Joseph Jr. Even if most folks call me Butch.

CHAPTER NINE

"Inside of a ring or out, ain't nothing wrong with going down.
It's staying down that's wrong."
Mohammad Ali

I HAD BEEN PLAYING BOTH FOOTBALL AND BASKETBALL with the same group of guys since junior high, so by the time we entered high school, we were like a well-oiled machine. We all knew each other and played well together, and we were expected to compete for the Louisiana state championship in *both* sports, which was a very big deal.

But it turned out that sophomore year was my first and last at East Ascension High School. Because of overcrowding and the fact that the junior and senior high schools served such a large area, a new high school was built in Ascension Parish, and the student bodies were to be split up.

After all the drama centered around those end-of-year awards, I was looking forward to settling down and just playing ball, but suddenly I was told that I would be spending the most important years of my high school sports career at a completely different school—St. Amant High School, home of the Gators. I was pissed off.

My father was, too. He tried every way possible to make me happy and allow me to stay at East Ascension High, but what it boiled down to was that, according to district rules, I would have to sit out of sports for a year if I transferred back to my old school.

How is it a transfer if I'm already here? I thought.

To a sixteen year old, sometimes you notice things in the grown up world that just don't make a lot of sense. This was one of those times. It seemed pretty simple to me. The school district needed to let me stay right where I was, and that was that.

Except it wasn't. Everything was changing, and I didn't think it was for the better. For one thing, I didn't think the other team would be as good as the team I was already on. I wanted to play for a winner, but not *just* a winner. A state champion.

You get attention from college scouts when you're an elite player, but when you play on the team that wins the state championship, that's icing on the cake. Every athlete wants that title, I don't care what sport they play or at what level. Everybody wants to be a champion.

And if you get to that championship game and lose, you're not thinking how great it was to get there. All you can think about is that you didn't win. You're not the champion. On that day, you were just the second best team, and that's never good enough for a competitive athlete. Or coach.

Believe me, I know. I had plans and goals, and I felt like they had just been upended, and I didn't like it one bit.

But that's how life goes. Just when you think you have it all figured out, you get a curve ball. A bad pass. A funny bounce. So, what do you do? What do you do when something bad happens?

Something unexpected? In my opinion, there are only two things *to do.* You cry about it or do something with it.

Change happens. There will always be situations when you are not in control, so sometimes you just have to roll with it. Adjust your game. And once you decide to turn those lemons into lemonade, you might find out that it tastes pretty good.

Sometimes you have to *make* it taste good. Add your own sugar. The one thing you always have control of is your attitude. A positive mental attitude will take you a very long way.

The great Langston Hughes once said, "I have discovered in life that there are ways of getting almost anywhere you want to go, if you *really* want to go."

You're preaching to the choir, Brother Langston. But it took me a while to get up to that loft. The coaches and the principals did what they could for me, too. It seemed like everybody wanted me to stay and play ball at East Ascension High School, except for the good Lord and the superintendent of schools.

I have to say that in all my years as a coach, I've met quite a few school superintendents at the high school level and athletic directors at the college level, and I think a few of them thought they *were* God. Except the ones I worked for, of course!

A change of venue wasn't the only change coming, either. I was about to drop a bombshell on my father that tested *his* ability to deal with change, and as it turned out, he didn't like it any more than I did. Like father, like son, I guess.

But my experience dealing with adversity at a young age taught me a lot, and I still use what I learned back then in my coaching today. When my father nearly died, that was a big-time change and major adversity, but my family and I got through it with God's help. So, there was never a question of whether or not I could deal with another school. That's just the way it was, and I had to deal with it.

The new school was in a white area, and so the school was mostly white, too. I would have new teachers, new coaches, new teammates, and have to make a lot of new friends. But there was something else new—the gym.

I don't think I'll ever forget the day I first walked into that gym. As a matter of fact, I remember like it was yesterday. It was the middle of summer and hotter than fish grease when I drove over to the new school to check things out. I pulled into the parking lot and just looked at the buildings for a minute. I had to admit that the place looked pretty impressive from the outside.

I saw a guy in coveralls come out the back door, so I ran over to catch him in case he was leaving. His name was Clark Lambert, and he was one of the janitors as well as a bus driver. He'd been working to get the school ready for its very first day.

I figured if anybody could tell me what was what, he would be the one. To this day, I always get good information from the custodial staff. Throughout my career, whenever I've been hired to coach at a new school, I always seek them out and introduce myself. They do a tough job for not enough pay, and just about every custodian I've met loves the school just as much as its most enthusiastic booster. And they know just about everything there is to know about how things operate.

It doesn't hurt to be friendly with whoever has the keys, either. You never know when you'll need to get into a locked door or figure out if some rumor is true or just gossip. I don't like gossip, but I love truth. And I always appreciate good information.

After we talked a minute or two, I asked him where the gym was. He pointed to a building with a big gold dome, which I would have thought was the administration building or something. It looked like a seat of power. Which I guess it was, when it comes right down to it.

"There she is," he said.

I just looked at that dome and then looked back at Clark. I guess my mouth was hanging open or something, because he kinda chuckled. "Go on over. It's open."

So I did. And the closer I got, the better it looked. But when I walked inside, it wasn't better. It was the *best*.

That was the prettiest high school gym I had ever seen, and it still is. And believe me, as a college recruiter, I have seen *a lot* of high school gyms. Inside and out, it was really special. It really wasn't even a gym; it was more like a coliseum. I was blown away. Just being in there got me excited about my junior year. It revived me.

I forgot all about how worried I was before, about whether or not the team would be any good, and just imagined playing on that court in front of a packed auditorium.

I had my ball with me, so I took a couple of jump shots. Felt really good. So, I went after it, running up and down the court, shooting from all my favorite spots. By the time Clark came back, I'd worked up a pretty good sweat.

"You're the first one," he said.

"First what?"

"First one to shoot on this court."

"*Ever?*"

He laughed. "First one ever," he said.

It turned out that Clark was from the area, and he'd heard of me. He told me everybody was real excited, expecting me to help bring in a state championship.

I saw an opening, and I took it. "You know, I'd like to work out here every day, Clark. But I get up real early." *Which was true. And I still get up early every day.*

"What, you want a key?"

"Oh, I'm gonna get a key?" I replied, and we laughed. He didn't give me a key, but he told me when he came in every day, and I was almost always waiting for him when he drove up in the morning.

I worked out there every day for the rest of the summer. I couldn't get enough. Sometimes dedication is as simple as being excited to do what you love, and I loved playing basketball. And I loved that gym. That was my house all summer.

One day when I was shooting, this guy walked in and just watched me for a while. I didn't know who he was, so I just kept shooting. After a couple of minutes, he called out to me. "You Butch Pierre?"

I stopped. "Yeah," I said. "Who are you?"

He walked over and stuck out his hand. "I'm Tommy Wall."

I shook his hand. "Good to meet you, Tommy Wall," I said, and then I just went back to shooting and doing drills. I didn't know who Tommy Wall was, but he watched my whole workout.

When I was finished, I grabbed my gear and walked to the door, but he called me back. "Hey, Butch, can I talk to you for a minute?"

I walked over to where he was standing. "What's up?"

"I just wanted to let you know that I'm the head basketball coach here."

"Really?"

"That's right."

"Okay."

"I'm gonna be coaching you," he said, "but I'm gonna need your help, too."

"What you need me to help with, Coach?"

"Let's sit down a minute," he said, and we walked over to the first row of bleachers and sat down. "I've heard about you and your family."

"Okay."

"All good things," he continued. "And what I want you to help me with is this: I've never coached black players before. My teams have been all white."

I nodded. "No problem, Coach," I said. "I can do that."

"You can help me out?"

"Yes, sir," I said. "I came here to win a state championship."

"Me too," he answered, smiling, and then stood up. "All right then."

Coach Wall put his arm around my shoulder like a father would do to his son and walked me to the door. When we got there, I turned to him said, "We're gonna make this work, Coach."

"I believe you're right, Butch."

Tommy Wall turned out to be one of my all-time favorite coaches. I loved that man, and everybody else did, too. He was a great coach, a terrific motivator, and he got along well with everybody. He understood how to establish relationships with his players. He made us into a team and a family. He was a real coach's coach, respected by all.

You know you have a great coach if you learn about coaching, just playing for the man. I wasn't planning on becoming a coach back then, but once I did, I found out how much I'd learned from Tommy Wall about coaching without even realizing it.

When August rolled around, the football team started practice. I was expected to start both ways, cornerback and wide receiver.

But I'd been doing a lot more than practicing my jumper in the gym all summer. I'd also been doing a lot of thinking. I went to my father just before school started and told him I needed to talk to him.

"So, talk," he said.

"Let's sit down."

He didn't ask why. He just followed me into the living room, where my mother was already sitting. I took a deep breath and just got it out. "I've decided to focus just on basketball," I said. "I won't be playing football."

My father didn't take it very well. "You're quitting football?" he exploded. "Who you been talking to?"

"Nobody, I just decided…"

"What's wrong with you? You got speed, power—you got it all! Why would you quit?"

"I just want to… "

"You're making a mistake, Son!" he thundered. "A big mistake!"

That was when my mom got into the conversation. "Let him talk."

"He's not talking sense!"

"It's his decision."

"He could play in the NFL!"

"Hey, he wants to play basketball, he's going to play basketball," she said firmly. "You just need to be quiet."

My father was so mad, he left the room, and then he left the house. He knew my mother was right.

But my father was also right. I *could* have played in the NFL. I was a better football player. But I loved basketball more, and I wanted to be as good at that as I was at football.

When my father came home, he'd calmed down considerably. That was the first time he'd exploded on me like that, and I think he knew it was wrong. But he'd played football, and he really wanted me to succeed. That's the hope of any parent, no matter what their child chooses as a profession. To go further than they did. To do better.

"You sure about this, Son?" he asked.

I nodded.

"Well, you need to tell the football coach," he said. "You know that's going to be an issue."

That was an understatement, to say the least. Football is *everything* in Louisiana.

"I'll tell him, Dad."

"You want me to go with you?"

"I got it," I said.

Even though it was painful for him to give up the dream of seeing his son in the NFL, I think he was proud I didn't need his help to take responsibility for my decision. I'm glad he offered to go, but it was better he didn't. He knew I had to follow my own path. Set my own goals. Strive for my own dream. And the sooner I did that, the better.

Before I went to the school to tell the coach, both my parents told me that they had confidence in me, and they trusted my decision, which of course made me feel like I had made the right one. That's called positive reinforcement.

I went into the coaches' office with my head held high.

The coaches didn't take it much better than my dad. "Who have you been talking to?" Coach Webb demanded. "Did Wall put you up to this?"

I guess he thought Coach Wall wanted me all for himself. "No, sir," I answered. "This is my decision."

"We'll see about that!"

Coach Bourgeois had been one of the assistant football coaches and also the junior high basketball coach when I set that scoring record. I almost told him he shouldn't have taken me out at halftime, but instead all I said was, "I guess we will."

They tried everything they could to get me to change my mind. They begged, pleaded, and threatened. One of the coaches even told me that I couldn't play basketball if I didn't play football, too.

"Wait a minute, now," I said. "How's that gonna happen?"

"I'm gonna call your father."

"You might as well skip that 'cause I already told him."

Coach Webb did call my father, and my father did sit me down and ask me again if I was sure. He agreed with the football coach that I was making a mistake. But I wanted a scholarship, and I thought the best way to get it was to focus on one sport.

And I just loved basketball more.

"I'm sure, Dad."

"All right," he said, and he never questioned it again.

That was one of the very few times in my life that my father told me he thought I was making a mistake. He always trusted my judgment, and while he would tell me what he thought was the right decision, he always told me it was my choice to make. And he never threw it back in my face, even if he was proven right.

So, was he proven right? Would I have made it to the NFL?

It's impossible to know. Every choice leads to another, and then another, and then another. Every day, we make dozens of decisions, large and small, and all we can do is choose as well as we can, and make the best of what comes.

Like Langston said, "...there are ways of getting almost anywhere you want to go, if you *really* want to go." I have a beautiful wife, and we have three terrific kids. If my choices led me here, then they were the right ones.

ATTITUDE

Attitude is an integral part of success. A great basketball player creates a winning attitude simply by playing great. He or she plays well, and by doing so creates the inevitability, probability, or at the very least, the possibility of winning every game.

A game has a predetermined expiration, but life is different. In life, things are not always so clear-cut.

A businessman's skills for success may not be as readily visible as a great jump shot. A student taking a physics exam may believe the answers are all correct, but that test still needs to be graded. The businessman makes a great deal but then has to run the business. The student passes the exam but then must write the thesis to get the degree.

Life is not a zero-sum game, and there is no expiration time, save the obvious. Life goes on, and if we want to achieve success as we progress, we need to create a winning attitude.

A winning attitude doesn't mean we always win. It means we *know how* to win. It also means we need to know how to lose.

Knowing how to win means understanding the fundamentals of the game we're playing, the business in which we're engaged, the subject we study. It means constantly being open to learning more about ourselves and what we do.

Knowing how to lose is how we react when things don't go our way.

CHAPTER TEN

"It is easier to build strong children than
to repair broken men."
Frederick Douglass

H UEY LONG'S MOTTO WAS 'EVERY MAN A KING,' and according to some people, at least, he acted like one. As governor of Louisiana, he had a well-known reputation for speaking his mind. A reputation for ambition and drive. Everybody who knew his name knew his reputation. Some folks thought he was a populist, and some thought he was a demagogue, but there's no doubt in anyone's mind that he created his reputation by word and deed and cultivated that persona his entire life.

Treat your reputation with respect because that will be the only thing some people remember about you. Sometimes it's all you got.

But if men are kings, they wouldn't get much done without queens. Most people don't remember that the entire slogan, which Huey actually borrowed from William Jennings Bryan, was "Every man a king but no man wears a crown."

My mother was my father's queen. She was always by his side. They complemented each other in practically every way you can imagine, from talent to temperament.

They each knew their role, and they each fulfilled their responsibility to their marriage and to our family. You might say they both knew who wore the pants in the family, but they both agreed with Huey about that crown.

My father was reelected every four years for three decades, and that kind of success doesn't happen by accident. My mother, besides working her own job until she retired, was like an unelected assistant to my father. She could type ninety words a minute on a Smith-Corona manual, go sixty with a pad and pen, and all those words, whether typewritten or written shorthand, came absolutely free of charge to the taxpayers of Ascension Parish. She could put those words together pretty well, too, whether on paper or in person. I always thought she could have been a great writer if she wasn't so busy with everything else. Also best creole cook in the world.

My mother also had a great memory for names, faces, and phone numbers, which any politician will tell you is an invaluable skill, or at least it was back in the days before we put our lives in the hands of our cell phones.

The people elected my father, but they knew they were getting my mother as part of the deal. My parents were partners in every sense of the word, and a great example for both my sister and me and anyone else who knew them.

I always told my mom that she was the smart one, and she'd just smile like I had told her a joke, but she never disagreed. She was a big help to my father in every way.

He needed it, too. It was a big job, or at least it was the way he did it.

As one of the first black elected officials in the parish, there was always a lot of pressure on my dad to produce results. The people he represented might not have expected too much from the white men who came before him, but my father was one of them, and so they expected a lot. And because he was just as attentive to what the white folks needed, they depended on him, too. He treated them all with respect, and he was respected by all in return. And like I said, *with respect comes responsibility.*

Whenever my father got a call about a problem, that problem was on the road to being solved by the time he hung up the phone. And there were a lot of calls over the years, at all hours of the day and night. Everybody in the parish had our number, and my father never failed to answer the phone.

When someone called looking for a job, he did his best to find one. He put a lot of people to work. When he was first elected, there wasn't a single paved street in our district, but he got all those gravel roads paved. He got streetlights put in, so the kids wouldn't have to go trick-or-treating in the pitch dark. He also got a community center built.

For twenty-eight years, hardly anything happened in Ascension Parish in the way of progress that my father didn't have something to do with, and he never asked for anything in return except for a paycheck.

And believe me, he could have gotten a lot more than that. Plenty of elected officials didn't always operate on the up and up, if you know what I mean.

Politics in Louisiana can be like boiling crawfish. You have to know when and how to stir the pot. My father knew how to stir that pot to get things done for his constituents, which meant he brought a lot of money into the parish over the years to do all those things that needed to get done. But he never stirred the pot for himself.

Politics in Louisiana can also be like a fish fry. There's always going to be folks coming by that buffet table with their plate out, waiting for someone to fill it up, even though they didn't catch anything, clean anything, or fry anything. And they don't plan on washing up anything afterward, either. All they want to do is fill their belly.

Some politicians show up only when they want votes and are never seen again until the next election. Some are just in it for themselves, plain and simple. You do a little something for someone here and there, and maybe a little something extra comes back to you from time to time.

My father never accepted any favors, no matter how small, because he never wanted to owe anybody anything. He was beholden to no one except the voters.

"Don't get in the habit of owing people," he'd say. "That's a bad habit to have."

And because he conducted himself in that way, his reputation was that of a man who got things done, and so it was a given that he would always do exactly that. It became part of who he was.

In every conversation and interaction he ever had, there was always the understanding that my father was a righteous man. That was his reputation, and it was undisputed. That was the secret to his success.

And the thing about success is that once you achieve it, you have to maintain it. Otherwise, you're just a fluke. And no one wants that kind of reputation.

Coaches live this their entire careers. Every game is a new opportunity for success or failure, every season another chance to prove yourself. One year, you're in the Final Four, and the next you're out of the tournament. The real measure of success is how you deal with either situation.

How you act on the mountaintop determines how you behave in the valley. Nobody likes a poor loser or an arrogant winner, and the way you take wins and losses reveals your character. And character is essential to both.

It's easy to be the toast of the town, but sometimes you're just toast.

Character is what we have, no matter what the final score, and since nobody wins all the time, your character will get you through the tough times. Character is your fallback position in life, just like preparation and ability are what you depend on in a game.

Talent or luck can save a win. Character can save your life.

My father worked hard when he was first elected, but he never coasted on his reputation. He kept working hard his entire career. We build our reputations early, and then we spend a lot of time living up or down to our creation. I tell my players to be very careful with their actions because those actions can follow them their entire life.

How we are perceived is not always in our control. But we can control what we do. As the Good Book says, 'by our actions we shall be judged.'

The Bible also says, 'a good reputation is worth more than silver or gold.' We create a reputation within our families, too. We develop our family role with expectations. A family is a team, and we all play a role in its success. We create expectations that our family expects us to fulfill.

Every year, my father would borrow $500 in December so our family could have a good Christmas, and then he'd spend the entire year paying that money back so he could do it all over again.

None of us would have been mad if he had wanted to skip a year and not work quite so hard over the coming months, but that wasn't my father. He created our expectations, and he never failed to live up to them. His role was to provide certain things, and that's what he did, without complaint.

He built his reputation and lived up to it every single day. He lived up to what was expected of him as a husband and father, and as a man and a politician. He understood the importance of his actions in every situation.

Sometimes, it's hard for a young person to get that, which is why mentors are so important. A young person needs someone to look up to, someone to set an example, someone who's been there before. Parents, teachers, coaches, mentors, all are very important in the development of young lives. Sometimes, a kid needs to talk to someone outside the family, or someone unconnected to the team. Someone with a little distance, but still able to provide good advice and counsel. Father Young was someone like that for me.

Most families in town were Southern Baptists or basically Methodists who didn't admit to drinking or dancing. We were one of the few Catholic families in Darrow, and to Catholics, especially in a small town, your priest becomes a very important part of your life. Catholics from all over the parish came to Darrow to attend St. Anthony's, so we were blessed that the church was only about four blocks down the main highway from our home.

I made my first confession when I was about thirteen years old, and if you know or remember anything about being a teenage boy, you know I had plenty of things to discuss. I really liked confession, too. There was something about it that felt so liberating: to be able to unload the burden of my sins to Father Young and start fresh as soon as our conversation was over. Well, after I'd done whatever penance he assigned, that is. And there was always a lot more to tell him the next time!

Father Young was easy to talk to, and we became very close. My entire family loved him. He had come to visit my father many times in the hospital during his recovery to give communion and pray and just to visit. Father Young was everything you'd want a priest to be— a spiritual advisor, a confessor, and a friend. Talking to my priest became a very special part of my life and still is to this day.

When I was growing up, I could tell my mother anything, but sometimes she would listen to what I had to say and decide I needed some spiritual guidance. "Go see what Father Young has to say," she'd tell me. So that's what I'd do.

Father Young lived in a house connected to the church, and the church was open all the time, so I felt like his door was always open for me, too. He was that kind of priest, and it was that kind of church. No door was ever closed, and no one was ever turned away. Father Young was always there for me, as he was for everyone.

During my senior year in high school, I really needed that. I turned my ankle right before the start of the season, which was a very big deal. I was a standout player and expected a scholarship, and there were going to be all kinds of scouts coming around. But now I was going to miss the first two games of the season. I rested up, and just when my ankle was feeling better, I twisted the other one.

What happened was I stole the ball in a game right after I started playing again and went up to dunk over another player, and he pushed me while I was in the air. I landed wrong and turned my good ankle really badly.

This time I could barely even walk.

Truthfully, I was probably doing a little showboating. I admit it. There were three high major college coaches there that night to see me play, including Dale Brown from LSU, which made it even more painful when I went down. But I was just so happy to be back on that court. I got caught up in what you call youthful exuberance. But all it got me was another injury. And a player can get a reputation for being injury prone, too. It's not just your own mistakes that follow you. Sometimes it's things completely out of your control. The only thing good about it was that it was near the end of the game, and I'd played well to that point.

It wasn't anybody's fault, really. That's just the way things happen, sometimes. But I got very depressed and emotional about it because I was really looking forward to showing those recruiters what I could do. I wanted them to see me at my best. I *needed* them to see that. I wanted a basketball scholarship more than just about anything I'd ever wanted in my young life.

The only thing I had ever prayed harder about was when my father was in that hospital. Now, life and death is one thing, and sports is something else. Everything I've accomplished as a player and a coach pales in comparison to the people I love. But to a kid like me in that situation, anything that prevented me from reaching my goal to play college ball felt like the end of the world.

If you've ever been young, you know that feeling. You don't have to be an athlete. It could be a test grade or a role in the school play or a girl you got a crush on. When you're young, you want what you want, and you don't always have the wisdom to know how to react when you don't get it.

The added dimension for an elite athlete is that you are supposed to be able to get it. People expect you to get it. That's why you train. That's what makes you elite.

But it's one thing to know you're capable of doing great things, and it's another to be able to do those things at the right moment. An elite athlete has to perform at the highest level when it counts. That's why you push yourself through thousands of hours of drills and practices. That's why you lift and run and shoot, over and over and over. That's why you sacrifice your time and your mind and your body to that court or that field.

You do all of that so that you can make that basket, or block that shot, or grab that rebound, or get that pass to your teammate. So you can do whatever you need to do whenever it needs to get done. So you can do it at just the right moment.

Timing, as they say, is everything. Ask a sprinter who lost a medal by a thousandth of a second. Ask a shooter who bounced one off the rim at the buzzer.

Then find the sprinter who made the podium by a lean. Or the shooter who hit nothing but net before that buzzer sounded. Those answers can change your life.

This was the first time I'd been hurt, and it was the worst time to get hurt. When the spotlight came my way, I was ready. And then I wasn't.

It was a big deal to everybody. The other players, the coaches, the fans. It was in the newspaper, people were asking me about it all the time, it was everywhere. I couldn't get away from it for a second.

Everybody had advice or some kind of remedy to get me fixed up, too. My Creole grandma crushed up an old dirt dauber, which was a wasp's nest that looked like a piece of rusty old pipe, mixed it up with some vinegar, and then spread that mess all over my ankle. I don't know what that did, but I was willing to try anything.

All of this really affected me. It changed my whole personality for a little while.

I didn't know it at the time, but I was getting a taste of the pressure my recruits feel when I bring them into big-time college athletics.

This was a high school team in small town in Louisiana before the Internet, and I felt pressure on top of my disappointment. I was putting a lot of it on myself, as all athletes do, but it was there.

So, you can imagine what these college players feel today, eighteen years old and their names are known all over the country, or even the world, and they're expected to perform on that stage and never make a mistake. At the age when you're supposed to be able to make mistakes so you can learn from them.

That kind of pressure can mess with a young man's head. I was finally getting my chance to show everybody what I could do, and suddenly, I wasn't sure I'd be able to do it.

So, what happens when a seventeen-year-old kid thinks the world is going to end? What does he do? How does he react?

In my case, I may have been down, but I didn't stay there. You can never stay down in a situation like that. If you do, you're lost. When you get knocked down, you have to pick yourself up. The longer you're on that floor, the harder it is to get back up. Some people even get comfortable down there.

So, what did I do? I went to my priest and got me some good old-fashioned spiritual guidance. And I prayed. A lot.

Father Young was great. He didn't talk down to me or say, "It's only basketball," or anything like that. He knew how important it was to me. He just prayed with me for healing and told me that everything was going to be okay.

And he was right. I ended up having a great senior year, got a scholarship to a fine school, and I played big-time college basketball. My mother even got to see me on TV, just like I had promised. It all worked out.

But in that moment of adversity, I could have gone either way. I could have let anger and depression take over, and things could have turned out differently. It was one of those moments that could have defined my life for good or bad, depending on how I reacted. One of those moments that can make or break a reputation. Fortunately, I had the support I needed, and I fought through it.

But there would be more injuries in my future, and there would be times when things didn't work out in the way I desired.

Sometimes, I think that was a trial run so I would be able to deal with what the Lord had in store for me later on. And I'm sure I'll see more adversity like that before I leave this earth.

Even so, I'm still going to pray, and I'm still going to thank the Lord for whatever He puts in front of me, no matter how tough it gets. If you thank God for the blessings, you have to thank Him for the other stuff, too. Because to tell you the truth, it's all a blessing. Just being alive is a blessing.

Sometimes things work out in ways that lead you to places you never expected to go. Better places. Different places. That's life. No one gets through unscathed. It's up to all of us to make the best of every situation. It's a cliché, but life is what we make it.

I'm grateful to this day that my mother insisted I go see Father Young when I was at my lowest point. Sitting out with an injury at that important time really could have had a negative impact on my thinking. I could have acted out and done something that damaged my reputation. Something that could have followed me around, maybe even changed my life for the worse.

My mother could tell, as she always could, that I was struggling, and she knew just the right words to say. Even today, every now and then, she'll ask me if I've spoken to Father Young lately, and if I haven't, she knows exactly what to tell me. "Better give him a call, Man."

I talk to Father Young at least once a year. I *always* do what my mother tells me.

CHAPTER ELEVEN

*"Coach was always there for me…by teaching me…
basketball, he taught me about life."*
Michael Jordan

LOOKING BACK, I think my father was probably right about my decision to quit football. I would have been an outstanding wide receiver. To tell you the truth, there's a good chance I would have done even better at football than I did at basketball, even though at the time I was one of the best high school basketball players in the state.

But, as they say, hindsight is 20-20. There's not one of us that can't look back over our lives and wonder 'what if.' What if I had done this or what if I had done that? Would things have been different for me? Would I have achieved greater success?

Those questions are a waste of time. The only reason to dwell on your past is to improve your future. You work hard and keep moving forward. You learn your lessons and move on.

We never know where life is going to take us, and the lesson I took from that time in my life is not that I made the wrong decision, but that I had the guts to make a choice, stick with it, and give it everything I had.

I not only made a decision, but I committed to that decision, too. And once I commit to anything, I do not stop. I do not give up. I'm like the terminator. When I want something, I go after it. That's how I played the game, that's how I coach, that's how I live my life. I want the best for my children and for my players, so I always do everything I can to set an example of commitment as a parent and as a coach.

That doesn't mean you don't make a change if circumstances warrant. Being committed doesn't mean you ignore the world around you. To achieve true excellence, you must commit, and you must be relentless in your quest. But you must also cultivate an ability to adapt.

In the 1991 NBA finals, Michael Jordan took a pass at the top of the key and saw an open lane to the basket. He drove two steps in and went airborne to dunk the ball, saw the Lakers' Sam Perkins on his right, and switched hands under the basket, flipping in a left-handed layup against the glass.

That's commitment in a nutshell. You set your goals, and then you do what you have to do to achieve them. You evolve. Sometimes, a right-handed dunk turns into a left-handed layup, but either way you get 2 points.

Going to one sport was an important decision for me at that age, but I was committed to staying the course. My goals were a scholarship, the NBA, and for my mother to see me play on TV. I switched my position, but the goal was the same.

I guess you can figure out which one of those goals turned out to be the most impactful, because that's the one that's still a big part of my life today. When my mother's in the stands, it's always special. But knowing she can watch me courtside even when we're far away makes all the hard work to get there worthwhile.

After I made the decision to focus only on basketball, things calmed down quite a bit. Coach Wall was very happy about it, obviously, but the other guys on the football team weren't. They wanted me on the field with them, which I understood. We'd been teammates since elementary school, and I was a star player. I had to do some explaining, but they supported me in the end because they were my friends and because they knew that once I put my mind to something, they weren't going to be able to talk me out of it, anyway.

And it felt good at the time, it really did. I don't know why people are so indecisive sometimes, because when you set a path for yourself, it almost always makes things better. A man who knows where he's going is a man who's halfway there.

I devoted myself to basketball, working harder than I ever had before. The school janitors, Hank and Clark, would open the gym for me every day to work out. Most of the time it was just me, but sometimes I'd bring some of the other players.

I enjoyed talking to Clark and Hank because I recognized they were hard-working men who got up every day and did their job without complaint, just like my father. I've always respected that kind of dedication. Often you find the hardest working people in the most unpretentious occupations.

And like I said, if you want to find out what's really going on at a school, just talk to the custodial staff. Almost always good, hard-working people. Status may draw my attention, but calluses earn my respect.

Coach Wall and I developed a great relationship. We'd talk about what kind of team we could have and how tough the district was, which was very tough, indeed.

We were in one of the most competitive districts in the state, so Coach Wall was looking for any advantage he could find. He'd ask me all about the other players and their strengths and weaknesses, letting me help him figure things out. He knew the other players looked up to me because I was a no-nonsense kind of guy when it came to basketball, and I could tell he was a driven man. Coach Wall wanted to do everything he could think of to win, and I thrived under his leadership and guidance. He was just the kind of coach I needed at that time in my life, and I think he needed a player like me, too.

Basketball really started to take over my life at that point. My grades were just average around that time, which was a big change from before, but I was obsessed with the game of basketball. As it turned out, most of the team was playing only one sport, just like I was, so Coach Wall had really high hopes for us. He could see we were really good players, but there was also that extra something that you don't always get with a team, at least not right away.

We developed a real kinship almost immediately. Just like Coach Wall and I had gelled right away, the team worked well together almost from the first day of practice. We became very close, and the entire school supported us all the way, from the students to the teachers to the custodial staff.

I really enjoyed my leadership role. I didn't know it then, but I was already showing an affinity for coaching. When the local sporting goods store gave me free shoes, I went to the principal and made sure my teammates got the good shoes, too. If someone didn't have a way home after a late practice, I'd give him a ride. And I made sure nobody had anything in his pockets that might get us into trouble if we got pulled over. Some things never change, I guess.

We didn't do as well that first year as I'd hoped. We had some decent guys, but we went only 10-20 my junior year, which I have to admit is pretty sorry.

We had Nat Spears at center. He was 6'7". We were tight. Chopper Williams was a little guy who almost never stopped talking unless he was eating, and even then it was debatable. His big brother Snake was 6'3". You already know Snake. Reggie Weems, Pernell Jones, Greg Perkins and I were all around 6'2". And our one white player was Shane Harris at 6'5". John "Hot Rod" Williams was 6'9", but he didn't play much back then, even though he'd go on to star in the NBA. His mama called him Hot Rod because when he cried, he revved up and dropped down like a dragster waiting on green. I heard it only once, but I have to admit it sounded pretty funny.

Even though the team didn't do very well, I averaged nearly 25 points a game and made first team All-District point guard.

Our biggest game that year was against Capital High in Baton Rouge, which had the best record in the district. Their top player was Tyrone Black, who would be District MVP that year and go on to play for the LSU team that made the Final Four in 1981 when he was a sophomore.

It was a packed house in Baton Rouge, the best vs the worst in the district, but we made a game of it. Even though we lost, I scored 39 points and kept us in it until the very end, which got a lot of attention. I still remember shaking hands after the game and the look in Tyrone's eye, which I gave right back to him: RESPECT.

We may have been the worst team in the district that year in terms of wins and losses, but we pushed the best team that night. We didn't make it easy for them.

But the best memory of all was after the game when I spoke to the team. Everybody played their hearts out, not just I, and I was pretty emotional about it. Sometimes no matter how hard you fight, you come up short. But if you leave it all out on the court, that's a win, no matter what the scoreboard says at the end. And that's kind of what I said to the team.

"Keep your head up," I said. "I don't wanna see nobody looking down at the floor. Ain't nothing to be ashamed of. Nothing! Next year we're gonna work hard and pack the house and win district and then come back here and beat their ass!"

The team was pretty revved up by that point. I may have even heard Hot Rod hit the gas. "We're gonna make everybody excited to see *us*!"

That was the emotional highlight of the season for us as a team, and for me as an individual. I had never given a speech like that in my life, but it all poured out as naturally as if I'd had it waiting my entire life.

That was the first time I realized I had a talent for real leadership. I had inspired my teammates on the court and lifted them up after a tough loss. It felt good to see their eyes filled with fire.

As a coach, I love to see that fire in my players, and I can trace it all back to that night. A tough loss that was a win in disguise. Once Coach Wall got us all calmed down, he led us in prayer, and we walked out of the gym together. Coach Tommy Wall put his arm around my shoulder and told me he was proud of me, which meant a lot. I remember that moment, too.

As a coach, you have a huge influence on your players. They look up to you, and from that height, your words and actions can hurt or heal, inspire or discourage. Had Coach Wall reacted negatively when we lost that close game, it would have affected us in an entirely different way. But he got the best out of us that night. And I got the best out of my teammates.

I was becoming influential in the community, but I really didn't understand it that way at the time. I was just a kid trying to do my best, who didn't want to disappoint anybody, and so the responsibilities of leadership kind of snuck up on me. One day you're doing wind sprints by yourself in a steamy gym, and the next day a dozen people you've never met all tell you they're looking forward to a win on Friday night.

We got even closer as a team, leading up to my senior year. We played in tournaments across the state, all of us crammed in my mother's car, having sleepovers, and getting into as much mischief as we could without getting into any serious trouble.

The school district finally built a gym at my old elementary school, so I was able to work out even more. The flip side of that was I barely studied at all. Every free moment, I was on the court. Fortunately, I was smart enough to get by, and later on, I would learn a hard lesson about the proper balance of mind and body.

Still, I was having a great time. My name was in the papers a lot in those days, which was nice, but I also started to realize that I wanted my team there with me. That was my budding sense of responsibility. I saw potential in my teammates that I began to work to bring out. If there was such a thing in high school as a player/coach, I was that person.

Don't get me wrong, I appreciated all the individual accolades and awards because I was so competitive, but I began to understand that none of it would amount to much without my teammates.

That summer, I went to a basketball camp at Southern Miss with Coach Wall. I went to his house the day before and spent the night. He had a big house in an all-white neighborhood I'd always thought of as kind of a racist area, but of course Coach Wall was a great guy, so I didn't worry too much about it.

Until the next morning, when the two of us stopped off at a store down the street from his house. We went inside to get something to drink for our trip to the college. The storeowner seemed to be a friend of his. Coach Wall introduced us, and I went to get a soda.

"What you fellas doin' up so early, Coach?" the storeowner asked.

"On our way up to Southern Miss for basketball camp."

"You want a couple of breakfast burritos for the road?"

Coach Wall shook his head and slapped his belly. "Sarah had bacon and eggs ready for us as soon as we woke up this morning."

I nodded. "Mighty good, too," I said.

The storeowner got real quiet. "When you woke up?"

"She made us a big breakfast."

The man looked at me, then back to Coach Wall. His demeanor had changed dramatically. "You let *him* stay overnight in your *home?*"

I nearly dropped my soda. The way he said *him* and *home* made the words sound like blasphemy.

Coach Wall put his pop bottle on the counter. "Why wouldn't I?"

The storeowner just looked at Coach Wall like it was the most obvious answer in the world. Which to him, it probably was. "'cause he's black."

There was just the slightest pause before 'black.'

Coach Wall turned to me. "Put your drink back, Butch," he said. But instead of taking it back to the cooler, I put it down on the counter. A little harder than necessary.

Coach Wall turned back to the storeowner. "Butch plays basketball for me down at the high school. He's welcome in my home any damn time."

The two men just stood there, staring at each other across the counter until I broke the silence. "Hey, Coach, let's go."

After the camp, we went back to Coach Wall's. He insisted I stay the night before I made the drive back home since it was pretty late. I was going to go straight to bed, but he asked me into his den where his wife Sarah was reading the Bible.

"Have a seat, Butch," he said. And then he told Sarah about what had happened at the store that morning. I could tell Coach was still mad about it, but there was only concern in the eyes of his wife.

"How are you, Butch?" she asked.

I was a little surprised by the question, but it was a nice surprise. To be honest, I was a little surprised by the entire situation. "I'm fine, ma'am."

"Are you sure?"

"Yes, ma'am."

Sarah was a beautiful woman, but the kindness in her eyes was what stood out to me at that moment.

"Well, you get some rest then," she said. "You must be pretty tired."

"Yes, ma'am," I answered, and Coach Wall stood up and patted me on the back as I left the room. I lay awake that night for a long time, thinking of how Coach Wall had reacted to that racist storeowner, and how his wife Sarah had looked so concerned. They were good people, and I felt good knowing them.

I remembered how Coach Wall had approached me in the gym on the day we first had met. How he'd just come right out and told me that he'd never coached a black team before and could use my help.

For all I know, I may have been the first black person with whom he had ever had a real conversation. He was a pretty young guy back then, so who knows what he'd done or where he'd been in life up to that point? We developed an even closer bond that day.

Tommy Wall was a great coach. He set goals and then did what he needed to do to achieve them. If he needed help, even from a player, he didn't hesitate to ask. He stood up for what was right and set a good example for his players. Win or lose, he knew how to play the game. He lived his leadership.

Some say leaders are born and not made, that our life experience will reveal those skills if and when we're ready. All I know is that when the game is on the line, if you can drive the lane and give it your best shot, then move forward, win or lose, all while setting an example for those who come after, that makes you a leader. That makes you a coach.

CHAPTER TWELVE

"I've got nothing to lose, it's just me against the world."
Tupac

I TOLD THE OTHER PLAYERS about my trip with Coach Wall and how he'd talked to the storeowner, and I think it impressed my teammates as much as it had me. It was another little thing that brought us closer together as a team and made everybody work just a little bit harder.

As a coach, you learn to recognize the things that motivate people. Different types of players are motivated by different things. That's why a good coach is a student of human nature. An observer. Something that works for one player might alienate another. And in college, at that age, most of these young men are still finding out who they are. What kind of player, and what kind of man, they can be.

As their coach, my job is to help them get there. To help them realize their potential. You can't change a person, but you can help them discover who they really are. Sometimes, I find out who my players are before they know themselves. That's another way that coaching lines up with parenting.

I know there's a lot of young men and women out there who roll their eyes when their mama or daddy says something like, "I know you better than you know yourself," but that's almost always true, especially when you're young. When you're a parent, you love your child and everything about them. You study them. You observe them. You can't get enough of them. There's not a parent alive that hasn't watched their child sleep or that doesn't know what their child is going to say before they say it. You will grow up and you will grow old, but you will never stop being their child.

I was extremely pleased after my visit to Southern Miss. I was not nationally known at that time, but the head coach, M. K. Turk, promised to come see me play during my senior season, and that was big. This was back in the days before social media and Sports Center and viral videos, so coaches had to see for themselves who the good players really were. And the best coaches were always looking to discover players no one else was thinking about. That's how you get an edge as a recruiter. You find great players before anyone else does.

Now that Coach Turk had found me, others would follow, and I welcomed the attention. I wanted to showcase my skills to a wider audience. It all goes back to those days as a kid in front of the TV, imagining how proud my parents would be to see their son on the little screen.

Soon after my visit to Southern Miss, I was invited to a week-long camp at what was then the University of Southwestern Louisiana, home of the Ragin' Cajuns. I was very excited to see how I measured up to the other players who were invited to participate, and also to be seen and start to establish a reputation for myself. I had a great time establishing my reputation as the best player there.

Years before at the school, Coach Beryl Shipley had been one of the first college coaches in the Deep South to recruit black players and integrate his teams, which didn't go over too well with some folks at the time. Coach Shipley said later that he was just tired of turning away good players, and I can't say I blame him for that. Every great player wants to compete against the best, and every great coach wants to coach the best. Beryl Shipley was a great coach.

When the state of Louisiana stopped him from using state money to pay for those scholarships, he got money from black businessmen to pay their way. But the NCAA found out and put the school on probation.

I had no idea about all the ins and outs of that situation at the time, of course, but I mention it now for two reasons: One, I built my reputation as a formidable recruiter by working within rules that can sometimes seem overly restrictive, so I can definitely relate maybe to pushing the envelope a little bit. Two, Louisiana sports, like the state itself, has a pretty colorful history, and by going to that camp, I was trying to make a little of my own.

The school's star player at the time was the great Hall of Fame shooting guard, Andrew Toney, who would go on to play for the 76ers. I knew the team would be looking to replace him, and sure enough, they were the first school to recruit me officially with a letter of interest. As you can imagine, that was a very big deal to me.

The assistant coach, Dave Farrar, came up and introduced himself the very first day of the camp. It was obvious he was impressed with my skills, which only made me work harder. I'm one of those guys who thrive on positive reinforcement. I can take criticism as well, but I admit I like to be recognized for my work.

As a coach, I would rather praise a player than criticize him, although some guys do their best work in a tough environment. And pressure does separate the men from the boys. Most of the time, you do no favors pulling punches. The truth may hurt, but truth is what's needed. Of course, there's a lot of ways to deliver that truth, and deciding on the best method for each situation and player is what separates the men from the boys in terms of coaching and recruiting.

The head coach was Bobby Paschal, who came after me hard. He sent a letter out to my house practically every day when they were recruiting me, and someone on his staff was always calling to tell me about all the great players that went to the school. He sent someone out to see every one of my games my senior year. Rules were different back in the day. I learned a lot about recruiting from the way they came after me. Coach Paschal was a calm presence in person, but there was never any doubt how bad he wanted to win.

Great coaches, no matter what their disposition, always have that inner fire, just like great players.

Speaking of which, I met Brian Jolivette while I was there, a player with a big heart and an even bigger mouth. He's one of my best friends today. He made sure everyone in earshot knew that 'the badass Butch Pierre' was in the house, which I didn't mind too much. I was cocky but cool about it. Brian was a real trash talker. We hit it off right away. I was voted MVP of the camp at the end of the week, and the whole experience set me on fire.

Northwestern State Louisiana also invited me to their camp, and it was there that I played against a truly great player. He was the opposite of Brian, very quiet and low key. But when he squared up against you, you knew he came to play.

I'll never forget the second day of the camp when we were scheduled to play five on five for the first time. I had heard about this other player who was supposed to be a big deal, but I hadn't seen him yet.

There was a commotion at the other end of the court, and all of these coaches and players had gathered around somebody, and so I figured that must be the guy. It was.

He was about my size and really muscular. He was a year behind me, but he didn't play like it. We squared off, and he went right at me, over the top and to the hole. I knew this dude was the real deal. A high level guy who was going to give me a high level game.

I hadn't been challenged like that in the camp to that point, so he definitely got my attention. The next time I got the ball, I went around him and scored, and the game was on. We really went at each other after that, and the gym was rocking the entire time. Being the two best players at the camp, I'm sure it was almost as exciting to watch as it was to play, because we really brought out the best in each other.

After the game was over, I introduced myself. When I shook his hand, I told him that he was the best guard I'd ever played against, and I meant it. I thought he had gotten the better of me, and I wasn't used to something like that. But it was definitely something I could respect.

I'd never said anything like that to another player before, but he earned it that day, and I believe I earned his respect, too. His name was Joe Dumars.

After that game, I was not surprised at all when Joe went on to great things in the NBA: Hall of Fame, Finals MVP, two championships. He did it all. Another guy who thought Joe was one of the best defender he'd ever played against was a guy named Michael Jordan.

There are very few players who have that kind of career, and I'm proud to have made him sweat a little bit back in the day. As you can tell, that camp had a major impact on me.

The last camp of the summer was at LSU, which was very exciting. If you grow up playing sports in Louisiana, you want to go to LSU. It's more of a football school because Louisiana is more of a football state, but LSU is still LSU. It's big.

I met Coach Dale Brown for the first time at the LSU camp, which was a very big deal. Coach Brown is a Louisiana sports legend, and one of the all-time great motivators. He was head coach at LSU for twenty-five years, and he's the only SEC coach at that time to take his team to the national tournament fifteen years in a row.

He had his own TV show back then, in the days when we received three channels and one extra if we put some tin foil on the antennae, so I was pretty excited to meet him. He knew who I was, which made it even better. Coach Brown was a character, so he might have been on TV even if he hadn't been coaching at LSU.

Playing against the LSU players was really special. Even better was that I matched up pretty well against them. They were bigger and stronger than I was, but I knew that would come to me over time. The point was that I could play, and every day, my confidence grew. I felt like I was sitting on top of the world.

It was at the LSU camp that I first dunked in a game, which was maybe the most exciting thing of all. Back then, you didn't see guys dunking in a game all that much, especially in high school. I'd been wanting to do it for a long time, and I guess just being there at LSU and playing in front of Coach Brown and the big crowd pumped me full of adrenaline. I stole the ball, saw a clear path, and, man, I soared!

I usually tried to be cool, but I know I was grinning from ear to ear as I ran back down the court. There's nothing like the first time you dunk in a game. The crowd really liked it, too.

Now everybody dunks. By the time I retire, there will probably be some kid in grammar school slammin' it. But back then, it was something.

My only disappointment was that there were two camps back-to-back, and I was there the first week, and a lot of really good players from around the state came the second week, so I didn't get to play against them. I wanted to be measured against the very best every chance I got.

Coach Brown told me to come back the second week on Thursday night for a pickup game, however, so I did get to play against some of those great players, and I held my own. I used that game as a motivator to show them I should have been in week two.

When Coach Brown told me he wanted me to play basketball at LSU, it was like all my dreams were coming true. When I went home and told my parents, they were even more excited than I was. I had my future all mapped out.

But life doesn't always work out like you want. You learn, you adapt, you keep moving.

I learned a lot that summer. Take my friend, Brian Jolivette, and Joe Dumars. Brian was very outspoken in his confidence, but Joe was real quiet about it. Like a silent assassin. I could see the benefits of both, and I learned through observation how to switch between them, depending on the situation.

That's another lesson in coaching and recruiting: adaptability. You do whatever needs to be done to be the best you can be on any given day and in any given situation. No matter what the task, there will be multiple ways to accomplish it. The greats work hard to figure out the best one.

The whole experience of going to these basketball camps made me a better player, but it also taught me a lot about recruiting. More than anything, a recruiter has to be adaptable. You have to be able to assess any situation quickly and determine the best course of action.

A major college recruiter has to understand who a player is and what he wants to be. I take into account a recruit's personality, his family, his friends, what he likes to do, his church, and his school. I ask myself what moves him, what he needs, what he wants, his mental and physical toughness, plus intangibles, and then decide if that player has what it takes to thrive on my team. If we can bring out the best in him and vice versa.

I've always been good at recognizing and evaluating talent and players that would develop into NBA prospects. But as the years go by, it gets harder and harder to find that diamond in the rough before anyone else does. I have to stay sharp and one step ahead of the competition, because it gets more intense every single year.

Adaptability means you are constantly evolving, learning, and improving your game, whatever your game happens to be.

There are days you'll be confronted with a Brian, and there are days when you'll face a Joe. There will be days when the only person standing in your way is yourself. Whatever the obstacle, your job is to figure out how to get past it. How to keep moving. How to accomplish your goals. Keep your eyes on the prize, and that prize will be yours.

ADVERSITY

"The ultimate measure of a man is not where he stands in moments
of comfort and convenience, but where he stands at moments of
conflict and controversy."
Martin Luther King Jr.

"When the going gets tough, the tough get going."
Knute Rockne

How we deal with adversity helps define us to the world and to ourselves. Nobody seeks adversity, but everybody deals with it. How you deal with adversity affects your path to success. It's easy to give up when the odds are against you, but those who achieve greatness find a way to use adversity. They turn negatives to positives. They find motivation in tough times.

Recently, the Drexel University Dragons achieved the greatest comeback in NCAA Division I tournament history by overcoming a 34-point deficit to beat Delaware.

I'm sure many had never heard of Drexel before that game, but they will be remembered now—for how they overcame adversity. Drexel literally turned a negative to a positive, reflected in numbers.

In life, it may take other forms, such as using the loss of a friend as inspiration to create a foundation in their name. Or in small things, like walking to work when your car is in the shop, thus improving your fitness. Turn your negatives into positives, and you'll slay the dragon of adversity.

CHAPTER THIRTEEN

"Do not fear mistakes. There are none."
Miles Davis

MY SENIOR SEASON WENT GREAT. We had a lot of fan support, and college recruiters were watching every time I hit the court. I had sustained injuries, but I recovered and played through them. I was single-minded in my focus, and nothing was going to stop me from accomplishing my goals.

In those days, the college coaches and recruiters who came to see me play could stay after the game and say hello. Nowadays, the NCAA more closely regulates contact with high school players. So, having coaches like Hugh Durham of Georgia or Jim Hatfield of Mississippi State or Dale Brown of LSU or Guy Lewis of the University of Houston walk up after a game and talk to me was an outstanding experience. I was an eighteen-year-old kid with a dream to play college basketball, and college coaches I respected were waiting around to talk to me.

It was a great experience. I was scouted at just about every game, both at home and away. It was unusual if there *wasn't* a big-time scout in the stands. It was very exciting for me to meet coaches from all over the country. My official visits weren't going to happen until the end of the year, so it was good to get to know some of the coaches a little before then. I had pretty much figured out which schools I wanted to visit, but I also wanted to keep my options open. It would be a big decision, and I wanted to do it right.

The scouts were great motivation, too. Not that I really needed it by that point. The deeper into the season, the better I played, and the better I played, the more motivated I became. I was on fire, obsessed. I was the best player in one of the toughest districts in the state, and I was named MVP. Personally, I thought we were the best team in the state, and I became more and more confident in my abilities. I was a big man on campus, and it felt fantastic.

Looking back on that time now helps me to understand the players I recruit today because I went through it myself. I know what it's like to carry the responsibility of a team and a school and a community on my shoulders. I don't mean to be overly dramatic, but high school sports mean an awful lot to people, and when you're a star player, you have to account for their hopes and dreams, as well. In other words, I was under a lot of pressure, and I loved every minute of it! It was a very special time of my life.

We played at New Iberia High School in the first round of the playoffs, which was about an hour and a half away. Even though it's almost always better to play at home, it seemed to give the first game toward the state championship an even greater importance.

Getting on that bus with my teammates and coaches was another bonding experience, like warriors going off to do battle. We arrived early and took some shots, warming up, as the home team glared at us from across the gym. Typical high school head games. I noticed a couple of their players were staring at me, so I gave them a confident half-glance before sinking a jump shot, the kind of look that said they didn't bother me at all.

I could play my own head games. That seemed to piss one of them off, and he came over to me like he was going to do something.

I stood my ground as he approached, passing the ball to one of my teammates and waiting as he walked toward me. I honestly didn't know if this guy was actually going to try something, but I figured my hands should be free, just in case.

"You ain't gonna score," he said, sneering at me.

I was so surprised, I almost laughed in his face, but instead I just looked at him like, *'we'll see who scores.'* Who did he think he was talking to?

By the time we were in the locker room, I had almost forgotten about it, but Coach Wall saw what had happened and was about to teach me another lesson in coaching that I never forgot.

He stalked the space between the benches where we were sitting for his pregame pep talk, and, man, he was on fire. "Did ya'll see what happened out there?" he asked, pointing to the door to the gym.

Some of the players nodded, but I'm not sure they knew what he meant. I wasn't sure myself, but I had my suspicions.

"That team out there dis-re-spect-ed Butch!" he growled. "And when they disrespect Butch, they disrespect this entire team!"

Everybody nodded at that. Whether they knew what he was talking about or not, everybody understands respect.

"That player challenged you, didn't he, Butch?"

"Yes, sir!" I answered.

"You're gonna accept that challenge, aren't you?"

126

"Yes, sir!"

Coach Wall went on like that for a solid two minutes, almost like we were in church. Call-and-response. He really knew how to get me going, and then he pulled the others in, igniting the team like kindling in a drought. By the time he had told us to get out there and whip some ass, we were loaded for bear and taking no prisoners.

I played the best half of my life. Dropped 30 in sixteen minutes without a miss. And the first player I blew past was the guy who had mouthed off to me before the game. It still makes me laugh to remember the look on his face after I scored every single basket.

At halftime, I patted him on the back as I left for the visitor's locker room. "Careful what you wish for," I said.

I didn't take a single shot the entire second half, just set my teammates up and passed off. I knew we had them. Since we were a new school, it was our first ever playoff game, so I made sure everyone was involved. Lesson learned, Coach Bourgeois.

Our next game was a lot closer to home, in more ways than one: East Ascension High School, where I would have been playing had they not built the new school and split us up. The local newspaper billed it "Butch Pierre vs Johnny Jones."

The future head coach and I were rivals but actually pretty good friends, unbeknownst to most of the fans. The thing was, we couldn't have gone to the same college because we played the same position, and we were just too competitive. Neither one of us would have settled for anything less than first team.

So, this was big, besides being a playoff game. I wanted to prove I was the better player, and he wanted to do the same.

The day before the game, I told Coach Wall I wanted to address the team. He didn't ask why or what I was going to say; he trusted me.

"I know it's been in the paper about me and Johnny, but that's not what this game is about," I said. "It's more than that."

I looked at my teammates. They were all my brothers at that moment. "It's about us," I continued. "It's about community. It's about getting to the championship game."

"Yeah!" someone shouted.

"I don't care about me. I care about us!" I said. "This team!"

"Yeah!" they yelled.

"I'll do whatever I can to help get us there. Whatever it takes!"

The team was yelling and Coach Wall was nodding.

"Take a challenge, back off a challenge, whatever it takes, whatever sacrifice I need to make, whatever I need to do, I'm gonna do!"

Everybody roared.

"Team first!"

"Team first!" they answered.

It was almost like what Coach Wall had done the game before, and the next day we won in a blowout. I played the entire game like I played the second half of the game before. I made my teammates my priority, passing off to them and setting them up as much as I could. As close as we had been before, we grew even closer as a team after that game. Everyone could feel it. I may have been the star of the team and the one in the newspapers, but by allowing everyone else their moment in the sun, I learned a valuable lesson about the true meaning of being a team. We all did.

Coach Wall was as proud of me as if I had scored every single point, even though I probably didn't fully appreciate why at the time. I felt good about helping my teammates, but it was not until later that I understood he was proud of what I had done, because, as a coach, he had taught me not just how to be a better player but how to be a better man. As a coach now myself, I get that.

Just like Coach Wall, I meet young men at a formative moment in their lives, and I try to teach them the game of basketball. But it's a lot more than that. They are at a point in their existence when life lessons surround them like the air they breathe. Every decision they make matters, and every decision resonates beyond what I teach them on the court. A good basketball coach does not teach just the game of basketball.

We played our quarterfinal game the following week at East Ascension's gym against Woodlawn High of Shreveport, which was a very tough, talented team.

They matched us basket for basket all night long. It was a battle, our hardest fought game of the year.

With fifteen seconds to go, we were down by one point. One basket would likely put us in the state championship game. Even though most people who were there thought that game was the *real* state championship, none of that would matter unless we could score. It's a sad truth, but nobody remembers who came in second except the second place finishers. That's why getting to a championship is so tough, and why becoming champion is so sweet. If it was easy, everyone would do it.

Coach Wall drew up the last play. It was for me. As we broke out of the huddle, I told Greg Perkins I might pass to him if I had to, since I figured I'd draw a double team.

Hot Rod inbounded the ball and passed it to me. Two of their guys swarmed me immediately. I passed to Nat Spears, who dribbled twice and then passed the ball back to me, as I broke through the two defenders.

They recovered quickly, as I advanced, blocking my path to the key.

Ten seconds.

I passed off to Perkins, who had an open shot.

Which he didn't take.

Perkins dribbled once and passed it back to me.

Six seconds.

I managed to grab the ball with four hands in my face, but I couldn't shake the double team, so I passed the ball to Parnell, who threw up a shot at the buzzer.

Off the rim.

To this day, I wish I had taken that shot, in spite of the fact I had two guys hanging all over me. A moment like that can change your life.

But even though I wish I'd taken the shot, that doesn't mean I'm filled with regret about the results. If the road I've traveled led me to where I am today, I cannot now question that path. I accept everything: the highs, the lows, the good and the bad.

As Satchel Paige once said, "Don't look back. Something might be gaining on you."

The very next day, my parents' phone was ringing off the hook. Recruiters.

But I'll go into that later.

At the end of that year, I went to the principal's office and told him I wanted to sign my scholarship letter in front of the entire student body as a way to thank them for all their support. It had been a great year for me but also a very tough year. I'd been injured and come back; I played well but there were difficult games, too. And there was the way we lost that last game. It took me a while to get over that.

But I wanted to share my good fortune with the school. I was very good at motivating myself because I was so driven to achieve, but at the end of the day, no one achieves anything big without the help of others, on or off the court.

The people who support you, on and off the court, become part of your game. Part of your team. So, I just kind of wanted everybody to share in my success a little bit. I was one of the first players from the area to get the kind of attention I was getting, and I felt an added responsibility to live up to how I was being treated. A lot of kids looked up to me, and I felt like the example I set could make a difference.

"That'd be just fine, Butch," the principal told me. "There's something else we'd like to announce at the same time, if it's all right with you."

"What's that?"

"We're going to retire your number."

That blew me away. That was big. I knew they retired college and professional numbers, but I'd never heard of such a thing in high school. I told him that was okay by me.

There was one area of my life that year which wasn't so successful, however: grades. I'd been so focused on basketball that I'd almost quit studying for the most part, getting by on my natural intelligence alone.

I did get by, but my grades still suffered, and, as a result, I would end up spending a lot of extra hours on math and English once I got to college. An off-the-court lesson I share with my recruits to this day.

Looking back, I learned a lot that year. Sometimes you're in the zone, hitting everything you throw up, and it sounds like the crowd is in your ear. Other times, you throw up brick after brick, and it seems like you're all alone out there. But you're not. You're never truly alone.

Whether we take that final shot or pass the ball, none of us is truly on our own. Even when there's no team, and no cheering crowds, there's always the Man upstairs watching over us. And that makes all the difference.

CHAPTER FOURTEEN

"Life is not a spectator sport."
Jackie Robinson

THE MORNING AFTER MY LAST HIGH SCHOOL GAME, all hell broke loose. Otherwise known as "college recruiting."

My parents' phone was ringing off the hook. It seemed like the calls were coming in about every couple of minutes, sometimes less than that. Sometimes, the phone would ring as soon as I hung it up. There was no call waiting back then, so I guess those coaches were just hitting redial until they got through. It was crazy, but the kind of crazy I'd been working toward for a very long time.

Even so, it surprised me a little bit. It's hard to prepare a kid for something like that. I was used to pressure situations on the court, but this was something new. It was a different kind of intensity. I was worn out from a long, hard season and went to bed the night before looking forward to taking a little break, but there was no break. There was only a shift in focus. I may not have had any more games to play, but there was still plenty going on.

Coaches were asking for home visits and inviting me for official visits. I was talking to everybody. It was non-stop. Many years later, I would be on the other side of things, and that helped me quite a bit. I know how a kid in that situation should be treated because I've been there. It can be overwhelming.

Naturally, I wanted Coach Wall to be involved, so he came over and talked to me and my parents and went over my choices. It's not like I hadn't been thinking about colleges during the season, but when you're an elite athlete, you learn to shift your focus, depending on the circumstances. You tune things out when you have to, and bring them back in focus when the time is right. Like when you're at the free throw line and people are screaming and waving, but you just have to concentrate and hit that bucket. Discipline and muscle memory takes over. I had been so focused on that championship game that I put everything else aside, but now the time had come to make a very big decision about my future. Now people were screaming and waving, and I had to listen to every last one of them.

Together, we narrowed my choices down from twenty schools to five, since that was the number of official visits allowed by NCAA rules. We decided on LSU, the University of Georgia, Mississippi State, the University of Houston, and the University of Southwest Louisiana Ragin' Cajuns.

The schools paid for everything and were allowed to bring me in for forty-eight hours, so every visit was packed with activity. With the help of my parents and Coach Wall, I put together a checklist for each school and a list of questions to ask. Each checklist was really two in one: one for basketball and one for academics.

At the top of my list for basketball was the coach. The coach is the top dog in any program; he or she sets the tone.

I wanted to play for someone like Coach Wall, a player's coach. Someone who lets the players play. A disciplinarian, but not a total hard-ass. I had such a good relationship with Coach Wall that I wanted that to continue. I wanted a coach who cared enough about his players to spend time with them and really get to know them. Someone who respected his players and earned their respect in return. I didn't want a buddy. I wanted a mentor. A teacher. A coach.

It's funny thinking about it now, but what I wanted in a coach as a young man is exactly what I strive to be for my players today. The reason I knew exactly what I wanted in a coach back then was because I had such good examples in my life—my father, Coach Wall, and others. What they taught me by example and otherwise, I now teach other young men. Life works by example.

Living by example is how you give back to the world. How you make your mark and how you leave things a little better than they were before you got here. You don't have to be a coach to make a difference. You can do it simply by living with integrity. Saying what you mean and meaning what you say. By keeping your standards high and doing your best to meet them every single day. Young people are watching all the time. They learn from us whether we realize it or not. What you do when you think no one's watching is important because someone is always watching.

Another thing that was very important to me in a coach was honesty. I like praise just as much as the next guy, but I don't want anyone blowing smoke.

I pride myself in keeping it real, and that's what I expect from others. I knew I was a good player, but I didn't want anyone telling me what they thought I wanted to hear just to get me into their program. Assistant coaches were a factor in my thinking, too, because assistants do a lot of the coaching. A good head coach delegates because he has to, and if the assistants are outstanding, that only shows good judgment by the man who hired them.

And, of course, education was important to all of us. Maybe a little more to my parents than to me. After all, I *was* still just a kid. I needed to have some fun. My parents wanted a coach who would look out for me. Someone who saw me as something more than just an asset to the team. Someone they could trust with their child.

I felt the same way when my kids went off to school. There's no way to describe what it feels like when your child leaves home for the first time. You feel proud and protective and terrified all at the same time. You want to hold them close, but you have to let them go.

Speaking of that, location was pretty important. I was excited to get out on my own, but family was important to me. How far away the school was would be a big consideration.

And of course I wanted to play for a team with great players who were NBA prospects, and I wanted to be a starter as soon as possible.

There were all kinds of other considerations. What was the campus like? What was the atmosphere? Who was the best player on the team and who was the worst? Were tutors available if I needed them? Who were the teachers? Where did the players live? How often could I go home?

All of the coaches sounded good, but I have to admit some of them sounded a lot alike. I remember thinking it was like listening to a bunch of used car salesmen. As a recruiter, I try not to fall into that habit. Sincerity mattered to me as a player, and I try to remember that when I talk to prospects today.

All five schools satisfied my basic checklist, except the University of Georgia was farther away than my parents liked. I liked the SEC because they were on television the most. There was no ESPN nationally back then, so getting on network TV was important to me. I was still thinking about that promise to my mom.

My first home visit was with Coach Paschal from the University of Southwest Louisiana, which went very well. My parents really liked him, and I've already mentioned how he sent all those letters. He was very persistent, which was another lesson I took from that time into my own recruiting. That first home visit probably went the best of them all, but I wanted to play in a bigger league.

Coach Durham and assistant Larry Gay from Georgia said all the right things, especially that I would play right away. That year, Dominique Wilkins played as one of the best freshman in the country, so he had great players. Plus, they really needed a point guard. At least, that's what I thought.

Coach Hatfield was the new head coach at Mississippi State. A real people person, he made my parents feel very comfortable. My mother also really liked Coach Farrar, one of the assistant coaches. "He's a disciplinarian, Man," she said. "Be good for you."

Guy Lewis from the University of Houston came next. He would coach Clyde Drexler and Akeem Olajuwon and a lot of other great players over the course of his long career.

Coach Lewis brought along a very serious assistant coach named Harvey Payton, whom my dad really liked. Probably because Coach Payton was a real no-nonsense, get-to-the-point type guy, just like my father. I remember he told my dad they expected me to help them win a national championship. "I wouldn't waste your time otherwise," he said.

The last visit was Coach Brown from LSU and his assistant coach, Ron Abernathy. My mother thought Ron was a fast talker and slick, too much like those used car salesmen I mentioned earlier, and I think he knew it, because he came back for a second visit and made a better impression.

As you can imagine, all of this was a lot to absorb. My mother likes this one and my dad likes that one, this one's too slick and that one's too far away, and on and on. After a while, I just wanted to get to school and play basketball again and not listen to any more sales pitches or opinions. But I also wanted the best fit for me.

So now, it was time to go to *their* house. My parents could have gone with me, but they thought it was better if I went on my own. "You're going to be on your own if you enroll, Man, so you might as well try it out that way," my mother said. My father just nodded. All five visits by myself.

At Southwest Louisiana, I loved everything. The food, the campus, the style of play. I spent a lot of time with Coach Paschal. He gave me the tour himself and even shot baskets with me at his house. I came back home very excited about my visit.

The first time I ever got on a plane was flying down to Houston, which was a very big deal for this small town Louisiana boy. But stepping off that plane was even better. Lots of balloons and two pretty girls, waiting to give me a tour of the campus. That was really something for a seventeen-year-old kid.

My roommate for the weekend was another recruit, Lyndon Rose. We're still friends to this day. The best player on the team, Rob

Williams, took us to a party and showed us around. He was from Houston, a city kid who was probably raised a lot differently than I was, to say the least. I had a great time. I played a pick-up game with Clyde Drexler and even ran into some friends from LSU, who were playing in a regional tournament there.

My friends were all pushing for Houston, and when they offered me a scholarship, I have to admit it was pretty tempting. I'd never seen anything like Houston before.

Mississippi State sent a private plane down to New Orleans to pick me up, which was another new experience for me. I've traveled on private planes quite a bit since then on recruiting trips, but there's nothing quite like the first time. I probably didn't fully appreciate just how amazing it was until I'd taken a few more trips in coach with my long legs, but it was still a lot of fun.

Al McGuire, who won a national championship at Marquette, was hitching a ride with us and told me to get in the cockpit to try it out.

"Seriously?"

"It's auto-pilot, kid, knock yourself out."

I sat down and kept things steady, but when I got cocky and started rotating the controls, Al took me down. "That's enough of that shit," he laughed.

It was another great visit, but it couldn't have been more different from Houston. It was a small town, like I was used to. Everybody knew everybody else, just like back in Darrow.

I went to a party there, too, and it was a lot different from the party down in Houston. It felt like the parties I went to back home. It felt like *home*.

Next up was the University of Georgia, which really went the extra mile. They filled my room with shoes, gear, and posters, and I had a locker with my name on it. I played against Dominique Wilkins, which was great. They had a lot of really good players, so that was a plus. The great recruiter Larry Gay gave me a great sales pitch, and even though I didn't end up playing there, he became a mentor to me and a real friend.

The Bulldogs might have gotten me except that the entertainment, instead of a party, was a movie for some reason. Not only that, but it was a horror movie, which is not my thing at all. I've always hated scary movies, even as a kid.

So, I sat in that theatre with my eyes closed and listened to the sounds of screaming women and power tools, and afterward, I was dropped off at my hotel, which was in a secluded area outside Athens, Georgia. I had a miserable night.

Whether I would have been a Georgia Bulldog if they'd taken me to see Richard Pryor: Live in Concert instead of *The Texas Chainsaw Massacre*, I have no idea, but it's possible.

LSU was my last visit, and being a Louisiana kid, I was biased toward the school. It's a great school, and LSU *is* Louisiana sports. But there were drawbacks, too.

I would be close to home but maybe a little *too* close. I would be a stone's throw from all my old friends, who wouldn't be playing basketball, and all my old hangouts, which would be tempting me every day. There were limited scholarships available, and I knew all the guys they were recruiting. I knew they gave a scholarship to a player that wasn't as good as I was, and it wasn't Johnny. It was going to be tougher to be a starter sooner rather than later. Also academics were not stressed like the other schools at that time. I wanted to leave school with a degree, since the NBA is never a sure thing.

Coach Brown still asks me questions about my dad to this day. I finally figured it out, but that's another story.

When I gathered my family to tell them my decision to attend Mississippi State, it didn't go as smoothly as I had planned.

My grandmother was not on board.

"You visit all you want, but you're not going to live there!" she said.

"Why not?"

"Mississippi?"

Of course she was talking about racism. She had lived a long time and seen a lot in her life, and to her, Mississippi meant slavery and Jim Crow.

"I won't let that bother me," I said boldly, with all the certainty of youth and inexperience.

She gave me a look that said, '*Boy, I oughta whoop your ass*', but it was my decision, and so she held her peace on the subject after she'd spoken her mind, *on a few occasions,* even though she disagreed. "You'll see," she predicted.

In the end, after I'd made my decision, I think we were both proved right. There was certainly racism in Mississippi, but I didn't let it bother me. Racism is everywhere.

I was a young man on a mission.

CHAPTER FIFTEEN

"You can't just sit there and wait for people
to give you that golden dream."
Diana Ross

I THINK THE THING THAT SEPARATED ME from the other recruits I met during my visits was the fact that I was serious about getting my degree. I may have had a lot of self-confidence, but I still understood that not every player makes it to the NBA. Just like every high school player doesn't make it to college. The higher you go, the tougher it gets. And the smart player, or the smart parents, prepare for any eventuality.

My seriousness of purpose came from my parents. They had instilled in me the importance of an education practically before I realized it was happening, so when the rubber met the road, so to speak, I knew I needed to take my education as seriously as I took my game.

That doesn't mean it all just came to me as soon as I graduated high school, of course. I was as cocky and sure of things as I had ever been, and I've already admitted that I coasted through some of my classes toward the end of my high school career. But deep down, the values of my mother and father had taken hold.

Values are like seeds your parents and mentors plant inside you at a young age. You may not see that harvest right away, but with the right care and nourishment, the bounty they produce will sustain you throughout your life, in good times and bad.

I remember meeting with Collis Temple Jr. He'd gone through a lot as the first black basketball player at LSU, but he loved that school and wanted to help recruit the best players. I met with him at his house near the campus, which was where he had met his wife and also where the Louisiana National Guard had to protect him. Talk about good times and bad!

Everything about him spoke to the kind of man I wanted to be. He had been a solid player and was now a successful businessman, respected in the community and a straight shooter.

Collis gave me the real story and treated me with respect. He let me know about the other players that were being recruited, which helped me make my final decision. Information is power. Collis's honesty was greatly appreciated.

"You have to look out for yourself," he said. "So, what else are you thinking?"

I liked that. He was asking not just to be polite, but because he was genuinely curious. Even if I didn't attend his alma mater, he was still interested in me as a young basketball player. As a human being who was about to enter a world he'd occupied himself until recently. If anyone understood what I was dealing with, it was Collis Temple. He even knew who my father was because of his political office.

"I'm going to make sure I get my degree," I said.

He nodded approvingly. We both knew a lot of players didn't think that far ahead, which was why a lot of athletes don't get that diploma. But what I said next seemed to genuinely surprise him.

"Then I'm going back for my master's," I added.

"Really?" he asked.

"I'll bring it back here and show it to you when I get it," I said.

He laughed. "All right," he said, and shook my hand.

And I did, too. That's another one of those values my parents instilled in me. Always do what you say you're going to do. Follow through.

A player who doesn't follow through on the court is going to miss a lot of shots, and a person who doesn't follow through in life is going to miss a lot of opportunities.

Collis was a role model for me. He'd gotten his degree, and at the time we spoke, he was back at LSU, working on his master's. He may have been surprised I came at him on academics, but it impressed him, too.

Speaking of follow-through, one of the reasons I finally chose Mississippi State was because the coaching staff followed through with me. I had decided on Georgia, but I wanted the coach to come out for the announcement ceremony. Not just for me, but for the community. I had gotten so much support from everybody that I wanted to pay them back.

The coach from Georgia was happy to hear I wanted to be a Bulldog, but he'd have to get back to me about the ceremony.

"It's kind of important to me, Coach."

"I'll call you back," he said.

As soon as I hung up the phone, it rang again. Coach Hatfield from Mississippi State. When I told him I'd decided on Georgia, he didn't just end the call abruptly like the coach from Houston had when I told him I wasn't going to attend his school. He, like Collis, was still interested in talking to me, even if I didn't choose his school. He stayed on the phone and asked questions, listening to my answers. The subject of the announcement ceremony came up. "Coach coming down?"

"I'm waiting to hear back," I said.

"Really?" he asked.

"Why?"

"If it were me, all you'd have to do is tell me what time."

I called Georgia and told them I'd decided on Mississippi State. Coach Hatfield followed through.

The toughest conversation I had about my decision, besides the one with my grandmother, was with Coach Bobby Paschal at Southwest Louisiana. He'd recruited me first and he'd recruited me best, and I knew he was going to be very disappointed I would not be one of his Ragin' Cajuns.

I drove all the way out to his house to tell him in person. It just seemed like the thing to do. He was disappointed, of course, but he invited me to stay for dinner, and afterward, we shot baskets outside and talked about things.

I was honest with him about everything. "I promised my mother a long time ago that she'd see me playing basketball on TV one day, and I'm gonna make that happen."

Following through.

Coach Paschal chuckled at that, but he knew there was nothing he could say or do to compete with a promise to my mother. His team just wasn't on national TV, and that was how my mother would see me play in the days before all those cable channels.

"Butch, just do me one favor," he said.

"What's that, Coach?"

"Call me if you're unhappy."

Once I'd made all the calls and told everybody my plans, there was something I had to take care of with my father. We'd made a deal a couple of years before that that if I got a scholarship, he'd buy me a car. Any car I wanted.

"A Corvette?" I asked.

He just looked at me with that way of his. "Was that our deal?"

"Yes, sir."

"That's your answer."

As always, my father's word was his bond. He *followed through.*

My sister graduated, got a great job and bought herself a brand new Buick Regal, which I really liked, and back in 1980, it was a very popular car. So, I gave it some more thought and switched from a Corvette to a brand new Monte Carlo, which was similar to my sister's car. We special ordered it from a family friend who sold cars, and it was a beautiful sight to behold. Black on black, with custom rims, T-top, and a fantastic stereo system.

It was a lot nicer than borrowing my mother's car, let me tell you. I'd been riding my Yamaha 650 to school or driving her car when it rained, so I was really looking forward to my first new car.

What's kind of funny is that it was delivered to the dealership on the day of my signing ceremony, and since Coach Hatfield was in town to attend, he went with me to pick up the car. I realized later that it might have seemed to some people that the school had bought the car for me or something, but all I could think of on that day was that I wanted that car as soon as I could get it, and I wasn't going to wait a day just to please somebody who had the wrong idea in the first place.

I was on top of the world. I drove my new car to school and went straight to the gym, which was filled with my friends, teammates, and other members of the community. It seemed like the whole town of Darrow was there under the golden dome, and maybe they were. It was all a blur. Coach Wall spoke before me, but I don't even remember what he said. I was just sitting there thinking about how good it all felt.

Once I had the mic, I thanked everyone for their support and named a few people, but I'm not sure I remember exactly what I said. It was pretty amazing just to be standing there, under those conditions. It was truly a once-in-a-lifetime experience.

I gave some interviews to the local media and signed my national letter of intent in front of the entire school, which was big. I wanted to share it with them, to make them all a part of it, because they had all been a part of my success.

The support you get from your family is important, but support from your peers does a lot of good, too. All the teachers, coaches, the booster club—they all helped me get to where I was.

It was almost like a pep rally, and afterward, I went to class and then played basketball with my teammates. And when they named me Athlete of the Year at graduation, it held a lot of emotion for me. Not only because of what had happened when I was a freshman, but also because of the support of my teammates. My teammates and the entire school had voted me that honor, and I was honored to receive it.

I had a great summer, playing basketball, driving my new car, and looking forward to college that fall. Not long before school started, I got a call from one of the assistant coaches. "You need to come up and take the ACT," he said.

I drove there the next day and picked up another recruit, Mike Green, on the way. We hit it off right away and decided to room together. We had a great time, and I think neither one of us took the test too seriously. Big mistake.

Because of my low score, I ended up in remedial courses that first year, which was not at all what I was used to and not at all what I was expecting. That was when I really understood how important education was. I mean, I knew before, but now I *knew.* Those remedial courses weren't going to count toward my degree.

At first, I was upset with the coaches, but in the end, I had to suck it up and take responsibility for myself. I learned a very valuable lesson the day my first class schedule came out. I learned always to ask questions and listen to the answers I got.

I learned not just to take things for granted but to pay attention and make sure I knew everything there was to know about my situation. The truth was the coach tried to tell me it was important, but I hadn't been listening. And in the end, I had no one to blame but myself.

To be honest, it embarrassed me to walk into those classes, which were filled with athletes who hadn't prepared themselves any better than I had. Fortunately, that would eventually serve to make me more determined to focus on my education, and my competitive instincts would come into play. Ultimately, I would work as hard as I could to excel in my education. But I wasn't quite there, yet.

Blowing off that ACT test would turn out to be a very good thing for me. Not only would it motivate me to focus my attention on my studies, it would also make me very meticulous in terms of contracts and other agreements.

It would also serve as a big lesson in learning what I didn't know. That's important in life. Not only to understand what you need to know, but to understand *what you don't know.*

To give an example of how green I was, I didn't even understand what people were talking about when they complained about how many hours they were taking. No one had ever sat me down and explained all the ins and out of college, and everything happened pretty fast. When people asked me my major, I would answer "business" because I had heard the other guys say that, but I hadn't really even given it much thought.

For all my high ideals, I was about to find out how things worked in the real world.

I didn't do very well that first year. My grade point average was terrible, and I was sleeping through my classes. Literally. I was tired all the time. Too many late nights. I had never been much of a drinker back home and always had good self-control, but those frat parties were pretty tempting, not to mention the sororities. I flunked my 8:00 a.m. biology class and then flunked it again, second semester.

I took terrible notes in my classes, was disorganized, and basically just lacked structure. My time management skills were lousy.

At the end of my freshman year, I was more than ready to go home and regroup, but before I left, I received an ominous warning from Assistant Coach Farrar. My mother especially liked Dave, because he was always direct. And he was extremely direct with me the day before I went home.

"You got a 1.9, Butch," he said. "You need a 2.0 and 24 hours."

"Okay, Coach," I said, eager to get out of there.

"You don't understand. Unless you take summer school and bring up that GPA and get 24 hours before the fall semester starts, you won't be eligible to play next year."

That got my attention. His words were like a cold slap in the face. I felt like I'd been living in some kind of dream. *How could this happen? Where had the year gone?* I wanted to go back in time and do things right. Start again. Except there are rarely do-overs in life. Another hard lesson for me to learn.

Just like before, at first I was upset that no one had bothered to mention that to me, but in the end I had to face the reality that I had no one to blame but myself. I was an A student getting mediocre grades. I could and should have done better. Had I applied myself, it wouldn't have mattered that I didn't know a 2.0 GPA and passing 24 hours was the cut off.

When you take care of business, your business is taken care of. No one does it for you.

ORGANIZATION

Some people plan their vacations, and some people wander. There's something to be said for both. Sometimes you need to plan down to the minute and mile, and sometimes you might want to roam around and see what you find.

But life is not a vacation. If you want to achieve greatness, you need to master three things: goals, details, and routines.

Goals: Have some.

Don't be one of those people without a destination in mind. Even though you *will* encounter all manner of obstacles and diversions, having a goal in your sights is essential. People without goals don't score.

Details: Sweat them.

I know, I know. Don't sweat the details. But if you want to get to your destination, you need to figure out a few details. Imagine loading your family in the car and running out of gas before you leave the driveway. Or worse, out in the middle of nowhere. Gas is a detail you need to sweat. Details matter. You don't have to be anal about it, although I will cop to that sometimes. You just need to be aware of what it will take to meet your goals.

Routines: Know them. Develop them. Use them.

Routines are great tools to get you where you need to go. Whether it's a workout that serves as its own motivator or a schedule that keeps you on track, develop routines to keep yourself on the path to success.

Greatness is no accident. It comes out of a lot of little things that all add up.

CHAPTER SIXTEEN

"I think people who have faults are a lot
more interesting than people who are perfect."
Spike Lee

I WENT HOME FOR TWO WEEKS and then it was right back to school. I was mad about that. Mad about my grades and about the time I'd wasted.

When I walked into my first summer school class, I was about to get even madder.

"I know you."

I looked up. The professor was looking at me.

"You're Butch Pierre, right?"

"That's right," I said evenly. *I'd barely sat down, and the professor was already on my case.*

"Point guard," he continued.

I looked down at my syllabus. *Dr. Robert Boling. What's his game, anyway?* "Yeah," I answered.

"You drive that nice black car," he said, "always washed and waxed. Always looking good."

I heard someone laugh in the back of the room. An uncomfortable laugh. There were about forty students in the class, and I had no idea why he had singled me out or where he was going with this, and neither did anyone else.

"That's right," I said.

"You need to come sit up front, Butch."

I shrugged and stood up, walking to the front of the class and taking a seat right in the middle, a few feet from where he was standing.

"That's better," he said. "Maybe now you'll get something out of this class."

My jaw dropped when he said that, but he just went on with the lesson like it was no big deal. But it was a very big deal to me. If I had been angry about summer school before, I was seething now. I stared at him the entire class, and as soon as it was over, I practically jumped out of my chair to confront him.

But I stayed cool. Whenever I got mad on the court, I always stayed cool, and I always played better as a result. I figured that winning was the best revenge. If you let someone make you angry, you give them control over you. So, I just put out my hand and introduced myself. "I'm Butch Pierre."

He shook my hand. "So?"

"So, I was wondering why you called me out like that."

He looked at me intensely, sizing me up. "Did it bother you?"

"Yeah, it did," I said. "It was embarrassing."

"If you have a problem with me, come talk to me in my office."

"How about right now?"

He shrugged. "Let's go."

I followed him to his office, no idea what was going to happen. Half of me wanted to back out of the meeting, and half of me wanted to tell him off. It had been a crazy freshman year, and the last place I wanted to be was in summer school, listening to some teacher talk about how often I washed my car.

What's wrong with a nice car, anyway?

By the time we got to his office, I was steaming. I followed him in, and he closed the door behind us.

What happened next was not what I was expecting.

"I see a lot of potential in you, Butch," he said, sitting down behind his desk. "Take a seat."

I sat down across from him, completely confused.

"I heard you were a pretty nice guy," he continued. "Intelligent young man."

"Uh…yeah, I guess."

"So, what's your problem?"

"Excuse me?"

"You heard me. What's your problem? Why are you in this class?"

His words hit me like a ton of bricks. What *was* my problem? Why *was* I in his class?

"I look at you, and I see a Mississippi State graduate," he continued. "I see a lot of potential, Butch. So, what are you going to do with all that potential?"

Something about the way he spoke to me made me trust him. He was a no-nonsense type guy, so I let everything out, all my frustrations with school, the ACT score, and everything that was going on with the basketball team. My year hadn't started well on the court.

I told the professor all about my freshman season, which had started poorly but ended pretty well. I had come to the school to play basketball, and I wasn't getting in nearly enough in the beginning. And to top it off, we were losing. Maybe I could have understood if we had a great team, being a freshman, but we were struggling and I wasn't doing anything to change that. I wasn't used to riding the bench, and I wasn't used to losing, either.

I had even been thinking about calling Coach Paschal at Southwest Louisiana. *Call me if you're unhappy,* he'd said, and I was definitely unhappy.

"You're not leaving in the middle of the season," my father said. *"You got to prove to them you deserve to play."*

I knew he was right, of course, and, during the second half of the season, I worked even harder and started getting in to play being a starter. So, things ended just fine, as far as I was concerned. Then they fired Coach Hatfield.

That was tough. Just when I was getting used to things and getting more playing time, they fired the head coach. Some of the players left, and I'll admit it crossed my mind, too. But when my dad found out, he reacted much differently than I had expected. All my life, he had been hard on me, but when push came to shove, he always had my back. He always took my side if there were outside forces to be confronted. In this case, he took the side of the coaches. He told me to trust Coach Boyd, who wanted me to stay.

The new head coach, Bob Boyd, kept contact with my father over that summer, and my dad really liked him. Probably because they were a lot alike. He was different from Hatfield, more of a strict disciplinarian. Even so, I guess I expected my father to support me if

I wanted to leave, but that wasn't the case. *"Listen to your coach, Son,"* he told me.

They let go Coach Hatfield's staff but kept Coach Farrar, which was a good thing for me. He'd recruited me, my parents liked him, and I liked him, and so that made me feel better about things. And Coach Boyd said all the right things to my parents. In particular, he stressed discipline. I remember him using that word quite a bit, actually. And my father liked hearing that word quite a bit. He liked Coach Boyd because they were very similar in that respect. Disciplinarians.

So, I'd had my mid-season crisis, but I fought through it. But then we lost the coach. I got through that. Then I discovered I might not even play unless I could get my grades up. It was one thing after another.

After I told him about my first year, Dr. Boling asked me what I wanted to do.

"What do you mean?"

"Don't forget why you're here, Butch."

That really hit home. I loved the school, but I didn't really have anyone to help me figure things out on the educational side of things. At that time, I didn't open up to the people in the academic center.

"I want to be a coach," I said.

"All right."

"But I don't want to major in P.E. I'm a business major."

He stood up and shook his head, walking around the side of the desk. "No," he said. "Don't ever let P.E. roll off your tongue like that. It's not P.E. It's *physical education.* You can take a Bachelor of Science in Physical Education and get your Master's in Education. That's how I got my PhD."

That was an eye opener for me. Like I said before, it's important to understand *what you don't know,* so you can push yourself to learn.

"I need your help," I said. "I need somebody to teach me this stuff."

Right then, he opened a desk drawer and pulled out information on educational courses and curriculum plans that basically showed me exactly what I needed to know. He explained each curriculum in detail. How many hours for this class and that class, and how everything would fit together to lead to wherever I needed to go. It was like he showed me how to put all the pieces of the puzzle together. So many hours this semester, plus summer school, plus so many hours next semester. He broke it all down for me, which was really important because it put my goal in focus and gave me a plan to get there.

"So, you do all that," he said, "and at the end of the day, you'll have your degree."

"Really?"

He laughed. "That's all there is to it."

That was exactly what I needed. It had never been explained to me like that before, by anyone. I put that curriculum over my bed and marked off each class as I progressed, and I did that until the day I graduated. I literally slept beneath my grades, and my grades turned around. That was motivation for me. I found my focus, and that allowed me to live up to my potential.

Dr. Boling became my academic advisor after that, and he was a great mentor. He saw in me a need I did not know existed, and by doing so, he helped me reach my true potential. That's the essence of an educator. That's the essence of coaching.

From then on, I followed his lead. Whatever he said for me to do, I did. That was a lot different from the other athletes on scholarship, but I didn't care. I put my faith in Dr. Boling. I stood in those lines when it came time to sign up for my classes, something very few athletes did. My assigned academic advisor even called Coach Boyd about what I was doing, and Coach Boyd called my father right in front of me.

Coach Boyd told my father that I was doing things differently than the other players, and he was concerned. I guess he figured my father would set me straight.

"Put him on the phone," my father said.

Coach Boyd handed me the phone.

"This is what you want to do?" my father asked.

"Yes, sir," I answered.

"Put Coach Boyd back on the line."

My father told Coach Boyd, *"If that's what he wants to do, that's what he's gonna do."*

So, that's what I did. And as a result, I was one of, if not the first black players at Mississippi State to graduate in four years. "On time," as they called it back in the day.

Butch Pierre graduated *on time.*

I've been a punctual man ever since.

Doing it that way not only guided me to a degree in four years, it helped me understand what it took to be an outstanding academic advisor, which really helped me when I went into coaching. That experience gave me an even greater confidence in myself and my ability to accomplish my goals. On time.

When you know how to fix a car, you feel comfortable driving as far as your vehicle will take you. And when you have confidence in yourself, you know you can travel as far as your dreams can reach.

Looking back, I can't believe how lucky I was that Dr. Boling challenged me in class that day. I was dragging myself to summer school, aimlessly, not really paying attention to anything, and all it took was one teacher to take notice and reach out. One teacher changed everything.

That's important for a coach to understand. Anything you say can be the one thing that wakes a player up and changes his entire game. Or maybe his entire life.

Because I trusted Dr. Boling and wasn't too proud to admit my ignorance, I learned a great lesson that day. A lesson that I've carried with me in everything I do.

I walked into his office ready to rumble, but the word of the day was humble, and that day changed the course of my entire life.

CHAPTER SEVENTEEN

"You can lead a boy to college but you
can't make him think."
Elbert Hubbard

A S TIME WENT ON, I settled into my college routine. I think there's a period of adjustment for most college kids, and I definitely went through mine. It kind of reminds me of a movie from years ago that my wife enjoyed, called *How Stella Got Her Groove Back*. That's what one of my players might call a chick's movie, and I would have to agree with that assessment. But the title says it all. Once I reached my sophomore year, I definitely got my groove back.

Basketball was very demanding on top of my academics, but I was determined to excel and reach my goals, no matter what it took to do so.

Most people probably think big-time college athletes have it easy. While it's true that there are a lot of rewards that go with the life of a student athlete, it also takes a lot of discipline and dedication. What you see on TV is a game; what takes place between the games is a lot of old-fashioned hard work.

The pace can be relentless. There are endless meetings and practices, plus you have to work out constantly to stay in shape. Playing college basketball is a full-time job. Add to that all the studying required to get my degree in four years, and there was very little time for anything else in my life. Basically, I became an expert in time management because I had to.

That doesn't mean I didn't have any fun or make friends. Some of the friendships I developed in school are still part of my life today. Some of the things I learned as an athlete are teamwork and loyalty, and that carried through to my personal life, as well.

I roomed with Jeff Norwood my sophomore year, and we had each other's backs both on and off the court. And I met a girl that year, someone who helped me blow off a little steam on the dance floor from time to time. I'd seen her around campus as a freshman and finally got around to asking her out the following year. She was one of those girls a lot of guys pursued, but most of them didn't seem to interest her. Some guys might have thought she was stuck up, but I just figured she was particular about how and with whom she spent her time.

I asked her if she'd like to study with me sometime.

"Study?" she asked.

"I'm gonna graduate in four years, and I could use a good study partner."

She looked at me for a moment like she was trying to figure out if I was serious or if I was shoveling her a line.

"No line," I said, reading her expression.

"All right," she answered, and so we became study partners. We did end up dating, though.

She was as serious about academics as I was, so we helped each other in that regard. She was just the type of girlfriend I needed at the time. Being with someone who studied all the time meant that I studied all the time, too. We encouraged and supported each other, which was important. Whether you're a male or a female, whomever you date at that stage of your life has a big effect on you. Your relationships can mean the difference between realizing your goals and setting yourself back. Ultimately, however, she was not 'the one' for me.

I had three important girlfriends in my life: my high school sweetheart who kept me out of trouble, my college girlfriend who kept my head in the books, and my wife Clemmie, the mother of my children and the love of my life.

There were always girls who were interested in me from an early age. It's like that with athletes. But there were only three girls that I took seriously. And the first two, as sweet as they were, only made me appreciate the one I married. Clemmie was the one who had everything I could ever want or need. But that came later. My sophomore year, in a way, was preparing me for Clemmie, and my profession, in a very big way.

There were lots of changes to deal with that year. Most of the recruiting class I came in with was gone. Michael Green and Tim Payton left. Jeff Malone, Kalpatrick Wells, Terry Lewis, Jeff Norwood, and I all played forty minutes a game, rarely coming out. We were in the best shape of our lives. But it was a young team in transition, a rebuilding year with a new coach and a new style of play, and we lost a lot of games that year, which was tough.

Someone joked that we may be losing, but we looked good doing it, and that was true. We lost close, and no team left without respect for our game. We gave everyone a run for their money.

It was frustrating for me at times, I must admit. I was playing forty to fifty minutes but shooting only six times a game. Even when I was perfect, that's 12 points, and, of course, I wanted more. I liked a faster pace, but I stuck with the coach's deliberative game plan. Most times, we scored in the fifties, which was very different from what I had experienced. Of course, 50 points will win if the other team scores only 49, so it's all relative.

It was good preparation for my coaching career, though. Very often a game plan requires a team effort and individual sacrifice. The fact that I went through it means that I understand how the players feel when I need them to make a sacrifice for the good of the team. Ask any championship player and he or she will tell you that individual stats don't matter if the team doesn't succeed.

We even had a few games that ended in the twenties. It was quite a season with a lot of ups and downs. One snowy night at Mississippi State against Georgia and the great Dominique Wilkins, they had the game in hand. Or so they thought, and he checked out of the game. He later walked over to the scorers' table, waiting to check back in the game because we were threatening to come back. We stalled the ball for eight minutes on offense to delay from him re-entering the game. From the scorers' table, he was yelling foul to his team because he wanted back in the game. No shot-clock in those days. We lost 26-23.

That same year, we upset Kentucky at home when they were in the top five. They may have been #1, which was a great victory for our scrappy team. That year taught me quite a bit about mental toughness and discipline. Our coach had control of every aspect of our game and knew exactly what he wanted out of each and every one of us.

It was also the year I drank beer, I mean really drank beer for the very first time. I blame it all on my roommate.

His parents were locals, and we hung out a lot, and one night he just pressed me on it. "Man, don't you want a beer?"

"Told you, man, I don't drink."

He just laughed. "No, you *didn't used to* drink," he said.

"That almost makes sense," I said, "but not quite."

"C'mon, man, one beer. *One beer!*"

He finally convinced me to have one beer. And then another. He still laughs about how I was buzzing after just two beers, but that was the first time I'd drunk since I was thirteen years old.

"As long as they don't ask me, I'll be okay," I said.

"As long as *who* asks you *what?*"

I looked at him a little drunkenly but very serious. "I never lie to my parents," I answered.

He looked at me like I had an antenna coming out of the top of my head. "Say what?"

"I said I nev – "

He busted out laughing before I could repeat myself, and pretty soon I joined him. But it was true. I may have been drunk, but I never lied to my folks.

Later that season, he and I went down to New Orleans and ended up pulling into my parents' driveway at sunrise.

My mother was waiting for us at the door.

"What do you think you're doing, Man?"

"I think I'm coming home," I answered.

"You been drinking and driving," she said. It was not a question.

After a moment, I pointed to Jeff. "He drove."

Jeff nudged me. "I thought you never…"

"Part of the way," I added.

My mother shook her head and stood aside, allowing us into the house, but she let me have it once the door was closed.

"You don't come in here like that after you've been out all night long, drinking and driving." I had never come home after midnight, and I never drank, so this was all a very big deal to her. And she was right. We never should have been driving.

My mother followed me to the bathroom and kept talking through the door, and then she followed me to the bedroom and kept after me there. Finally, my father woke up and walked into the hallway. "Is he all right?"

"He's all right."

"Then leave the boy alone, Gloria," my father said. "He's in college now."

My father turned and went back into his bedroom. My mother looked from him to me, unsure of who needed to be fussed at, but since she'd given me quite a bit, she decided to go after my father. I think maybe he lured her away from me on purpose, sacrificing himself for the good of the team!

The next day he pulled me aside and asked me if I remembered our talk. I did.

And just before my twenty-first birthday, I had a beer with my father for the very first time. That was big.

In a way, I'd been waiting for that moment my entire life. In the eyes of my father, I was a man. Like I said, we didn't always see eye-to-eye, and he was a hard taskmaster. He could be downright mean, or at least that was how I saw it sometimes. But he was my father, and I was his son, and now we were also two men having a beer together, and it meant a lot to me.

Jeff and my other friends back at college were always surprised when they heard how I told my parents everything, but that's just the way it was. I'll bet most of them wish now they had had that kind of relationship with their parents. As adults, we learn to appreciate our parents more and more as time goes by, especially when we have children of our own. I've had the benefit of a close relationship with my mom and dad for longer than most, and I'm grateful for that every day.

I've been telling that story to my own kids since they were twelve years old. I may have left out the part where I was drinking *before* I turned twenty-one, but that's a minor detail, in my opinion. My twin boys reached the age of twenty-five before either of them drank and they still have not, although I'm pretty sure my daughter may have had one or two drinks before she reached that age.

The reason for my certainty is because when I asked her if she'd ever taken a drink, she said, "Dad, don't ask me that," real indignant-like. That's how you know. As self-assured a young lady as she was and is, I've never yet seen anyone under the age of thirty pull off righteous indignation with any believability at all. But she always did what she was supposed to do, so I'm not disappointed. She's probably the toughest one of my kids, to be honest, and I'm sure her brothers would agree. I guess she takes after her mother that way.

CHAPTER EIGHTEEN

"I'm not a businessman, I'm a business, man."
Kanye West

TOWARD THE END OF MY SOPHOMORE SEASON, we played at LSU, so you can imagine how badly I wanted to impress my hometown crowd. Even though I was on board with Coach Boyd's style of play and had been giving it everything I had, I still didn't like it all that much. And knowing that I would be playing in front of all my old friends, I think it got to me a little bit.

A local paper did an article on me for the front page of the sports section, and in the interview, I said I wasn't used to the new style of play, but that was what the coach wanted. Hopefully, you can imagine how the coach felt when he read that, because I was young and had no idea at the time.

We lost the game, but I played well, so I was happy about that, at least. Then I got called into the coach's office the next day. "Are you happy on this team, Butch?"

"Sure, Coach," I answered. "I mean, yes, sir."

"It doesn't seem like it to me," he said, and he placed the newspaper article down on his desk. "So, let me ask you again. Do you want to be on this team?"

Well, to me that was an entirely different question than the one he'd just asked. It was true that I would have been happier with a faster game and scoring more points. "I just think I play better getting up and down the court," I said, "sir."

"You know, if you don't like it here, you don't have to be here."

Things were escalating a bit, and I knew they could go too far unless I told him what he needed to hear. So that's what I did. I told him what he needed to hear, but it was also something I needed to say. Because unless I could say it out loud to my coach and believe it, he was absolutely right. There was no reason for me to be there unless I was committed.

"I'm a team player, Coach," I said. "You won't have any problems out of me."

He looked at me for a good long while and then stood up and offered me his hand across the desk, finally smiling. "Glad to hear it, Butch."

And I was glad to say it.

I've never been afraid to speak my mind to anyone, no matter who it is. Whether you're a governor or a janitor, all men are the same to me. So, I had no problem telling him how I really felt about our style of play and also that I wanted to stay.

My only misstep had been the fact that he had to read about it in the paper first. Another lesson I would remember when I became a coach: If you've got dirty laundry, wash it before you wear it in public.

That's good advice for life, not just basketball. Words matter. How and when you express yourself matters. How you present yourself to the world matters. So, always present yourself well, because you never know who's watching. Now more than ever.

Coach Boyd, as much as any of my mentors, made me the coach I am today. Under his tutelage, I became a better player and got myself together, academically and otherwise. I became my own man during that year, for many reasons.

I think he had that effect on the other players that stuck with him, as well. That core group of guys stuck together.

My father really liked him, probably because they were similar in some ways. Some would call it 'old school.' My mother was of another mind, however. When we played Southwest Louisiana in a tournament, I saw they were playing the kind of basketball I wanted to play, and I considered a transfer, which my mother was all for. My father thought I was developing well and thought I should stay where I was.

All of that was another great lesson, because they were both right in a way. My father was correct in that I was doing well where I was, and my mother was correct that I could have thrived by making that move. Sometimes in life, we face a choice that's difficult because both paths have potential. It's easy to decide on your direction when things are obvious, but life doesn't always make it so clear-cut.

In this case, I stayed with Coach Boyd. He had placed his confidence in me, and I returned that trust. It helped that they were recruiting two local guys I knew, and two of the best players in the state: Jerome Baptiste and Greg Lazar, both pure Creole and Louisiana to the core, 6'8" and 6'9".

Maybe some choices become clear-cut once you make them.

I was their host when they came to visit, and we had a great time. Their parents spoke Creole, and my father is French Indian and Catholic, so we had a lot in common. Jerome asked me if he could room with me, and I just looked at Jeff and smiled. He laughed, because he knew we needed these guys, too.

Even better than gaining two great teammates was the fact that Coach Boyd hired John Brady as his assistant to get those two recruits, and Coach Brady would eventually become a very big influence in my life.

Great coaches and mentors influence others in many ways, sometimes by design and sometimes by happenstance. The fact that they are mentors by both nature and experience means their very presence makes things happen. It's like what they say about luck: When you're good, you make your own. If you're the type of person who has a positive impact on those around you, good things will happen.

And I believe it works the other way, too. When a young person is receptive to growth, they will naturally be drawn to mentors and coaches whose presence in their lives will produce positive results. And as that young person grows, he or she will become a natural mentor to future generations.

A great coach produces not only great players but also great coaches.

Coach Boyd facilitated my growth as a player and introduced me to John Brady, who helped me grow into the coach I became. Both were open to helping someone like me, a young man looking to soak up every bit of knowledge and experience I could handle. Was I lucky or good? I'd like to think I was both, but even so, I needed the guidance and experience I received from both of those men.

Being in the right place at the right time doesn't mean much if you're not open and ready for the experience. Those coaches helped me get there.

So, things were working. After that rough first year with summer school and then rebuilding during my sophomore year and all that, by the time my junior year rolled around, I had gotten my GPA up to where I wanted it to be and had my academic path all lined up to graduate in four years.

But just as I was always pushing myself on the basketball court, I also wanted more out of academics. After my freshman year, I decided to turn a negative into a positive and signed up for summer school again, even though I didn't have to. I continued doing that every summer. Some of my friends thought I was crazy.

"You mean you want to go to school in the summer?"

"Don't you wanna have no fun?"

"Man, you gonna miss out."

I have to laugh at that last one. Some of those guys who told me I'd be 'missing out' ended up missing out on a lot of opportunities later in life. The fact is that most college kids want to have fun and don't always do what they need to do. Sometimes because they don't care, and sometimes because they just don't know any better. Like my first year when I had no idea about how my GPA could affect my athletic career.

That's where mentors enter the picture. People who have been there before and can guide you along the way. That's why every good coach is also a good mentor. That's why every good coach is also a teacher.

I took summer school classes to make sure I stayed ahead of the game, and it paid off for me big time. A dog that runs hard every morning gets to relax in the afternoon.

That summer before my junior year went really well. We had Larry Eustacey and Coach Brady as assistants and Richard Williams on staff. Kermit Davis Jr. was a graduate assistant. After that rebuilding year, we looked to have a good team, and I was excited. Those Cajuns came up for the summer and went home every weekend, just like good old Louisiana boys.

Everybody was working hard. Sometimes maybe a little too hard.

Running outside in the Mississippi heat and then lifting weights on our schedule was tough. Legendary Al Miller's "Miller Time" as he would say strength program was no joke, and I saw that those new players were having a hard time. I felt responsible for them, which I think was the beginning of my affinity for coaching. I had showed them around the campus their very first trip, and they felt close to me ever since, like an older brother who had been around a little longer and who they could admire. And I liked that, being a mentor. I wasn't really thinking of it so much in that way, but later on, I recognized the significance of our relationship. Looking back at my life experience, it's easy to see the signs that pointed to a career in coaching. So I went to the line for them.

Dogging it is one of those macho things where you don't want to ease up in front of your teammates. Even when those other players have a year or two on you in both experience and physical development. You never want to look like you can't keep up.

I went to Coach Boyd and let him know that maybe the coaches should ease up on the two freshmen from Louisiana just a little bit. I told Coach Brady the same thing.

"You went through it," he said. Coach Brady was just a young guy back then, not that much older than I, really, and we had easy rapport from the very beginning. I was respectful of his position as coach but felt like I could be honest with him, too.

"I know these guys, Coach," I told him, and I did. Born and raised in Louisiana and going home for Mom's cooking every weekend was something I knew very well. Being young and homesick can break your spirit a little bit when you add all the physical and mental demands of elite basketball. It's a tough transition from high school to college, even without athletics on top of it. "They're different from me, Coach."

Coach Brady could see that I was serious about the team and sincere in my concerns, but ultimately it was up to Coach Boyd, who was a tough coach with his own mind, same as any coach. I just didn't want to lose two good players, and I could see they were struggling. My opinion was that everybody has to go through the fire, but it doesn't hurt to adjust the temperature now and then. But it wasn't enough.

At the beginning of the year, before the start of the season, both players disappeared. I was rooming with Jerome, and one night he asked me if I could disappear for a while, so he could bring a girl up to the room. Now that was strictly forbidden in those days, but guys did it anyway from time to time, because that's what guys do. You can't have a dorm filled with four hundred male college students and expect that nobody was gonna ever break that rule.

And I guess maybe he knew about a time when *I* broke it, so it wasn't like I had any room to tell him no. "All right, man," I said. "Just don't get caught."

"Gimme till 12:30," he said.

That was pretty late for me because I had to get up early for class, but I told him okay and left him to it. I got back right on time, and he was gone, and his bed was made up real nice and neat, so I figured he must have done his business and taken her home. I brushed my teeth and climbed into bed, but something just didn't feel right to me. Who has sex with a woman and hangs around to make the bed before he takes her home? No college kid I ever heard of.

I jumped out of bed and checked the closet. All his stuff was gone. I went to check Greg's room. Same thing. They'd both packed up and gone back to Louisiana, and they ended up transferring to schools closer to home.

Back then, nobody had personal trainers and everything else the elite players show up with nowadays. There were no nutritionists and sports psychologists and all the other types of support systems that exist today in big-time college athletics. Even though they were both great players with NBA potential, that night they were just two kids a long way from home. I understood the feeling.

Still, it felt bad. Neither one had said anything to me beforehand, which hurt my feelings a little bit until I realized they were probably just embarrassed and couldn't face me.

Jerome in particular would have known I'd have tried to talk him out of it and probably succeeded, at least for a while. Both guys looked up to me and didn't want to disappoint me, I guess.

And I *was* disappointed, to be honest. Before they arrived, I had been rooming with Jeff, whom I trusted completely, even to drive my car, and anyone who knew me back then knew how much I loved that car. But Jerome wanted to room with me, so I said okay. And I already mentioned how I tried to look out for both of them. Every big school had recruited them, but those two guys from south Louisiana felt real comfortable with me. So, I felt like I did my part to bring them to the team. I guess that was my first experience as a recruiter.

Despite my disappointment, I learned from the experience. The whole situation was another lesson for the coach I would become. Ultimately, you do your best to train and educate and support your players, but they will still make the final decision on a lot of things you just can't control. Just like your children. You raise them as best you can, you give them all the tools they need to succeed, but they're always going to make decisions for themselves that you may or may not agree with. Decisions that may or may not disappoint you. That's part of the game. Part of life.

You can't shoot the ball for your players once they're on the court. Those two guys wanted to go home, and that's what they did.

Adversity happens. You have to deal with it and move on. But there was plenty more adversity to come.

MENTORS

Finding one and being one.

We all have people in our lives, on our "team," who are indispensable. People who we couldn't do without because they always have our back and are always available with advice or comfort. Everybody needs someone to talk to from time to time, but how much better is it when that person also has good advice for us?

Mentors and role models are incredibly important to achieve success in any field, whether it's sports, business, or just personal. Whether you realize it or not, you have these people in your life. Even if you haven't designated them as such, they are there, and they guide you, if only by example.

Finding a mentor or role model is easy. Just think of who you look up to or who you want to be more like, and that's it. Hopefully, you choose someone accessible because mentoring requires personal interaction, but a role model can be anyone, even someone you've never met. You just have to see admirable qualities you want to emulate.

Being a mentor is harder. It requires commitment and example. You have to be there for your mentee, and you have to set a good example for them. Being a mentor, in my opinion, can be even more valuable because it keeps you on your toes. No coach wants to disappoint a player, no parent wants to disappoint a child, and no mentor wants to disappoint a mentee. Being a mentor is an incredibly rewarding experience.

I have had many mentors and have mentored many. I highly recommend both.

Greatness takes teamwork. Finding and being a great mentor is essential to your success.

CHAPTER NINETEEN

"Hold fast to dreams, for if dreams die,
life is a broken-winged bird that cannot fly."
Langston Hughes

L ATE IN THE SEASON, I broke my fifth metatarsal, which is the long bone on the outside of the foot that connects with the pinky toe. I missed the last nine games of my junior year and the SEC tournament, and our team missed the NCAA tournament.

It was especially disappointing because we were doing really well up to that point. The team did okay without me but would have been better with me because I'd been the starting point guard since my freshman year. Jeff Malone was having a great season, however, averaging around 25 points a game, and ended up a top ten NBA draft pick after his senior season.

Needless to say, my season was not what I wanted or expected it to be. Wearing a boot cast on the sideline while your team loses is a pretty terrible experience.

But even before my injury, I'd had my ups and downs that season. I got caught with a girl in the dorm one night after a game and got kicked out of the athletic housing as a result. It was after a game and after midnight, and I should have snuck her down the back stairway, but instead we took the elevator.

When the doors opened in the lobby, I saw Coach Akins, the athletic dorm director, making his rounds, coming right toward me. I quickly nudged her back into the elevator and stepped out like nothing was wrong.

"What are doing up this late, Pierre?" he barked.

"Just getting some air, Coach," I answered, which sounded even more stupid *after* I'd said it. It didn't help that he saw me push the button for the basement after I'd stepped off.

His eyes met mine, and I knew he had me. Coach Akins hit the stairs to the basement, running, and caught her getting off the elevator, and just like that, I was out of the athletic dormitory.

I wasn't actually all that upset about it, except I missed that extra-long bed they provided the athletes. And it wasn't as convenient for meals with my teammates since my new dorm was a few blocks from where we ate. But I started meeting a more diverse group of students since I basically had to fend for myself a little more than I had done before. In the athletic dorm, a lot of things are taken care of for you.

I met more white students during that time and made friends, and even took a few brothers to some mostly white parties, which was a new experience for several of us. There's a lot of segregation that happens because people just naturally hang around with those they relate to most easily. I think it's good to get out of your comfort zone from time to time. Talk to people you wouldn't normally talk to. A good part of my job as a coach and a recruiter has been communication, and that time helped prepare me for what was to come.

On the negative side, I was drinking more than before. Sometimes I'd even have a beer on the drive home over the weekend or holidays, which was a stupid thing to do, I admit. There's no excuse for it, but it is what it is.

I'd made the drive home to Louisiana so often, I guess I got a little too comfortable in my driving routine. And a little too cocky in other ways, because I got more than a few speeding tickets that year, as well. I'd become friends with a highway patrolman who would always take care of them. I don't know what he did with those tickets, but all I had to do was hand them over, and I never heard of them again.

That's one of the dangers of being an elite athlete, particularly at the college level. It's easy to become dependent on special favors like that, benefits not enjoyed by other people. You don't have to do the same things other people have to do. You can almost forget about real life, in a way. Everything's done for you. Your problems are handled. Things like speeding tickets magically disappear. But it's dangerous because you never get a chance to see yourself as a normal person, doing normal things. Because you're elite.

Because you're young, you're still developing your personality, your work ethic, everything. People fawn over you, and it can be just as intoxicating as that beer you have while you're driving, even though you know it's wrong.

The last time I was stopped for speeding on my way home for the weekend, the highway patrolman saw a six-pack of beer in the back seat with two missing. He asked me how many I'd drunk, and I said one. I was alone in the car, the beers were still cold, and I had the nerve to tell him one beer. He wrote me out a ticket after I passed the sobriety test.

For some reason, I mentioned that I'd be giving the ticket to my friend, my 'fixer.' I don't know how I expected him to react, but, like I said, I'd gotten a little cocky about those tickets. The highway patrolman looked up at me for a moment and then went back to his work. He tore off the ticket and handed it to me without another word. That wasn't the last time I saw him.

When I stopped by the station to deliver that ticket to my friend, he was a little less happy to see me than usual. There was no talk of basketball, either.

"Can't fix this one," he said.

Before I could ask why, he turned and went into an office. After a moment, the highway patrolman came out, the one who'd written the ticket. My friend's *supervisor.* Turned out he knew who I was the night he had stopped me.

"Don't get any more tickets," he said and handed the ticket back to me.

That was the last time I got caught drinking and driving.

There were other things that happened that season that weren't exactly positive. I was late for curfew after we lost at Vanderbilt. I was only about thirty minutes over, but rules are rules, and Coach Boyd was a disciplinarian. He left a note on my door to call him when I arrived.

Curfew was midnight, and I had gotten back about 12:30, so I figured I shouldn't wake him up, but that's not how the coaches saw things. If I was thinking logically, I would have realized that the only way he knew I wasn't there was because he had checked, which meant he'd written that note in the last half hour, which meant I wouldn't be waking him up out of a deep sleep. Now that I'm a coach myself, I understand these things a lot better.

I was also mad that we had lost, to be honest. Another player and I hadn't played as well as we usually did, and since it would have been big to upset Vanderbilt at home, I was upset at how things ended. And the fact that the coaches knew I could play better than I did only added to that. They mentioned it after the game, too.

Coach Boyd asked me the next day if I had gotten his note.

"What note?" I lied.

I knew the way he was looking at me that he didn't believe for a second that I hadn't gotten it. I have looked at players in exactly the same way. Any coach that's been around longer than five minutes can tell when a player's feeding them a line.

"I called your father this morning," he continued, ignoring the fact that I'd just lied to his face. He was a disciplinarian, but Coach Boyd also knew that when some immature kid was digging himself a hole, sometimes you just take the shovel away and move on. "Better call him and tell him you're okay."

So I did. He asked me what had happened, and I told him the truth, which was that we had met a couple of girls and went to a party. Someone else was driving, so we got back late. And that was it.

Except that it wasn't it because Coach Boyd didn't start me the next day for a nationally televised game at Kentucky. So, I learned that no matter who you are, your actions have consequences.

We lost by 25 points, and Coach Boyd finally put me in with about five minutes left. Knowing him, he probably didn't want to play me at all, but I think he wanted to prove a point.

Before then, I was cheering the team on from the sidelines as loudly as I could, showing the coaches that I wasn't one of those players who threw tantrums or sulked or any of that nonsense. The way I saw it, if I did the crime, I'd do the time, even if I didn't think it was fair. My attitude was going to be positive no matter what the circumstances.

When Coach Boyd called my name, I jumped off that bench and ran up to the scorers' table and ripped off my sweats like a man on fire. I went into that game and played as hard as I could for those last few minutes, both for my self-respect and to show the coaches they should have put me in sooner.

Coach Boyd was probably testing me, anyway, to see if I'd mope around like I was still upset or something. It makes me laugh now to recall how fast I ran out onto the court just to prove nothing could keep me down. He'd have yanked me right back to the bench if I hesitated, anyway. It's not like I was going to make up 25 points in five minutes so he could have left me out the whole game. But since he wanted to see how I would react, I gave him a good show.

Kentucky was a top five team at the time, and we were underdogs, so it would have been a safe bet that we would have lost the game even if I'd started. But even so, you never know what would have happened. We were a good team that year and came within a second or two of beating them at home earlier in the year.

In my mind, I was a lot more upset about that game than I let on because I think the punishment was too harsh. I was a good player that didn't cause any problems on or off the court. I went to class, made good grades, did everything I was supposed to do. But the first time there was problem, he sat me out.

I tell that story because it made me a better coach in this way: I have learned to treat everyone fairly, but I have also learned that fair does not mean equal. There are always going to be differences in people and in circumstances. Everything is a judgment call.

That's where Coach Boyd and I differ a little in our coaching philosophies. I respect him like no other, but he treated everybody fairly *and* equally, without regard for circumstances. The way I see it, you're better off looking at the whole situation. The whole person. Just like those two kids from Louisiana. Treating them equally meant there was no easing up on those workouts. They had to do everything the same as the juniors and seniors. Whereas I would have eased up a little and worked to help them get to the same level as the older guys. I would have treated them fairly but not necessarily equally.

There are exceptions, of course. Sometimes a coach needs to make an example of someone for the good of the team. Sometimes team morale is the most important thing to work on, and sometimes individual morale takes precedence. Every problem demands a specific solution. Nothing works *all* the time. I expect my players to trust me and to do what I say, but I also recognize that I can adapt when the situation warrants. Some players do better when you ride them hard, and others respond better to positive reinforcement. In my opinion, a coach needs to know the difference.

On the other hand, Coach Boyd called me into his office after we got back from Kentucky and told me how much the team needed me. How he expected me to step up and how he knew I *would* step up. What he knew I was capable of doing.

The whole coaching staff was there, and telling me all that in front of everyone really meant something to me. That was the right button to push with me.

The very next time we played, I had the best game of my college career. Scored 22 against Tennessee, and we won a game we were supposed to lose.

So, I guess in a way, our coaching philosophies are not really all that different. Even though he was a real tough disciplinarian, he had the knowledge and understanding to find out what best motivated me to achieve excellence. And I guess I've found over the years that some of my players thought of me as a hard-ass, too. It all depends on your perspective.

I'm sure if I had moped around after being sent into that game with five minutes left, Coach Boyd would have assumed I was just a selfish, immature player who could hurt the team as easily as helping it. But because I kept a positive mental attitude, he saw the potential in me and helped me realize it.

After that, I had a better understanding of him as both a coach and a man, and my respect for him has grown over time. I never doubted he respected me as a player, but it took me a year or two to understand that he also cared about me as a human being, and that made a big difference in my growth as a player, my potential as a coach, and my evolution as a man.

But of course the worst of all was being injured. It was a terrible time to get hurt, and, frankly, it depressed the hell out of me. I couldn't practice or really even walk, so I drove everywhere. I was miserable.

My whole family was praying about it, and nothing made me feel any better. I was no longer in control of my destiny, and that was a tough thing for me to deal with, especially after all my hopes for that season. After all I'd hoped for my life.

For the first time, I had to face the cold reality that I might not make it to the NBA, something I'd dreamed of my whole life. Something I'd wanted more than anything. Something I knew in my heart I was capable of achieving. It wasn't the same as someone who never played the game dreaming of what it would be like to play in the NBA or hit a homerun in the World Series. This was a dream I was perfectly capable of achieving.

What happens when you get that close to your dream, and it's snatched away? What happens when the thing you love the most in the world is taken away? What do you do then?

At a time like that, a real life-changing moment, the rubber meets the road. You find out what you're made of when life knocks you down. Things can go wrong in a hurry if you're not careful. That's when some really bad habits can develop. Habits that can change the course of your entire life. Drugs, alcohol abuse, you name it. I wasn't going to take that road. I had to get myself together.

I talked things over with my parents quite a bit during that time. We prayed together, cried together, and prayed some more. The fact is that the higher you go, the tougher it is to reach the top. It never gets easier. At that level, the competition is fierce, and those who make it are few. And when you come so close and don't quite get there, that makes it even harder. Never give up on your dreams, but make alternative plans.

That was a hard pill for me to swallow, but I got through it. I got myself together. I manned up and faced reality. God always has plan!

As a coach, I explain all this to my players at some point. I give them the straight talk they need to hear, because they're just like I was. They're all sure they'll make it to the NBA. But a lot of them won't, and they have to be ready for that. They have to make other plans. There are other places to play, foreign leagues, things like that. Coaching is a great way to stay in the game, which is the route I took. You have to consider other options, even while you fight as hard as you can to make your dreams come true. Because you never know what's coming your way. You fight and you fight, and you keep moving forward. Like Satchel Paige said, "Don't look back 'cause whatever's back there might be gaining on you."

Fight your fight the best you can. Fight your fight and move on.

I got hurt again in my senior year. A hairline fracture to my tibia, which turned out to be tough to diagnose. It seemed like shin splints for a while, so I just tried to rest between games and practices and to keep on playing as best I could. I might have been compensating for the previous injury, and those shin splints turned into a fracture at some point. I really don't know. However, it happened, and it meant my basketball career was over.

I didn't want to give up, of course. I kept thinking I could still compete, and, the truth is, today I still believe I could have played in the NBA. That's the mindset you develop as an elite athlete, and I still have it. Every time I stepped onto the court, I believed I could win. You have to think that way to compete at a professional level. But on a human level, you have to accept reality.

I had been hurt in high school and played through the pain until I was back to full strength, but back then there was time to heal. Now my time had run out.

After graduation, I received calls from the Dallas Cowboys and San Francisco 49ers, asking me to try out. I accepted their invitations and did pretty well, but, deep down, I knew I wasn't going to play pro football. Basketball had been my life since I was a kid. That decision was made a while back.

Whether I had chosen basketball or basketball had chosen me, neither one was done with the other just yet. Not by a long shot.

CHAPTER TWENTY

"Challenges make you discover things about
yourself that you never really knew."
Cicely Tyson

THAT LAST YEAR IN SCHOOL WAS TOUGH, but I kept moving. I began to read more, study harder, and take a good look at the world around me. I became more observant. I started paying more attention to what was going on outside my life on the court, because I wanted to prepare myself for whatever came my way. I wanted to figure out where I would be in the next few years if I was no longer playing basketball.

In my years as a coach, I've always tried to prepare my players not only for each and every game but for bigger things, as well. Part of my job is to see the bigger picture, even when they can't, and to get them ready. I want my players to succeed not only on the court but in life, too. And I see it as my responsibility to prepare them for that. I want every one of them to play in the NBA if that's their dream, but I also want to help them find a way forward if they travel a different path. Lots of players just aren't ready for it to end, and that's normal.

Speaking for myself, I didn't want to go into the coaches' office and ask them what I should do, and I didn't want to go home and explain to people what I was doing back there. A lot of people back home were invested in my success, too. I had received incredible support from the community, and I didn't want to let them down. So, it was hard. Like I said, it was a life-changing time, and I had to find my own way through it. As much as my parents loved me, as much as the community supported me, no one could make those decisions except me.

I've seen guys that just couldn't handle it. They let everyone around them say it's okay when it's not, and they kind of revel in that pity. They get soft. They have a beer, they smoke some weed, and they let everyone around them feel sorry for them. And they feel sorry for themselves, too. It's easy to surround yourself with people who are bad influences. People who distract you. I came close to that at times, I admit.

I was devastated, but I tried to keep a positive attitude. I hid my feelings from my parents at times, but they knew I was hurting because they were hurting just as much.

So much of life at that age is just feeling your way through, finding solutions to problems you never knew existed until they stop you in your tracks. As a kid, you have tunnel vision. You know what you want and you go after it. When an obstacle comes your way, it's new to you so you deal with it.

I was lucky because of my upbringing. I don't know where I would have ended up if I hadn't had strong, moral parents that set good examples and gave me the love and support I needed. Sometimes it was tough love, but tough love is still love.

Life is all about choices and consequences. One always follows the other. You learn from both victories and losses, and hopefully, you get better as you go along. I'm still learning things every day, and every lesson makes me a better husband and father and a better coach.

When one of my players gets injured, I pay close attention because of my own experience. I watch them. I observe. Maybe they never had a problem with drugs, but such a problem could develop. When circumstances change, people can change. I want to see my players change for the better. I want my players to evolve. I want them to become better players but also better men. I'm there for them because so many good people were there for me.

I took a full load that fall semester, and I would need to take twenty hours to graduate in the spring, but I was determined to do it. I spent a lot of time with the trainer that year because he taped my ankles before every practice. Paul Mock was a good trainer, personable as well as knowledgeable. Trainers spend a lot of time with injured players, and sometimes there's a lot of time to talk. Paul was almost like a counselor to me.

"You may be one of the first black athletes to graduate in four years at Mississippi State, Butch," he said one day.

"One of the first or the first?" I asked. I always wanted to be number one.

"One of the first."

"Then I'm gonna be the first," I answered.

I got excited about that academic goal, which was a good distraction, because it really helped me power through what turned out to be an excruciating season.

Midway through, I was in so much pain; I could barely walk to class. And by then, it was too late to redshirt, so I played hurt the entire year, but I couldn't play up to my potential. It was probably the most miserable three months of my life.

Coach Boyd was very supportive during that time. He even let me store my things at his house when I went home for the summer. By then, we'd gotten to the point where we talked quite a bit. One day, he told me he thought I'd make a good coach, which kinda pissed me off at first because I wanted him to say that I could still make it to the NBA. But I guess he'd seen injuries like mine before, and he knew they could take quite a while to heal sometimes.

Which turned out to be true in my case. Once I played my last game at Mississippi State, it would be a full two years before I was able to play again. As you can tell, I still held out hope, even as I hobbled through that last season.

After they finally had diagnosed my injury as a hairline fracture of the tibia, they told me simply to stay off it as much as I could. The doctor didn't put me in a cast or anything like that. And it was impossible to know exactly when the fracture occurred and whether or not I came back too soon after my previous injury.

Getting the definitive word was pretty hard. As you can imagine, there was a lot of anger and second guessing. Even though I was pressing forward with academics and thinking about my future plans, when the door finally closed, it closed hard. I went home and spent a month on the Mississippi River, running parts on a grain elevator. I thought maybe that would take my mind off things, but that didn't work. The mental and psychic wound was too fresh, and, like my ankle, it would take time to heal.

Word got out, of course. I'm from a small, tight-knit community, and there are really no secrets in a place like that. Everybody just assumed I would play in the NBA one day, just like I did.

People were good about it, though. They gave me my space. A local high school offered me a coaching job, but I wasn't ready for that. I had a long talk with Coach Boyd, who told me I could be a graduate assistant at Mississippi State and work on my master's degree. He even told me I could stay in his spare bedroom while I did so.

I turned him down. "Thanks, Coach, but I think I'm going to go home and think for a while."

He understood. "Let me know if you change your mind, Butch," he said. "You'd make a great coach."

I went to church and talked to my priest. He thought coaching was a good idea, too. My Aunt Cleo had a similar opinion, but she expressed it in her own unique way, of course. "Carry your ass back to school, boy," she cackled. "S'a no brainer!"

My mother thought I should go play in Europe, but I wasn't healed up enough for an elementary school playground at that point.

Of everyone I spoke with, my father was the only one that thought I should just take the high school job. "Can't be no prima donna, Son. Got to get a job, get your own place. Start paying some bills for a change!"

There was some of that tough love I was talking about. He pissed me off, to be honest, but there was some truth to what he said. I had never paid any bills to speak of. He'd supported me until I received my scholarship, and then the school supported me, mostly. Maybe I did need to take the job.

But something Aunt Cleo, an educator, said was floating around in the back of my mind. When I told her I needed a break from school after sixteen years, she'd said, "Once you quit, there's no going back."

The more I thought about it, the more I agreed with her. It might not have been true for everybody, but it was for me. If I didn't stay in school and get my master's degree now, I might never do it.

I talked it over with my father, and he thought that was probably right. "But I'm gonna need your help," I said.

He just looked at me, waiting for me to ask. Ain't nothing easy about my father, not then and not now. Grandchildren softened him up a little, but only to a point.

"I'll be on scholarship, but I'll still need money for housing and food and things."

"And *things*?"

"C'mon, Dad."

He nodded, mulling it over. I think we both knew what he was going to say, but he still needed to come to terms with it in his own mind.

"How long?" he asked.

"Two years," I answered.

"Two years," he said. "But after that, you're getting a job."

"Grad assistant *is* a job," I said.

"A job that *pays*," he said, before seeing the tiny smile forming on my lips. "Boy, don't try me."

"No, sir!" I said and left the room before I busted out in a big smile for my mother, who was waiting for the word from on high. She gave me a big hug. I think she was as relieved as I was that I'd found my path forward.

I called Coach Boyd.

"It's Butch."

"Change your mind?"

"How'd you know?"

"Cause you're a smart young man," he said. "Why do you think I said you'd make a good coach?"

I took him up on the job, but I didn't move into his house. I figured I'd want at least a little separation from the job and my own space. Maybe even a social life. He was pretty smart to make the offer, though. If your grad assistant is living under your roof, when does he clock out?

It was a little strange at the first coaches' meeting, hearing them discuss the players and their abilities and personalities. Making a few jokes about them.

I had to know. "Did ya'll talk about *me* like that?" I asked.

One of the other coaches laughed. "You were even worse," he said.

I turned to Coach Brady. "*You* liked me, right?"

He smiled and paused before answering, long enough to make me sweat. "I liked you all right, Butch."

Well, *that* gave me a different perspective on coaching. It's like the first time you see one of your teachers at the grocery store or you hear them cuss or something when they don't think any students are listening.

Turns out they're people just like you, with opinions and everything. And they might just make jokes about you behind your back now and then.

I took to coaching right away. Fell in love with it, to be honest. I eventually came to believe it was what I was meant to do. I loved watching film and discussing the game, how certain players did well or how they should have done something differently. I really enjoyed analyzing the performances. It was like I was living vicariously through the players. I could understand what they were doing before they did it because I had been there myself.

I threw myself into the job. I helped out around the office, spent time on the floor with the players, and basically did anything that needed to be done. My father would call it *making myself useful.*

That's part of my philosophy of life, actually. Make yourself useful. Or better yet, make yourself indispensable. Do your job so well that no one can imagine anyone else doing it. Make yourself a necessary part of the team, no matter what your profession. If you're needed not wanted, you'll never be out of a job.

Coach Brady and I bonded on scouting trips. Even though he was a full assistant coach and I was a grad assistant, he never talked down to me or discounted my opinion. Speaking of which, I learned pretty quickly when to share my opinion and when to shut up. I understood the hierarchy in coaching and gave it my respect. But even when I didn't share my opinions, I still had them. Plenty of them.

I began to develop my coaching philosophy even during that first year. I soaked up everything like a sponge. Seeing the game from a coach's perspective was amazing to me.

If I had known as a player what I was learning as a coach, I would have been an even stronger player, of that I'm sure. I started to act like an assistant coach, even as I began to think like a head coach. I believe all assistant coaches need that mindset, because you never know when an opportunity will present itself. Years later, when I was thrown into a head coaching position unexpectedly, I was as ready as anyone had ever been to take over that job in those circumstances.

Success requires preparation, and I had begun my preparation for the rest of my career. I found my true calling.

In '84, Mississippi had a choice between a kid from Atlanta and a local kid from Mississippi. We couldn't recruit both, but we needed one. The local boy was tall, 6'9", but what Coach Boyd would call "a little soft." I had played with him in the basketball camps and thought he was going to be a great player, even though the big city kid was probably tougher at the time.

The local was one of Brady's recruits, and since I went on trips with Coach Brady, he asked me which one I would take.

I told him I'd take the local kid. "I think he's gonna be big time, Coach." I thought he was a late bloomer, maybe a little bit timid, but he'd grow out of it.

Coach Boyd offered the scholarship to the guy from Atlanta. The Mississippi kid, the one I'd recommended, who was "a little soft," went to Alabama, and Derrick McKey went on to kick our ass every single year and play in the NBA for fourteen years after that. Derrick was all-conference at Alabama, SEC player of the year, and he would have been an easy sign for us. A player like that makes a big difference.

I just have a feel for talent, I guess.

CHAPTER TWENTY-ONE

"Never was anything great achieved without danger."
Machiavelli

S INCE I HAD FOUND MY CAREER PATH, I was anxious to get down to it, and I worked my tail off. There were a lot of people invested in my success, and I didn't want to let them down. My parents, my coaches, and even the guys I played with always expected me to be the best at whatever I did, so that's what I always set out to do.

It really just boils down to pride. When you have pride in your game, pride in yourself, you have the confidence to take on whatever comes your way.

That's something I try to instill in my players, leading by example. But there's a verse in the Bible that reminds us what pride can do if we don't maintain a sense of humility. During my last year as a graduate assistant, I almost took a very damaging fall.

A girl I was friendly with called me at home one night and suggested we go out for a ride. Maybe have a beer or something. I didn't ask what *or something* meant, because I was a young man in college, and she was a pretty girl, and that was all I needed to hear to get me out of the house.

I don't mean to say I understood that anything more was going to happen than just a drive in the country, but I'd be lying if I tried to tell you other possibilities hadn't crossed my mind. Still, I would have been perfectly all right if a drive was all it turned out to be.

It ended up being a lot more than that but not in a good way. See, the girl was white.

A young black man in Mississippi doesn't have to go very far to find trouble, sometimes. Just run out of gas out on some country road late at night with a white girl, and see if trouble doesn't find you right quickly. And find me, it did.

We were about twenty miles from campus and five miles outside the nearest town when I heard that engine sputter and realized I had misjudged my gasoline situation. We'd been talking and laughing and having such a good time, I just missed the gauge, somehow.

I let my foot off the gas and coasted as far as I could until we finally came to a stop. I shook my head in disgust. I really couldn't believe I had actually run out of gas.

She was fine with it, though. Not mad or anything. She even joked about whether that was my plan all along.

"C'mon, now," I said. But hearing her say that made me a little uncomfortable, to be honest. She had come to all the basketball games, and we were friendly, but I really didn't know her all that well.

There was a house up the road with a light on, so I told her I'd see if someone there could help us out. I figured it would be better if I went alone, seeing as how neither one of us knew the area or the people in it.

Luckily, the guy who answered the door at that house was a basketball fan, and he not only offered to give me a ride into town, he even let me borrow a gas can.

We passed my car on the way, and I told her we'd be right back. The guy driving, who was also white, didn't say anything about her at all, just kept talking basketball, so I relaxed a little.

I couldn't help but remember my mother's reaction back in high school when two pretty white cheerleaders had shown up at our house with beer on their breath. She politely but firmly sent them on their way, but as soon as that front door closed, she went ballistic.

"Don't you *ever* put yourself in that situation again, Man!"

"What situation?" I asked.

"You know exactly what I mean," she yelled, and of course I did. But she explained it for me again, anyway. It was a variation of the talk all black parents have with their children, especially their sons.

The basketball fan pulled into his driveway and let me out. I promised to bring the gas can back and walked up the road to where the car was. It was pretty dark, so I didn't see the man standing around back of the car until I was almost up on him. It was a white police officer.

I remember I immediately slowed my pace just a bit to appear more casual. It was almost instinct. I briefly wondered why his car was parked a few lengths behind mine, with no lights on at all. It was then I noticed she wasn't in the car but leaning against the back fender. Neither one of them said a word as I walked up with the gas can.

"Hello," I said, trying to sound friendly and unconcerned, but my heart was racing. It was just the kind of situation my mother had told me to avoid.

"Right now you're here at home, in a safe place, where your father and I can protect you! But it's not always going to be like that."

"I can take care of myself."

She just shook her head. "Don't be stupid, Man."

"This your car, boy?"

I was glad it was dark because I knew my eyes probably flashed a little anger when he called me 'boy,' and I didn't want him to perceive anything but respect in that moment.

"Yes, sir," I said.

"What you doing out here?"

"Ran out of gas," I answered.

He sneered and moved a step closer to me. I was at least a head taller than he was, but he was the one with the gun on his hip. "I guess I can see that can you're holding, boy."

There it was again.

"I mean what are you doing out here with *her?*"

Of course, I knew exactly what he meant. She started to say something, but he shut her up with a look and then turned back to me, waiting for my answer.

"We just took a drive. Neighbor up the road gave me a ride into town for gas," I said. "He's waiting for his gas can as soon as I can get it back to him," I added.

The officer looked past me. I turned my head and saw the house light was still on.

"This your *girlfriend?*" he asked.

"Friend," I said, hoping the correction wouldn't upset either one of them.

He turned to her. "That right? He your friend?"

She nodded. I saw fear in her eyes, which wasn't at all what I wanted to see. If she panicked and decided she might get in trouble herself, who knew what she would say? What if she made something up? Finally she found her voice. "We're just friends," she said.

"You sure you're all right?"

This cop was really making me mad now. It was like he wanted to stir something up. Almost like he was telling her to give him an excuse to arrest me or something.

Not exactly the *or something* that had gotten me out of the house earlier.

She looked at me and then back to the cop. I held my breath. To think that I'd put my life in the hands of a girl I barely knew was really stupid.

"Don't be stupid, Man."

"I'm all right," she said.

The cop looked at her for a long time and then turned back to me. "It's dangerous to leave her out here by herself," he said. "Pour that gas in, and I'll follow you back to campus."

I quickly emptied the gas into my tank, returned the can, and drove back to the gas station. The officer watched as I filled the tank and then followed us all the way back to campus, where he waited until I dropped her off before he finally drove away.

The only words I spoke to her after the gas station were, *"Sorry for making you wait."*

I saw her around campus after that, but I avoided her like the plague. I had lots of white friends, but none of them were women for the next several years.

When I finally got home, my hands were numb from having been so tightly clenched on the steering wheel. My adrenaline was off the charts.

That was the first time something like that had happened to me, and I was determined to make it the last. I never told my mother what had happened because it would have just made her worry, but I never forgot her words again after that. I tell recruits about that kind of thing all the time.

"One mistake could destroy your career, maybe even end your life," I say. And I see who gets it and who doesn't. It's in their eyes. I can read them like a book, just as my parents could always read me. I was just like them, and I know they'll make mistakes, just like I did. "One wrong choice can affect the rest of your life," I tell them. "So make good choices."

Hopefully, they'll be as fortunate as I was and learn those hard lessons without too much tragedy. Hopefully, they'll understand the importance of those wise words I got from my mother. *"Don't be stupid, Man."*

I continued working on my master's degree and received it by the end of my second year, right on time. Which meant it was time for me to get a "real job," as my father would say. There was a coaching staff shake-up around that time, and almost everyone got fired. I was hoping to stay on and maybe get a permanent job at the school, but there was one problem. Earlier in the year, there had been a snowstorm. One of the assistants asked me to go outside to the bus and bring in his bag. It was probably about two degrees or something.

A lot of times as a graduate assistant, you get asked to do things like that, and most of the time you would just do it. Women go through this a lot more than men, I'd bet, being asked to make coffee when it's not their job, things like that.

But something about the way he asked me to carry in his bag just rubbed me the wrong way, and I said, "Nah, I don't really think I want to do that."

And there I was, a few months later, asking him for a job.

He didn't say, *"Nah, I don't really think I want to do that,"* but he might as well have. He said something about how he wanted someone from Mississippi with more experience in the assistant coach's job, but the truth was that he'd never looked at me the same way after I refused to carry in his things or at least that's what I thought. And I think that was his way of paying me back. I had a master's degree, and it wasn't my job, but I probably should have just made a joke about it and carried in that bag.

It wasn't a tragedy, but it was a choice, and it came with consequences. The consequences were that I had to go back home and take a job running parts down at the grain elevator. I put the word out I was looking for an assistant coaching position and went back to work. There was no way I could do anything else after the promise I had made my father.

Fortunately, I got a call from Paul Peck at Kentucky State University Coach Farrar's recommendation, who was looking for an assistant basketball coach. He knew all about me and my family and my basketball career, and he thought I'd be a good fit for the program.

I would have to scout, get the players in condition, assist the coach, advise students, plus teach three classes on top of all that, in addition to whatever else they needed me to do.

"You'll have to wear a lot of hats, Butch. You up for it?"

"Coach, I've never been more ready," I answered.

For performing all of those duties and quite a few more, I would be paid $17,442 a year. And let me tell you, it didn't sound like much even back then, but I was grateful to get it. Everybody's got to start somewhere.

When I told my father, he shipped me out with $1,000 and a U-Haul full of furniture: a couch, dinette set, mattress and box springs, washer and dryer. I was now officially on my own. I understood that no more financial support would be forthcoming. He didn't even have to say it. I was on my way to Frankfort, Kentucky, to coach some basketball.

DISCIPLINE

Life is all about balance. We have to balance our personal and professional lives, and sometimes it's easy to tip too far to one side or the other.

I've coached some great offensive players who couldn't defend the goal. Others could block shots all day but not hit a jumper to save their soul. A great coach looks for balance in his team. Pair your great defender with an outstanding shooter and great supporting players, and your team has a better chance of success. It's all in the balance.

Discipline will help you achieve balance in your life. If you have personal habits that interfere with success in your professional life, discipline will save you.

One of the greatest transformative players I had ever coached came to me with sloppy discipline. Jabari Smith had great skills, but he showed up as a junior college transfer overweight and oversleeping, which made for a terrible first year. He was one the best kids I ever coached, with good values and real leadership potential, but he couldn't succeed until he found the discipline in his workouts to get in the proper shape to take advantage of his natural gifts. Once he found discipline, he achieved greatness as a player.

As children, we think we don't want discipline. We *think* we want to do whatever we feel like doing. But we really don't. Children crave discipline, because discipline grows out of love from their parents.

Love yourself. Find your discipline. Achieve greatness.

CHAPTER TWENTY-TWO

"All kids need is a little help, a little hope, and
someone who believes in them."
Magic Johnson

I QUICKLY FOUND A PLACE TO LIVE and started my new job. Finances were pretty tight, but I managed to make it work. I could eat almost for free in the school cafeteria, and we had a booster who provided free dry cleaning services at his establishment, so I didn't have to worry about clean clothes. Once my rent and utilities were paid, I usually had about $250 left over to pay for gas for my car, and that was it. It was almost like being in college again, because I had so much to learn about really being on my own.

I had never even written a check, if you can imagine that, because I'd never had my own checking account!

But I looked at my ignorance as opportunity, just another aspect of life to learn about, and I threw myself into it with the same enthusiasm as any other problem to be solved. I went to the school's academic advisor, and he recommended a fantastic book on contemporary business. Reading that book was almost like taking a business course. It defined and explained everything from supply and demand to the differences between a recession and a depression.

I read that book three or four times and probably highlighted a third of it. Finance was like a whole new world to me. I realized I needed to manage my money wisely because otherwise that $17,442 wasn't going to get me very far.

I actually didn't need much money left over at the end of each month because I had no time to do anything but eat, sleep, and my job, which included being the strength and conditioning coach, recruiting, coaching, and managing the players, on top of teaching my classes, which meant creating a syllabus for the accreditation committee, SAC's study and testing, and all the rest of the things a teacher does.

I opened an investment account with a broker and put in the minimum each month —$50—into a mutual fund called Investment Company of America. And every month when I opened those statements, I could see the numbers move up a little bit, but it didn't seem real to me, somehow. Finally, I withdrew most of the money just to see if it was real. Once I had it in my hands, I put it right back in my account.

I mention this because it's one of the lessons I learned early and which I've tried to share with both my children and my players. No matter what your business is, you have to take care of business. It doesn't matter whether you're a coach or a teacher or a janitor or a barista. One day, you'll be out in the world on your own, earning your own money, and you need to be smart about it.

A young person who understands the value of money will also understand that the value of the hard work is the engine that causes the money to end up in your pocket in the first place. And once you understand the value of hard work, you'll never go hungry.

Obviously, some people are born with a silver spoon in their mouths while others are born in poverty; some have talents and skills that are more highly prized than others. But whatever you do with your life, you and only you are responsible for that life. Take care of your business, and your business will take care of you.

And as my father always told me, before you can take care of somebody else, you have to be able to take care of yourself. So, if you want a family someday, do right by yourself so you can do right by them.

As soon as I was hired, I met with Raymond Burse, the president of the school and a real sharp guy. He was a former Rhodes scholar and related well to the athletic department. He had been a recent hire himself and made lots of changes when he took over, always looking for ways to improve the school in some way. He had tremendous leadership skills, and I learned quite a bit just by observing him during the two years I was there.

As a matter of fact, several of the friendships I developed there have lasted to this day. I had so many responsibilities that I needed all the help I could get, and there was always plenty of support when I needed it. Dr. Shirley Reese, a teacher in the physical education department, showed me the ropes there, and Dr. Diane Murphy, who would go on to be the athletic director at Columbia University, helped a great deal, as well. Both were new hires like I was but were more experienced teachers.

An English professor got me playing golf twice a week, a game I'd never played but which would really help my career in the future because so many athletic boosters and other influential people play golf. I had always been good with people, so building relationships came naturally to me.

On my first recruiting trips, I traveled all over the state of Kentucky in a big boat of a car owned by the state, with only an AM radio and no heater in the middle of winter. But I loved it because the state of Kentucky was crazy for basketball. Still is. Sometimes, I'd show up early at some tiny school out in the country with a gym that looked like it *might* hold five hundred people if you keep the doors open. No one around but me. Come game time, two or three thousand people would be hanging from the rafters, screaming for their team so loudly they could probably hear them down in Nashville.

That love for basketball inspires me to this day. It's the greatest game ever invented.

As much as I enjoyed looking for players, I also really liked meeting other coaches and getting to know them and their ways. I wanted to know what made a successful coach successful. I felt like I could learn from anyone and everyone. I soaked up the experience like a sponge.

I went to high schools in Chicago, spent a week touring Florida's junior colleges, and did a week in Kansas. I got used to feedlots, the smell of manure, and speed traps. I signed Thor Shaffer down in Florida, a small 6"3' point guard, friendly white kid who agreed to come to a historically black college and ended up one of the most popular players on campus. He was my very first signee. He was a tough kid being raised by a single mother, which I took as an added responsibility.

I went to see Lamon Berry at home on the south side of Chicago in a pretty rough neighborhood when he was on break from his Florida junior college. He was one of the best JC players in the country.

On that trip, I took my own car, which was a lot more impressive than that school car I'd been driving. I spoke to Lamon and his mother in their living room, but I couldn't get into a rhythm with my pitch because his big brother and several friends kept jumping up and rushing over to the window.

"What you guys keep looking at?" I asked.

"We keepin' an eye on your car, Coach."

Overall, my first recruiting season was quite successful. I signed four down in Florida and one up in Boston, all high Division 1 players seasoned in junior colleges and ready to go to a four year school. All juniors, all impact players.

Even so, that first rebuilding year, we went 5-20, which was a real tough thing to go through, both for me personally and for the team. It was what you'd call a character-building season.

As a matter of fact, you could call my entire tenure there character-building. We had a decent budget for recruiting, but we didn't have anyone to answer the phones or sweep the gym. So you know what I did.

I answered the phones and swept the gym. I had those players up running and weight lifting at 6:00 in the morning and on the court by 8:00. I made calls and answered phones and made sure the gym floor was spotless before each day's practice.

I developed a great work ethic because I had to, and I'm grateful to this day for the experience. Before long, I'd take a job for twice the pay and half the responsibility, but I still missed those days back at Kentucky State.

It was also where I met Clemmie, which makes those days extra special. I had no time or money for bars or restaurants or anything like that, so we spent our free time either in church on Sundays or having dinner with her parents at their house or watching TV at my apartment.

The first time I went to the NABC (National Association of Basketball Coaches) convention was in 1987, down in my old stomping grounds, New Orleans. I met Dwane Casey, who was then an assistant at University of Kentucky Big Blue Nation as it was called. He'd been around a little longer than I and was a good source of information.

On my second day there, Dwane mentioned he'd seen a beautiful girl back in Lexington, Kentucky, and couldn't get her out of his mind.

"This is New Orleans, Coach," I said. "Lot of women down here."

"Not like this one," he said. "But I got her license plate. I'm gonna have a police buddy of mine get her phone number for me."

I just laughed. "Do what you gotta do, I guess."

Later, I got a phone call from Clemmie. "You know a basketball coach named Dwane Casey?"

"Yes."

"That's him. He called me today out of the blue, said he was a basketball coach. I told him my boyfriend was a basketball coach, too."

"Oh, man."

"He didn't stay on the phone too long after I mentioned your name, though. Did you give him my number?"

There was a long pause. "I'll have a talk with him," I said.

"You do that," she said. I could almost hear her smiling as she hung up.

No doubt Dwane had fed her a line that was also the truth—that he'd seen her drive past and just had to meet her, and he was a big-time college basketball coach and all that to try and impress her.

I have to admit, it impressed me. Dwane was a hard worker, and a very resourceful recruiter. I wasn't surprised that that carried over into his single personal life. I'm just lucky in this case that I'd gotten there first.

I learned a lot at that conference and not just to keep an eye on these guys around the woman who would become my wife. I closely watched what other successful coaches did, and then I endeavored to do likewise. Whenever I saw a successful coach at the conference, I'd introduce myself and pick his brain. It's amazing what you get when you just come right out and ask for it. I tell my players, "Don't be shy," and sometimes they laugh about that, but it's amazing to me how many players can be so dynamic on the court and so reticent in real life. You have to go after what you want in life, just like you go for a loose ball or an open shot. You may not always get what you were after, but you'll never succeed unless you make the attempt.

Plus, people like to be asked for guidance. They like to be helpful. Some of the coaches who gave me advice would become fierce rivals in recruiting and job openings, but we had respect for each other and so were willing to compare notes at the conference. And gradually, I became one of those coaches that younger guys would approach for advice and counsel.

I always try to be as helpful to the young guys coming up, as so many coaches and mentors had been for me, because I know how it was when I was in that position. In the same way I can mentor my players because I was in their shoes, I mentor young coaches.

That's what some people call paying it forward, but to me it's just another way to take care of my business. Doing for others what you want done for you is also a solid, moral teaching.

I've been attending the conference for many years now. For the first fifteen years, I went to just about every seminar and coaching clinic they scheduled. I listened, I asked questions, and I learned.

It was also very important for me as a black coach to meet other black coaches. Even though there are plenty of elite players who are African-American, there is a real dearth of black head coaches and assistants at elite schools. There are a lot of reasons for that, but the simplest is that people just have a tendency to hire people who look like them. So, if most of the athletic directors are white, chances are a lot of the head coaches are going to be white, too. And that means a lot of assistant coaches will be white.

While those stats sound depressing, I wasn't going to let them depress my career. My skin has been the same color from the day I was born. If I have to work harder because of it, then that's what I'm going to do. My dad would say, "Better is not good enough; you have to be the best." I'm not the type to let factors beyond my control keep me from what I want.

Meeting other black coaches was important not just from a networking standpoint but also on a psychological level. I've always been very competitive, and if I see someone accomplish great things, it only fuels my ambition. If they can do it, why can't I?

I met Wade Houston at the conference, who was then an assistant at Louisville. Leonard Hamilton, one of the best recruiters I've ever known, who's now head coach at Florida State. These were great guys and great at their jobs. Tubby Smith, Clint Bryant, Melvin Watkins, Jerry Dunn, Jimmy Collins, Al Skinner, Sherman Dillard, the list goes on. All excellent coaches and recruiters, different in style and personality, but I learned from all of them. I would see Larry Gay every year, who had recruited me when he was an assistant at Georgia.

I first met Tubby Smith at the NABC Final Four conference. He was easy to talk to and free with advice, which I still seek out today. When he met my father for the first time, he told me he reminded him of *his* father. Hearing that made me proud, and my dad felt the same way.

These men were all mentors by example. Even if they weren't actively mentoring me, they showed me the qualities I aspired to as a coach by the way they lived their lives and performed their duties. I try every day to be such an example to the young coaches I meet and the athletes I coach.

That's why it's so important for me as a coach to be an example both on and off the court, in both my personal and my professional life. Because there's always someone coming up, someone watching and learning from the way I take care of my business. I want to make sure I always mentor by example.

CHAPTER TWENTY-THREE

"Yo nací para tus ojos para nadie más."
Beyoncé

I'M NOT GOING TO SAY that constantly noticing how other men looked at Clemmie sped up my timetable toward asking her to marry me, but it certainly didn't slow me down any. We had a great relationship, and there are only two things that happen in that situation: Either you keep going or your paths diverge. There was no way I wanted that woman's path to be anywhere but right alongside my own.

Her folks were like my own in some ways and very different in others, but our backgrounds were similar in the most important respects: We both had been raised by two loving parents in households that loved God.

That said, it did take a little getting used to going from Creole Catholic to Southern Baptist. I'll just say that down in Louisiana, we like to drink and dance, and Southern Baptists, well, they have a different viewpoint on such pleasures, which they call sins. But we made it work, as you do when love comes calling.

Clemmie's entire extended family, the Caises and the Beattys, all attended the same Baptist church in Lexington, where I spent every Sunday before we had dinner with her parents, who owned a successful construction business in the area. I liked spending time with her dad, another man who mentored by example. He was definitely a good influence on me as a young man living and working far away from my own father.

I never got anything but positivity from her parents, who, a few months into our relationship, had come by my apartment for a dinner/inspection tour and discovered how neat and organized I kept things. I fixed dinner, too, which impressed both my future wife and her parents.

Clemmie told me later she thought that sort of thing might continue after we were married, but our wedding pretty much ended my cooking career, except for crawfish boils, gumbo, and the occasional fish fry, which of course I could never give up.

My future in-laws ran their business together and were partners in every way. Clemmie's mother ran the business side of things from their home while her father worked out on construction sites. He was a lot like my father in that he knew at least a little about almost everything. People respected him and came to him for advice, another similarity with my own father. And like my mother, Clemmie's mom was one-half of the backbone of the family. She was the one who brought everything together. Their personalities complemented each other in just the right way.

Clemmie and I did, too. I've always been an outgoing person. I can talk to anyone and feel comfortable almost anywhere, from church on Sunday to a bar on Saturday night.

With her upbringing, Clemmie was more of a homebody, but that was just fine with me. As I mentioned earlier, I saw her as my ideal partner. Her own person, to be sure, but also the perfect coach's wife.

Clemmie's the type of woman who impresses with her presence. Every time she enters a room, she makes me proud to be her man. To be honest, she just makes me look good.

Still, it took me a while to get there. I felt the heat during that first year. She would introduce me to her friends as "the man I'm going to marry," and I would just smile or laugh, but I wouldn't say those words. "He just doesn't know it yet," she'd explain, and there would be more laughter. But she was right. My fate was decided as soon as I laid eyes on her. It just took me longer to figure out.

Meanwhile, my career path was progressing. I got a raise my second year, and we went from five wins to twenty, which was quite a turnaround. I began to get noticed by other schools as a hot young recruiter, so I put my resume together and took it out for a spin. I was always on the lookout for something better. A better job, a better win-loss record, a better life.

An opening for assistant coach came available down at Southwestern Louisiana, and everyone I knew who also knew the coach was throwing in my name. I wanted that job bad. Coaching back home where I'd grown up and played was just what I was looking for. I interviewed with the coach, Marty Fletcher, and it was a pretty short interview. I was sure I didn't get the job, but Clint, one of the people who'd put my name in for the job, told me to be patient. "Nothing's decided until it's decided," he said.

On the home front, Clemmie was getting impatient for other, ultimately more important things.

"Are you going to marry me or not?"

I stood up. We'd just been on our knees together, praying for that job.

"Someday," I answered, hoping that would end the conversation.

"When?"

It was just like her father had told me. *My daughter's a strong woman. Smart. Stubborn. You can't tell her what to do.*

"So, how do I handle her?" I asked, kind of joking but not really.

"You'll have to figure that one out yourself," he laughed.

He would prove to be right about that, as he was on most things. I've never been able to "handle" my wife, and it probably took me about ten years just to understand her. But it would, of course, be worth every moment.

I looked at Clemmie, who was waiting for a better answer than "someday." I figured any woman who'd get down on her knees and pray with her man that he'd get a coaching job that would likely take her farther away from her parents than she'd ever been, deserved a better answer than the one I'd given her.

"It's a date," I said, and she practically leapt into my arms.

We set a date for June, and I took her home to meet my people. My dad's mother, who was ninety-two at the time but only a little hunched over from her straight up 6'4", took Clemmie's hand in her own and blessed her in both Creole and English, which was big for my father. "She one 'a us," she told him, and that was all he needed to hear.

Two weeks before we were to be married, I started to get cold feet. We'd gone through Catholic pre-marriage counseling, which was a little rocky for a good Southern Baptist girl. It was big for my parents, but Clemmie didn't like signing a pledge to raise our children Catholic. She had opinions on everything and so did my parents, to be honest.

"Do they drink?" my father asked.

"Nope."

"What about music?"

"They're not too big on that, either."

He furrowed his brow. "I'm guessing they don't do too much dancing."

I shook my head sadly.

My father sighed. "We're gonna hafta talk about the reception."

We compromised by planning a ceremony with both a preacher and a priest, among other things, and since our future children would be able to decide how they wanted to live someday, anyway...

It was tough, but we got through it. But all the back and forth got me overthinking things. *Was I ready to settle down? Was I ready to start the rest of my life?*

For the first but certainly not the last time in our relationship, Clemmie took me to the woodshed. "You're looking a little unsure lately," she said.

"I was just thinking we might be rushing things a little bit."

Clemmie got right up in my face. "My parents spent a lot of money on this wedding, and I sat through that Pre-Cana stuff for yours," she said. "You think you're backing out now? I don't think so."

She stood on her toes and kissed me and then walked out of the room. I doubt she heard me say, "Okay."

I sat down. My future wife had spoken and that was that. Just then the phone rang. It was Coach Fletcher. "Heard you're getting married," he said.

I looked at Clemmie, who was bustling around in the kitchen. "Looks like it."

"Got time to sign a contract?"

I nearly jumped out of my shoes. As it was, I actually stood up from where I was sitting and practically yelled into the phone. "I'll drive down right now."

He laughed. "Hold your horses, son. I'll fly you down. Ticket'll be at the airport."

I flew down the next day, realizing only as I boarded the plane that I wasn't entirely sure what position I'd just accepted, what my duties would be, or what I would be paid.

I shouldn't have worried. Coach Fletcher took me to dinner and offered me $30,000 a year, which was ten more than I was getting now. I would have been equipment manager for that big a raise.

"What do you want me to do, Coach?" I asked.

"Assistant coach," he said. "You recruit, coach, manage those recruits, manage the team. Our team."

"Exactly what I wanted to hear," I said.

He laughed. "Well, you're exactly what I need."

I went back home, Frankfort, Kentucky, and prepared to get married.

My dad paid for a second reception. There was no way that man was going to watch his only son get married without liquor, dancing, and rhythm and blues.

He hired two Greyhound buses to bring in all our family and friends, and there were plenty on the bride's side, as well.

Having all my friends show up for the bachelor party was fantastic. I hadn't been with all those guys at once for a long time, and I may not ever get them all in the same room at the same time again unless somebody dies.

We had the rehearsal dinner the night before, which was beautiful. The next morning, I played nine holes of golf with one of my groomsmen, Barry Robert, who happened to be white and one of my best friends since junior high, at 8:00 and was in the packed church at 2:00 in time to get hitched. In between, there was a lot of laughing and crying and everything.

The alcohol-free reception took place at a fancy horse farm in Lexington, very exclusive and maybe a little extravagant. We took a carriage ride through the park, and then everyone went inside where a tuxedoed piano player took over.

"Least they got some music," my father whispered.

But I don't remember anyone getting up to dance. Maybe it really is against the rules for Baptists, or something.

Once that reception was over, the buses showed up, and two busloads of people took everyone about twenty miles away to Frankfort, where we did it up, Louisiana-style.

The band was hot, and the champagne was cold, pouring out of a fountain in the center of the room. Before I knew it, those Southern Baptists from my wife's church were on their feet, cutting that rug like nobody's business. I wasn't checking or anything, but a few of them may have gotten right with the Lord over by that champagne fountain, too.

I looked over at my father and mother dancing together and thought back all those years ago when she'd sit by his bed, practically willing him to heal. He couldn't move like he could as a younger man, but he looked pretty damn good out there on the dance floor.

I may have gotten a little misty-eyed watching them that day. When I caught my father's eye, he looked like the proudest man on the face of the earth. Especially since he'd gotten all those Baptists moving their feet.

"Your mother was a Baptist before I got to her, you know," he called out.

"I know."

Clemmie's parents had stayed behind at the horse farm to settle their bill, and when they walked in, I thought they might have a joint heart attack. There was their little girl up on stage with all the groomsmen, dancing and laughing and looking more like the entertainment than the guest of honor. Later, her father asked if she'd drunk from the fountain.

"How could you ask me that, Daddy?" she said, just like my daughter would answer me many years in the future.

A father can always tell, but he seemed okay with that answer. Everybody knows a bride can do no wrong on her wedding day. That's a rule for Catholics and Baptists, alike, I believe. Two days later, we loaded up another U-Haul and headed back to Louisiana.

CHAPTER TWENTY-FOUR

"…if you do it well I'm sure there was someone
cheering you on…a mentor."
Denzel Washington

ONCE WE'D GOTTEN SETTLED, we managed to go to Las Vegas for a few days to finish up the indulgences that Baptists weren't supposed to enjoy. "I'll make you a Catholic yet," I told her.

Lafayette, Louisiana, had been one of the wealthiest areas of the state because of oil and gas money, but we arrived in the middle of an economic downturn, so there were a lot of people who'd lost everything. We felt blessed to be there, however. A brand new job, a brand new marriage, and a brand new life.

Clemmie had worked as an insurance agent back in Kentucky and found a job right away in the same field, and of course I knew lots of people, met lots more, and was eager to get started. They'd done a good job recruiting before I got there, but the team hadn't been winning, so there was pressure on us right away to change that. The coach was very offensive minded and loved the shooters, but I was always looking for good defensive players, as well.

I stayed for eight more years, and we were always known for our strong offensive roster. We had lots of talent during my tenure. Kevin Brooks would be a first rounder in the NBA. Sydney Grider was an outstanding leader and a 3-point scoring machine. Aaron Mitchell, Marcus Stokes, who played overseas after college, Bobby Thigpen, who now coaches high school basketball in Texas, Johnny Womack, Eric Mouton and lots of good players went on to become good men.

Coach Fletcher loved those threes, and we ran a wide open offense, but with these young guys that sometimes meant they needed a little extra discipline, which I provided as needed. I had other ideas about the best ways to win games in addition to scoring, but I was always very well aware of my position as assistant coach. As I mentioned before, I acted like an assistant coach, even as I began to think like a head coach. Loyalty and an understanding of the chain of command is very important in an assistant coach, so I voiced my opinions where I could and bit my tongue when necessary. That's what a good assistant does, and I was a good assistant coach.

My time there also taught me a lot about coaching philosophies and how to win with different game plans. I was used to coaching players to be disciplined with their shots, but we normally recruited shooters and played a lot of different defenses, which I also understood.

I was always looking for ways to win. If that meant accepting a different game plan than what I would have drawn up myself and working with what I had, then that's what I did. But having been an unselfish player back in school, even though I loved to score, it was a challenge sometimes.

I remember that first year when a couple of us assistant coaches split into teams to scrimmage. Toward the end of the game, the best player on the team, Kevin Brooks, who was playing for me, just up and quit. We were a little behind at the time, so that was when I needed a player like him to step up. It was a selfish thing to do. He knew he wasn't in danger of losing his starting position, so I guess he just decided he was tired. It was just practice and they were losing, so he didn't need to go hard all the way to the end.

I stopped the game and laid into him. From the look on his face, I could tell no one had ever called him out like that. The entire gym was silent, as I told him I expected a 110 percent every day in every way. Especially from him.

"I won't accept anything else!" I blew my whistle. "Let's go! Get back to it!"

He looked at me and nodded, finishing strong. No backtalk, no attitude, just giving me what I demanded. After that, the other coaches, and, more importantly, the players, all knew what I was made of. It was a good way to establish myself in their eyes as serious about my job and serious about winning. Right then and there, I saw my role as both coach and disciplinarian.

My first season there, we went 17-12, which was an improvement over the previous year, but we all knew we needed to be better. Even so, I figured my job was safe. It wasn't so for everybody, however.

I was always the first one in every morning because I liked to get in a full workout before my day started, just as I do today. As I was finishing up in the weight room, I heard a door bang open, and another assistant stormed out of Coach Fletcher's office. I watched him leave, no idea what just had happened.

Coach Fletcher stepped out. "Can I see you in my office, Butch?"

I followed him in and closed the door. "What's going on, Coach?"

Apparently, there had been a boosters' meeting Coach Fletcher hadn't been told about. During the meeting, some of the boosters discussed firing the head coach. Somehow, it was reported in the local sports pages, and the assistant coach's name had been mentioned as being there.

"I can't have any disloyalty, Butch," he said, "That's a firing offense."

"Lemme stop you right there, Coach," I said. "This is all news to me, but I'll tell you two things: I would never attend a meeting like that without your knowledge, and if anybody suggested something like that to me, you're the first one I'd tell. Loyalty's big for me, Coach. I'll quit before showing you disloyalty."

He got wide-eyed at that. "No, no, Butch, I need you here," he said.

He did, too. He knew it and I knew it. It was a good opportunity for me to tell him how we could move forward. I had some ideas about how we could win, big time, and I told him all about it.

As for the assistant, he held a press conference and quit shortly thereafter, which was a big deal because he was very popular with the players, many of whom he'd recruited. Whenever the guy that brought you in leaves, it can be tough for young players. Coaches are like father figures, and that loss is hard for some to take.

It was another good lesson for me. Stay loyal and pay close attention to the boosters and media.

I went off on a recruiting trip, doing my part to build on what we'd accomplished, but I rushed back as soon as I could to make sure the team held itself together. I spent a lot of time reassuring players who were thinking about leaving that we'd be all right.

"We gotta stick together,' I told them.

Coach Fletcher and I bonded with the players through that adversity, and we managed to get through the season's turmoil with a 17-12 record, but by the end of the year, two more assistants were gone, which made me the longest serving assistant coach with the team.

I'd had a pretty successful start in terms of recruiting, but it required a lot of travel. Even though I was away from home quite a bit, Clemmie was always very supportive. I think I could not have done the job I did without knowing she was back home waiting for me.

I quickly learned I had to be very aggressive as a recruiter, which some people didn't like, but that was what was required to do my job properly. We were competing against elite schools with bigger budgets, and there were a few gray areas back then that I took full advantage of when needed. I never broke any NCAA rules, but I fought as hard as I could for my players and got more than my share. It was a tough game, and I learned not to be shy.

In those days, you could really get out there and recruit. You had to; there were no cell phones or computers, really. It was all telephone calls from the office and personal contact. You had to get out there and meet people. I spent more time than I can say with the families of prospects. Had a lot of homecooked meals. Attended a lot of church services. Met a lot of parents and grandparents. Single mothers. Brothers and sisters. Anybody in the life of that young man was a person I wanted to get to know. I became like part of the family.

I also got to know a lot of coaches, and I paid attention to them. Lots of AAU coaches, middle school coaches, high school coaches. I'd even go see an elementary school coach if they had someone special. I found a lot of young guys before anyone else because I worked hard, kept an open mind, and just plain hustled.

One of those AAU coaches I came not only to depend on but to love was Big Dave Thibodeaux. He was a big Creole teddy bear who spoke two languages like my grandmother and was just a little taller. I got to know him a little bit in high school, some more in college, and we were practically brothers by the time I'd been coaching a few years. He was absolutely an indispensable resource, but more important, he was my friend.

Dave knew everybody in Louisiana basketball and states beyond, with a great eye for talent and a way about him that made you want to follow him into battle, no matter what the fight or where the war. Guys came from all over the state to play for him. Elite players who could have played in any tournament in the country came down to South Louisiana to play in his. I spent holidays with him, watched Monday night football with him, took turns cooking dinner with him, and was proud to be in his wedding.

He never had much money, but he had great influence in the community. If you were running for local or statewide office, you went to his modest two-bedroom house and talked to Big Dave. If you needed community support for some project or issue, you went to see Big Dave. He was one of those people beloved by everyone. If I ever needed anything, I could always call Big Dave, and he could do the same.

When I was at LSU, I remember there was this player that Dave kept telling me to watch. Every time we spoke, no matter what the subject, Dave would steer the conversation back to this kid. "Gotta get him, Pierre," he'd say. "Somebody else do, you be really sorry." He called me every day, telling me I had to sign that player.

That player was Darrel Mitchell, who helped take us to the Final Four in 2006. Big Dave died a few years ago. He knew more about basketball than anybody I ever knew. He taught me never to overlook the grassroots guys, the troubled guys, the kids who might not seem like much but who just needed the right coach or environment to become great players and men. Some needed a life coach and that was me.

He was a big part of my growth as a recruiter. A lot of guys looked down on the AAU coaches but not me. I made my reputation finding guys before anyone else, and all it took was a word from Big Dave to remind me that no player was too small.

There was some resentment of my success here and there, of course. When you get a top prospect that means everybody else came in second. And second place might as well be last. In the competitive atmosphere of big-time college sports, there's always pressure, but since most recruiters were also players at one time, that desire to win was only amplified. Recruiting is high pressure, high stakes, and high stress. I loved it.

But as good as I was at my job, there were very few times I missed out. Nobody wins them all.

When that happens, you pick yourself up and move on. You figure out who you can get to replace the one that got away. I never bitched and whined because another guy took away my recruit. I really can't stand that kind of attitude. Be disappointed all you want, but if you got a job to do, get back to it. You have to overcome adversity. You have to use adversity to make yourself better. Just like that season when we lost that popular assistant coach, we moved on and took care of business.

The way I always looked at it, if I didn't sign a prospect, he was never mine in the first place. So nobody ever stole anyone from me. Nobody ever out-hustled me. Sometimes you win, and sometimes you lose. Always fight, never complain.

To paraphrase Tom Hanks in a movie about another sport, there's no crying in basketball. Big Dave taught me that, too.

WORKING SMART

Success and failure are two sides of the same coin. Sometimes the difference is large, and other times it's infinitesimal. I've been on both sides of a blowout, and it's never pretty. But if you win or lose by a single point or by a few dozen, the result is the same. W or L.

But wins and losses both come from your efforts or lack thereof. It's all in the work you do. Work dumb or work smart. The result will always be one or the other: success or failure.

How you deal with those outcomes determines your ultimate success. Sometimes, we learn more from our failures than our successes, but we always need to pay attention so we can learn no matter which outcome we achieve. In recruiting, working smart means not wasting time if the outcome has already been determined. That decision has already been made before the recruiting process began.

Working smart means getting every last bit of lesson from both wins and losses.

Working smart also means recognizing and crafting the business of YOU.

You might not think you're a business, but you are. You put an image out in the world that has value. People see you, recognize you, and decide how to treat you, based on your business model.

Craft an impressive business model. Mean what you say and do what you promise. Maintain your personal integrity in all things and the business of *you* will be a success.

Success and failure are inevitable. Treat them as they require, and the business of you will achieve greatness.

CHAPTER TWENTY-FIVE

"We must find a way to look after one another,
as if we were one single tribe."
T'Challa
The Black Panther

———

*O*PPORTUNITY KNOCKS.

That's a handy phrase to consider in all aspects of your life, but there's a lot more to it than some folks realize. Because while opportunity might knock pretty loudly one day, the next day, it might just give a little tap. Some days, it might just whisper in your ear while you're busy with other things, easy to overlook or ignore. Some days, it might not make a sound at all, just brush past you on its way to somebody else who might grab it before you even knew it was there. The point is: Opportunity may or may present itself in an obvious way, but you always need to be ready to answer the door.

In other words, to cultivate your ability to take advantage of whatever opportunities come your way, it takes a lot of preparation and a constant state of readiness. Big-time players are always ready to take the shot. An open look is a beautiful thing, but it doesn't last long. An open lane closes quickly.

Preparing yourself for that shot and being ready to take it when it comes means learning to recognize the moment. Understanding who you are, where you are, and what's going on around you. It means self-awareness.

This was something I had to learn as a player to play my very best game, and it's what we all must learn to live our very best life. Because sometimes, all it takes is one element, one decision, one relationship to make everything fall into place.

One great player can turn around an entire program. I've seen it dozens of times over the course of my coaching career. The right player can elevate the level of play for an entire team. But everybody on that team has to be ready to step up. Each player has to recognize the opportunity. Each player has to be ready to play his or her part in its success. Every player has a unique relationship to each other and to the team.

Early in my coaching career, Michael Allen was a real difference-maker. I recruited him in 1990 at Southwestern Louisiana, now the University of Louisiana at Lafayette. He was strongly considering Georgia, but he came down to Lafayette because I had developed a relationship with him. I recognized his potential and was ready for the opportunity. So was he. Michael ended up being a three-year starter, MVP of our second Sun Belt Championship team, and Conference Player of the Year.

Along with Todd Hill, Tony Moore, Cedric Mackyeon, Tyrone Jones, Bryan Collins, Barry Bowman, Shawn Griggs, and Marcus

Stokes, Michael was a big part of a very talented team that went to the NCAA tournament in '92 and '94.

It was during those early years that I began to really understand how opportunities were all around me. Any chance meeting could turn into a job interview or lead to a recruit who could take my team to the tournament. And it was always about self-awareness.

Being self-aware doesn't only mean you're *aware of yourself*, it also means you're *aware of your environment*. It means you can see how you relate to other people from their point of view. It means you understand how others affect you and how you affect them. This is true both on and off the court, and it's definitely something that can be developed.

True self-awareness is like having excellent peripheral vision. You're not only aware of yourself, you're aware of your surroundings, too. Your *context*. A great player doesn't just see an open shot for himself, he can see an open shot for his teammate, as well. Those no-look passes by Lonzo Ball or LeBron James are because both those players possess exceptional self-awareness on the court.

They're also a lot of fun to watch. They each present an image not only of hard work and excellence but one that's entertaining. In a way, they are presenting their brand to the world. You may like their brand or dislike it, but it's there.

A by-product of self-awareness is learning how to present yourself to the world. We all do this, whether we realize it or not. Every time you set foot outside your door, you are being watched by somebody. Unless you live out in the woods somewhere, you *will* be observed, and your behavior *will* be noted.

As a man of faith, I know I would be observed even if I *did* live out in the woods, but since most of us live among other human beings, we need to understand that we project an image to those with whom we interact, like it or not. So it's important that we act accordingly.

I have spent just about my entire basketball career in the public eye in one way or another. That's just a byproduct of athletics, especially nowadays.

Whether it was playing in front of my classmates back in the high school gym or big arena college games, or coaching from the sidelines on national television, I have learned how important it is that I present an image and behavior that makes me proud. That makes my children proud. That makes my parents proud.

All those years ago, when I promised my mother she would see me play on TV one day, I had no idea just how much that reality would shape my life. Because even if I had never fulfilled that promise, I still would have the same goal every single day in everything I do: to make my mother proud. To never embarrass her or myself. And now that I'm a father, to present a positive image to the world that my own children see as a positive example.

How you present yourself reveals how you see yourself. If the way you dress and behave shows a lack of self-regard, don't think others will respect you, either. As a basketball coach, I may be in shorts and a t-shirt at practice, but on the sidelines during a game, I'll be in a suit and tie. Either way, I present myself to the world as a man who cares about his appearance. Who takes a minute before he leaves the house in the morning. I present an image to the world that I believe in myself, and I expect others to believe in me, too.

Even if your job is solitary, even if you interact with only a single person each day, you should always present yourself as well as you can. I can't tell you how many players and coaches and families and fans and taxi drivers and custodians and journalists and recruiters I've met over the years. Thousands and thousands of people I've spoken to and interacted with, and I always try to leave them with a good impression.

I don't kiss up to people or act phony or anything like that. I just try and give each one of them my respectful attention for as long as we're interacting. Even if it's the only time I ever speak to that person, I try not to leave them with anything negative. Especially if it's the only time we speak. Why leave a bad impression if it's the only impression they'll ever have? As I tell my sons, remember a fifteen-second handshake is an INTERVIEW.

I'm not perfect, far from it. There have been times I've been in a rush to catch a plane or too busy to stop and chat with a fan. I've been short-tempered with friends and family and even strangers from time to time. I just see no reason not to make my best effort to be positive in all things as much as I possibly can.

For one thing, as a recruiter it's just good business, because you never know who that person might know or can introduce you to. My job is to find players who can help my team, and I've found them in all sorts of places and through all sorts of people.

But it also goes back to presenting myself in a positive way. Even if you're not in the public eye, you'll still be in public. Which means you're still projecting your image out in the world. Your brand. Protect your brand.

Sometimes, five or six recruiters will all show up to look at the same player at the same time. How am I going to stand out from the others?

One way is by reputation. I've always been known as a hard worker, because that's what I've been my whole life. I'm honest and direct. Sometimes, I'm probably too direct, but I don't like to waste anyone's time. I say what I mean and mean what I say.

Your reputation is a direct result of the image you present to the world. One feeds the other. If you want to be thought of as an honest broker, the easiest way to achieve that is by being one.

You've probably heard the phrase, 'you never get a second chance to make a first impression.' While that's true, I guess I would add, 'but it's never too late to make a good impression better.' Or even a bad impression good. If you get off on the wrong foot with someone, just put your best foot forward from that moment on.

If you miss your first six shots, you try and hit the seventh. Or maybe you start passing. But you never give up the game before the buzzer sounds.

I admit that I achieved this positive attitude over time. I was probably a little too cocky in the beginning. That's what comes from being young and thinking you're invincible. But I realized pretty quickly that there was a certain way I needed to conduct myself if I was going to succeed. I became meticulous in all things, from the way I dressed to the rental car I drove. Perception was everything. The way I presented myself was important to the families of the players I recruited. Since I was basically asking them to trust me with their child's welfare, I always presented myself with total professionalism.

Since I knew I would actually be looking out for their son, I just presented myself as the right man for the job. My "brand" was honesty and hustle, and I tried to live up to that every day in every way.

I may have been a little too honest sometimes, but I couldn't change who I was. I know some guys who would rather tell the parents and the players what they wanted to hear, but I could never do that. It wasn't my style.

As a player who'd gone through the whole recruitment process just a few years before, I knew everything they were facing. I could relate, which became another one of my strengths as a recruiter. All I wanted back when I was being recruited was the straight story. I didn't need anyone to hold back or blow smoke or any of that nonsense. Just tell me what I need to know.

Many times during my college career, I was fortunate enough to meet someone who saved me a lot of time and effort by just telling it like it is, so I try to do the same thing for the guys I recruit. That's who I am.

Speaking of which, being true to yourself is important. Everybody has to find a way to succeed by utilizing his or her own unique strengths. That doesn't mean you can't do something unless you have an innate talent for it, however. If it doesn't come naturally, you just have to work harder.

My first couple of years as assistant coach were dominated by lots of travel and long hours. I worked very hard to establish myself. To establish my reputation. My brand. Clemmie was great about it, the perfect coach's wife. But that wasn't all she was. She had a thriving business career of her own and really took to Louisiana. I owe a great deal of my success to her support. It's not always easy to be married to someone who works as much as I did.

I learned a lot from Coach Fletcher, who was always a positive influence on everyone around him. He believed strongly in positive motivation. His way would not have been mine had I been the head coach, but it worked for him, and I learned a great deal from him.

I remember one game in particular when one of our best shooters went cold, missing his first five shots from the floor. Had I been the head coach, I might have taken him aside and told him to start feeding the others since he was having an off-night.

Coach Fletcher didn't say a word until the kid passed on his next open shot. He called a time out. "What's the problem out there?"

The shooter just looked at Coach Fletcher, no idea how to answer.

"You're my shooter, son," he said. "You pass up an open shot like that again, and you'll be ridin' the bench. Understood?"

The shooter nodded.

"Now get out there and do it."

That kid went back in the game and made five straight three's. I was blown away by that. Coach Fletcher showed me the power of positive motivation in that one simple instruction, but even more than that, he opened my mind to new possibilities. We had always worked extremely well together, but it was even better after that. I was really growing as a coach.

I became his disciplinarian, because my natural inclination was to be a little tougher on the players than he was. Probably because of how my father had raised me. Even so, he got results. There's always more than one way to succeed, you just have to find what works for you. You have to find your own path to greatness.

Coach Fletcher and I had different approaches, but we worked well together. We complimented each other. I learned a lot from him, both as a coach and a father. I observed him on and off the court. I saw how he treated his family, and it was the same way with his players. Always positive and respectful.

I've continued to grow each year as a recruiter and a coach, just like I did as a player. I've had my good seasons and very few bad ones. The one constant is forward motion. I strive to be better each day than I was the day before, no matter what the task. I keep an open mind, and I'm always looking to learn something new. The people I meet and talk to in the course of my job are always showing me something I can use to better myself, and I hope I have the same effect on them.

Coach Fletcher liked to say, "Don't bring me problems. Bring me solutions." And that's exactly what I did as his assistant coach. Working for him was a great opportunity for me, and I took full advantage. And I always put my best foot forward.

CHAPTER TWENTY-SIX

"The measure of a man is how well he
provides for his children."
Sidney Poitier, quoting his father

E ARLY IN MY COACHING CAREER, I was often the one on staff
in charge of conditioning, which I really enjoyed. I was
determined to stay in excellent shape myself, and that was a
good way to stay on top of that type of thing as I got older. There's
nothing like pushing a bunch of nineteen and twenty year olds to
their physical limits to keep a guy in shape. But I also used it as an
opportunity to determine the toughness of my players, both
physically and mentally.

Guys will always have certain physical qualities that can adversely
affect their performance in certain situations, but if they're mentally
tough, they find ways to compensate. Like a small player who
achieves great vertical leap or a big man who develops his agility.
Sometimes these things come naturally, but either way, there's a lot
of hard work involved. And hard work comes from mental toughness.
Pushing far beyond the "norm.' How your mind responds under
physical and mental adverse condition. I'll take a guy who's maybe a

step slower but mentally tough over a guy who was born fast but doesn't work as hard, every day and twice on Sundays.

I liked to run my players every day and run them hard, both to get them in great shape and to see who excelled when things got tough. There were usually guys who surprised me, guys I thought would wilt but who only got stronger as the day wore on. And there were guys who went the other way; the players with great physical gifts who couldn't go the distance.

My job was to get them there. *All* of them. This game isn't for slackers. There's being in great shape, and there's being in great *basketball shape.* Two very different things, believe me. Basketball IQ, skill level, and having a great feel knowing how to play, that's another story.

Being in charge of conditioning, I got to see all those things up close and early on. I got to see the potential strengths and weaknesses of the team before anyone else, so I could advise the head coach, and we could address potential deficiencies. Individually and as a team. Being in charge of conditioning helped sharpen my skills evaluating and developing talent. I took great pride in the strength and stamina of the teams I coached.

To be great, a player needs to recognize both their strengths and weaknesses, and my job was to guide them there. To help them turn liabilities into assets and weaknesses into strengths. As a parent and a mentor, I do this is life, as well. Every lesson I teach on the court is a lesson that can be applied anywhere. At home, on the streets, from the classroom to the boardroom. From your first job to a first date, there is always a path to a positive outcome. A path to success. A path to greatness.

Nowadays, teams usually have a strength and conditioning coach whose only job is to get the players in shape and keep them there, but back in the old days, I enjoyed pulling double duty. Doing more than most. That was *my* path to greatness.

Back in 1991, the number one junior college recruit everybody wanted was Carroll Boudreaux, a big Creole kid born and raised in Cecilia, Louisiana, about 15 miles from where I coached for the Ragin' Cajuns and about 75 miles from where I was born and raised.

You might think that was a strength in my game, and you'd be right. But when I say everybody wanted him, I mean *everybody* wanted him: Oklahoma, Nebraska, Arkansas, UNLV, and of course, LSU. Those were my liabilities.

So, why did the most heavily recruited player out of junior college choose the University of Southwest Louisiana? Because I did what I had to do. I turned my weaknesses into strengths and my strengths into deciding factors. I could relate to his Creole mama and developed a real relationship with her. I told her I would take care of her son, and she knew I would because I proved it.

Right around that time, Clemmie was pregnant with our first. She was about six months along as the signing date approached, but no matter how busy things got, every night I took my stereo headphones and played Beethoven or some other classical music right up against my wife's belly for fifteen minutes. Every time I did that, I could feel the baby move, which I can remember to this day. There's no feeling like it that I've ever experienced. I can't do it justice with words.

Then one night, I didn't feel her move. I wasn't too worried at first. Maybe my daughter was just a little tired that night. I'd had a long day myself. But I woke up at 4:00 in the morning, and something didn't set right in my mind. I asked Clemmie if we should go to the doctor, so we went. They checked her out and told us the baby was fine.

"Go home and get some sleep," the doctor told me.

Every night, my daughter had been moving with the music, and then she didn't. And I was supposed to just go home and get some sleep? I don't think so.

"I think something's wrong, Doc."

"Go home, Mr. Pierre. Your baby's fine."

That wasn't good enough for me, and I made such a fuss that another doctor came in to check on Clemmie. He looked concerned. "Her intestines are twisted," he said. "We have to get the baby out now."

Just like I can't adequately describe how I felt placing my hand on my pregnant wife's belly to feel my child moving inside her, I can't really tell you how that felt when I heard those words from the doctor. I've heard people say, 'my bad, man,' but it was more like I suddenly felt like I was burning up.

They rushed Clemmie to surgery, where my daughter Langley was born three months premature, just 3 pounds, 1 ounce. They flew Langley by helicopter to New Orleans Tulane Hospital, and she stayed in the hospital for several months before we could take her home. Every day, her grandmother and Clemmie would drive in to see her from opposite directions, two hours each way. There was a lot of love directed at my child, and she needed every bit of it. I have always told her she was a very special child to survive all of that, and she has proved me right every day since.

The next day, I was supposed to see Carroll Boudreaux play, and all the other coaches would be there. But I really didn't want to leave my daughter. The doctor told me to go. "She'll be fine now," he said.

Clemmie cried, which was something I had seen only once or twice before. Nothing wrong with that, she just holds her emotions that way. "Go," she said, because she knew it was my job, and she knew how hard I worked. But it was a hard thing for her to say, I could tell. I had more respect for her in that moment than I can say.

I turned back to the doctor. "You sure about that?"

He nodded. "She's a fighter," he said and then looked at Clemmie. "Both of them are." He smiled. "They're in good hands. Trust me."

That man, who had taken over for his colleague and made the correct diagnosis, who had trusted a parent's instinct over the word of another doctor, and then taken immediate action that saved the life of my child, said exactly what I needed to hear. His word was good enough for me because his actions had already shown me the quality of his expertise and the strength of his character. I trusted him just as he'd trusted me. Plus, I had another mouth to feed.

I went to the game, signed Boudreaux, and solidified my value to the team. That was big. It was pivotal to my career. It showed I was an up and comer, and I became one of the highest paid assistant coaches in the conference. In the years that followed, I would become one of the highest paid assistants in the entire country. And it all started with the birth of my daughter and a doctor who trusted a father's instincts.

That's why you always have to be vigilant, focused, and prepared. Always do right, and you'll never go wrong.

I was wrung out emotionally, but the thought of Clemmie's strength and what she'd been through drove and inspired me. My daughter did, too. Like the doctor said, they were both fighters. So, I went back into battle and fought for them, for our growing family. I fought to better our lives, and this time at least, I'd been victorious. We were still in our little two-bedroom apartment at the time, so building my career and reputation and getting the salary increases that came with that was key.

When Carroll's mother heard the story of my daughter's birth, she shared in my emotion. She kept asking me if anything was wrong, a mother's instinct, I guess, and when I finally told her what I'd been through, we bonded in a way that told her she could trust me to do right by her child. A mother's word means a lot to her son. Maybe that was the deciding factor.

The year my daughter was born, I helped assemble one of the greatest teams I've had the privilege to coach. In over thirty years, there have been five teams that I thought had what it took to make the Final Four and compete for the national championship, and that was one of them.

We had seven or eight players who could have played anywhere in the country. They could score and defend, and we had a great bench. I knew from the start they were going to be good. It was a special team to me and a very special year, for a lot of reasons.

Besides Carroll Boudreaux, we had Marcus Stokes, Byron Starks, Todd Hill, Eric Mouton, and Michael Allen. I still talk to most of those players today.

By the end of that year, we decided to build a house. We'd saved up some money, and it was time. Clemmie's dad was a contractor, and he taught me a lot, and of course my own father knew how to build things, too. I read up on things and felt pretty confident, so I decided to serve as my own general contractor. We bought a lot, had some plans drawn up, and were all set for the next phase of our lives.

Then Clemmie woke up in the middle of the night. "I'm not feeling good," she said.

We both looked at each other, realizing at the same time. I rushed to an all-night drugstore and got a pregnancy test. Positive.

We hadn't planned *this* one, but it was a good surprise. A life surprise. "At least, we'll have more room once the house is built," I said.

We went to see the doctor the next day. Clemmie was on the table getting an ultrasound. "You need to see this," she said.

I got up to take a look at the monitor. *Two* heartbeats.

The doctor, the same one who'd told me to go home and relax the night Langley was born prematurely, took me aside and apologized. I accepted his apology, and then he asked me why.

"Why, what?"

"Why did you come back to me?"

I put my hand on his shoulder. "Doc, I know you're going to be *extra* careful *this time,*" I said.

And he was. I knew there wasn't a doctor on Earth who would care for Clemmie and her babies like that man would after our previous experience. It reminded me a little bit of Coach Fletcher and that three-point shooter. Sometimes, even the experts just need a little vote of confidence to bring out their best game.

While Clemmie was getting dressed, I stepped outside in the cool air and looked up at the beautiful blue sky, and I cried. I was already a father, and now there were two more on the way. And I was building a house. Except having three kids in diapers was bound to get pretty expensive. I canceled the house.

Meanwhile, Langley finally came home from the hospital, and she was an unbelievable baby. Happy and healthy and strong after a very rough start. The Cajuns won the conference and the conference tournament. We went to Hawaii and played some of the best teams in the country, including North Carolina whom we took right down to the wire. That was the only time I ever saw Dean Smith without a tie on, and when I mentioned it to him after the game, he shook my hand and told me he was going to wear one next time, for sure. His team would go on to win the national championship that year.

We got our bid and went to the NCAA tournament, starting off in Tucson against Oklahoma. I watched Louisville and DePaul practice and told Coach Fletcher we could beat either one of them, and it was true. We weren't ranked, but I thought we matched up against anyone.

It was obvious to us that the players were a little nervous, so Coach Fletcher ran the same practice we always did, and then blew the whistle, yelling, "Ball!"

Every player took a half-court shot, followed by every coach on staff, and the players had a little fun before the biggest game of their lives. I thought it was a great technique to relax everyone.

Jerry Tarkanian, who was watching, came up to me afterward and said, "You're gonna win the game."

I just smiled. "I know, Coach."

And we did. We beat a really good Oklahoma team. It was fairly close, but our guys were loose and confident.

Then New Mexico State beat DePaul, and it seemed like anything was possible. I figured we would beat New Mexico State and move on to the Sweet 16, but it just didn't happen. It was a great game, and we had the lead, but in the last few minutes, they snatched it away from us.

It was heartbreaking because if we'd held on, those players would have built up some momentum in the tournament and could've gone all the way. It was especially tough for the seniors, and to be honest, the team never quite gelled the next year. There was still a lot of talent, but I think the toughness of that year's team was never quite duplicated.

I learned a great lesson from one year to the next, something I would begin to tell my players in the future whenever they neared that level of achievement. When you have your chance, make the most of it. Because getting back is a lot harder than it seems.

Clemmie was pregnant with twins during the tournament. My twin sons were also born premature, weighing only 2½ pounds each, but Josh and Joseph had to stay in the hospital only for ten days before we were able to bring them home.

I knew having three kids in diapers would be very expensive, so I took the money we had set aside to build the house and bought an eighteen-wheeler and started a small trucking business, hauling oil field supplies for extra money.

Clemmie ran that business for two years, which was a lot of work, but it paid off in the long run. We also started a college fund for our children, which is one of the best investments we ever made. As parents, we made sacrifices for our children and our family and each other.

We also made mistakes, but we learned from them and did whatever needed to be done. Clemmie and I became two sides of the same coin, partners in life and love as our family grew.

And like my family, I was growing as a coach. There was always more to learn, both about coaching and the politics of coaching. For example, during my first three years at Southwest Louisiana, I was recruiting, but my coaching was mostly behind the scenes and out of the public eye. I realized that to progress in my career, I needed to be more visible, so I began to do more coaching from the floor. I took charge of the defense during games, which helped my profile. If you want to move up in the world, you need to be aware of the world you're in.

I also began to study budgets and the administrative side of things, which a head coach deals with more than his assistants do. Since I aspired to be a head coach, I reminded myself to *think like a head coach but act like an assistant.* That's all part of preparation. Focus on both short and long terms goals. Prepare yourself for who you want to become.

Becoming a father was also part of my growth. I began to see the players as I would my own children. Having children changes a person, and it changed me. It matured me in many ways. The mistakes a new parent makes are similar to the mistakes a new coach sometimes makes.

As an example, I had two players in successive years with relationship problems. The first was an NBA prospect I had recruited, who fell in love with a girl and moved out of the athletic dorm and moved in with her. I thought this was not a wise decision, but it was his choice to do so. When his level of play diminished noticeably, I confronted him about it and he resented it.

I wasn't telling him to break up with her, I just wanted him to understand why he wasn't playing well. In my mind, if you want to fix a problem, you have to understand its causes. He was too young to be living with her, and it was obvious to me that he was using her as a crutch for his problems in life and basketball. That was a bad choice for him and too much responsibility for her. I was pretty direct with him about all this, which was probably a mistake. I should have known not to get in between a young man and his girlfriend.

"During basketball season, your focus needs to be on this team," I told him. "They need you." I also told him he needed to study so he could graduate, and all of that would inevitably put pressure on his relationship. "If she's the one, she'll understand."

He didn't listen and had a terrible season. His grades suffered, too. No NBA.

The following year, another of my star players had the same problem. I learned from the previous year and approached him more carefully. I was measured and thoughtful in my concerns, and as a result, he responded in kind. Things worked out much better than before because I had learned and applied a valuable lesson.

Both players ended up marrying their girlfriends, although only one of them stayed married. Guess which one?

It took about fifteen years, but the first player eventually told me that he wished he'd listened to me. I understood. I was a young man, too, I told him.

"I guess sometimes we learn things the hard way, Coach," he said.

Sometimes we do. But easy or hard, every lesson has value.

CHAPTER TWENTY-SEVEN

"We're here…to throw little torches out to
lead people through the dark."
Whoopi Goldberg

I T TAKES A LOT OF HARD WORK to build a successful Division I
basketball program. Finding top players is one thing; getting
them into your program is another. But even then, the hard
work is just beginning. I've had really talented guys that just didn't
gel, for some reason. We had a great recruiting year after our trip to
the tournament but still finished 7-22 the following year. We had a
highly recruited team with lots of potential, but the maturity level
just wasn't there. I don't mean individual maturity, although with
young players that can be factored into the equation.

I mean the *team's* maturity as a unit. Their collective toughness
and experience. Sometimes a group of guys could all be NBA-level
prospects, but they just don't mesh. Maybe it's getting used to each
other or a new coach or a different style of play. Maybe it's how they
respond to each other or the coaching staff.

Maybe they just miss their families or have other such
distractions. For whatever reason, that next season was especially

tough, both because we had just come off a great year, and we had so much unrealized potential. In a situation like that, there's a lot of pressure on the coaching staff.

Of course, there's always pressure to win in big-time college athletics, but it gets even more intense as you achieve success. The higher up you go, the tougher things get. It's like that in life, too. Whenever a CEO or other high-level supervisor has to make a tough decision and complains about it to one of their friends or subordinates, that person will often say something like, "That's why you get the big bucks."

It's become a cliché because it's true. The higher you go, the harder it gets. But everybody still wants to climb to that mountaintop. Like that other cliché, if it were easy, everybody would do it.

That's why I don't complain. I made good money, but I earned every penny by doing a difficult job well. There's nothing like the view when you reach the top, and complaining is just a waste of time that I could better use to fix the problems in my way going up that hill. Problems that will often be blamed on the coaching staff, right or wrong.

Nobody wants to hear excuses, not the public, not the boosters, not the media, not the fans. Everybody wants a piece of your success, but nobody wants to hang around if things go bad. But that's all right. That's the job. When it's good, it's great, and when it's bad, well, I still wouldn't do anything else. I put my heart and soul into coaching because that's what it requires. I think that's why the best coaches are usually family men. Often men of faith. Because that kind of commitment requires a lot of love and support.

Even so, there's not always a lot of stability in coaching. Assistant coaches move around a lot. Sometimes lateral moves, hopefully upward moves. But a lot of moving. I'd say the average contract for most assistant coaches was probably three or four years at most, and I had already been in Lafayette for twice that. I received job offers after every season, but there just had not been anything that felt right. And I was loyal. I loved the school and I loved Louisiana. If it's not broke, don't fix it, right?

I stayed and we worked our way back to a winning record, but when Melvin Watkins took over as head coach at the University of North Carolina at Charlotte after seventeen years as assistant to Jeff Mullins, he made me an offer that felt right. Clemmie and I prayed on it, and we decided to make the move.

It was very emotional for us both. We'd been there a long time and leaving the school was like leaving family. I took Clemmie to see President Authment, who was understandably reluctant to see me go. When we walked in the door, I was set in my decision, but he asked me to think about it another day. "Sleep on it, Butch. See how things look in the morning."

I agreed, but as we left, Clemmie could sense I was unsettled. She literally stopped me in my tracks. "Do you want to stay?" she asked, her voice serious.

I looked at this woman, the love of my life, the mother of my children, the one person alive, who, outside of my parents, knew me best in this world. We shared everything, which was why I'd brought her with me in the first place.

"No," I answered honestly. "I really don't."

"Then you should go back in there and tell him," she said. "Don't let him hope for something that's not going to happen."

She was right. Clemmie has a way of boiling things down to what's right or wrong and then making a clear-eyed decision. She has that mother's instinct for ripping off a BAND-AID® fast because she knows it hurts less that way. Clemmie was talking about tough love.

I turned around and went right back inside. I told President Authment I had to think of my family and my career, and I didn't want to lead him on, not even for a single night. He tried everything to make me stay. Years later, I think he never forgave me.

"I gotta move on, Dr. Authment."

Dr. Authment nodded his head sadly. He said he understood.

A year later, Coach Fletcher was let go. Some said I should have stayed and maybe the school would have offered me the top spot, but I believed in my heart that had I been there, Coach Fletcher wouldn't have been let go. It seems like a Catch-22 situation, looking back on it. If I had stayed, the job wouldn't have opened up. But because I left, they wouldn't give me the job.

The way I see it, they could have offered me the job, no matter where I was. It was one of those things I'll never know, so it doesn't do any good to dwell on it. Whether you miss a shot or make a shot, you still have to run back down the court to defend your goal. Still, it would have been a good fit, and it bothered me that they didn't see it that way, too.

Even so, my year at Charlotte prepared me for bigger and better things to come. Melvin and I went way back, and he trusted me with a lot of responsibility as he took over the top spot. I was responsible for recruiting, conditioning, and a lot of coaching, as well. Melvin had waited a long time to move up, and I'm sure he'd been thinking of how he'd make the transition for quite some time. He put together a great staff, and we all clicked right away.

Being in a different environment after so many years in one place, with more responsibility, doing a lot of things a head coach usually did, really prepared me for the next level. I jumped right in and got to work, learning the lay of the land, figuring out the power brokers, getting to know the area.

One player followed me up from Southwest Louisiana, even though I went out of my way not to encourage it. The problem was that a player often feels closer to the assistant coach who recruited him because an emotional connection is made at such a young age. For some players, that bond is so strong, they insist on transferring if that coach leaves. Which is what this player did, even though it meant he had to sit out a year to do so. Whether the loss of that player had any effect on the school's decision not to offer me the head job when it opened up a year later, I have no idea. But it's certainly possible.

But as I said before, I don't like to carry old baggage around with me because it just gets in my way moving forward. I have to swim in the same water as everybody else, so I'm aware of the politics, but at the same time I have a job to do, and my focus is always going to be putting together the best possible team. I'm proud to say I've won at every level, with big budgets, no budget, and everything in between. My record speaks for itself.

We had a really strong recruiting year, and I brought in some quality players, players that formed the core of our winning season.

Clemmie and I bought a beautiful home in Charlotte, she quit work to stay home with the kids, we won the conference, and then went to the tournament. Life, as they say, was good. And then, everything changed.

That was a pivotal year for me. I had more responsibility, but I welcomed it. The more that's expected of me, the better I like it. We had good players of good character, and we got close really quickly. I hunted and fished quite a bit in the area around Charlotte and introduced the team to my famous crawfish boils, which were always a big hit at the new house. We beat Georgetown in the first round of the NCAA tournament, but then lost to Utah in the second round.

Judy Rose was the new athletic director that year, and we got along very well. Diane Murphy had been my boss when I was at Kentucky State, and in my experience, a woman brought a different perspective to a department, in a good way. Women seem to always focus on working toward a proper balance of academics and sports, and as an elite athlete who made the effort to graduate in four years, I appreciated that.

Melvin taught me a lot on a personal level. He really understood how to communicate with the alumni groups, the movers and shakers who can make a real difference to an athletic program. Even though he'd been a star player there, one of the captains of their 1977 Final Four team, with his jersey retired during his final game, and an assistant coach there for seventeen years, there were still some boosters who didn't want him to get the job.

That's unbelievable to me, but there weren't a lot of black head coaches, even at the college level at that time. But Melvin talked to those supporters and really won them over. He took them to the tournament for two years in a row before leaving to coach at Texas A&M, and I bet those naysayers were crying when he left.

One of my most significant weaknesses is probably my propensity for truth telling, meaning I have not always been as diplomatic as I should have been. That's a polite way of saying I can be pretty blunt when I want to be.

But Melvin showed me you can be truthful and diplomatic at the same time. He didn't try to "settle scores." He just let his performance do the talking and proved the naysayers wrong. As a black coach, that was impressive to me. When you start a few steps behind the pack, you have to run a little faster to the finish line. When you can do it with grace, without complaint, and still win, that's an example I want to follow in my own life and pass on to those who follow.

Like me, Melvin was a good family man. He was one of the first coaches to tell me how he prepared to be a head coach, and he encouraged me to do so, as well. "Don't be afraid to voice your opinion, Butch," he told me. "We both know you're not shy."

I laughed at that. Being shy was never my problem. But I understood his meaning. What's the point of forming strong opinions if you always keep them to yourself? But there's a time and place, and a *way,* for everything. Coach Watkins worked with me and treated me as a peer in a way a lot of head coaches don't always understand. He was the head coach and I was his assistant, but he was also a mentor. It was almost like having an older brother as my head coach.

Another coach who had a big impact on my life during that year in North Carolina was Joel Hopkins, who coached at Mt. Zion Christian Academy in Durham. He was an outspoken guy who seemed to know everybody, so right off the bat, I could tell he was a good person to play golf with. But more than that, he was a really good friend. He did great work through his church and was a positive force in the lives of a lot of troubled kids. He also had contacts all over the country and a lot of knowledge about sponsorships and agents, both of which were really becoming a bigger and bigger part of the game and therefore my job as a recruiter, in ways they hadn't before.

I never signed any of his players, although he had some great ones. One in particular I remember as someone I would have loved to have signed. Joel called me up one cold morning, telling me I better get myself to one of the gyms around town he'd borrow to showcase his players to watch a little five-on-five.

It was early and freezing outside, but if Joel Hopkins said I should come, I was there. I forgot how cold it was outside when I saw this kid burn up the court. He was from Florida, about seventeen years old with another year of high school. I was probably the first college recruiter to see him play. He was one of the best players I'd ever seen. We took the kid out to eat afterward, along with one of the church deacons.

"What do you think, Coach?" the deacon asked me.

I looked at the kid across the table, then back to the deacon. "I'm not gonna recruit him," I said. "Be a waste of time."

The deacon looked at me with his dropped jaw, but Joel was smiling like a cat who'd just swallowed a cage full of canaries.

"Why not?" the deacon asked, but he was the only one at the table, including the kid, who didn't already know the answer to that question.

"Cause he's going straight into the NBA," I said, looking at Tracy McGrady, which was exactly what happened. Ninth overall pick right out of high school.

When Joel Hopkins told me I needed to see somebody play, I always knew it would be worth my time. He changed recruiting, he really did. It became more and more about summer camps and AAU leagues and shoe companies sponsoring clinics and tournaments, and Joel was always out in front of the curve.

But even though the corporate influence was growing larger and larger, it was still all about relationships with him. Joel could relate to anyone and always tried to uphold his Christian values, and that's how I've lived my life, as well.

I take players home to meet my family all the time, to see my values and get to know me as more than just another recruiter. Like Joel, I can relate to a kid who grew up in the hood or the suburbs, with a white or blue collar background. Raised in a two-parent family or a group home. I've met parents and family members who were drug dealers and engineers, car salesmen and factory workers. I relate to them all. I can talk to anyone, and a lot of that I learned from Joel, who was a real gunslinger. He wouldn't take no for an answer, but he always showed respect for whomever he was talking to, and he was one of the smartest guys in the business. He was a game changer in recruiting, figuring things out before almost anyone, as recruiting moved away from the high school coaches and toward the agents and big money corporate sponsorships.

Joel would take a kid from the streets and really develop him as a player, and it changed the game. He taught those kids real values and showed them how to use their talents in a positive way. Joel was a grassroots guy, and grassroots always leads recruiting. He steered them through rough waters, filled with people who would take advantage of them, and showed them how to maintain themselves and their families over the long term.

Some people didn't like all the money pouring into the game then and still don't now, but Joel recognized it early and always managed to swim with the sharks without getting bit. It's like living moral values when confronted by immorality. Maybe you can't change the world, but you can take charge of your place in it. And by doing so, who knows? You might change the world, anyway.

PERCEPTION

People think self-awareness is being aware of your*self.*

Sounds *self*-evident, doesn't it?

Not so fast.

Imagine waking up blind. Or are you just blind*folded*?

That's it, you're blindfolded. And tied to a bed. You begin to thrash around, trying to free yourself. You feel hands on your arms and legs, holding you down. You feel a needle go into your arm, and you start to relax. You believe you've been abducted, but now you've been drugged, and it doesn't matter so much. Someone begins to remove your blindfold. Except the blindfold is actually a bandage. You're tethered to a hospital bed because you were in a fire, and your scorched eyes are too sensitive for the overhead lights, which have now been dimmed. The doctor explains, and all is well. You're alive and healing.

How could you be so wrong? You lacked *context.* You needed to know where you were in relation to the world around you. You needed *perception.*

When we understand perception, we can improve our self-awareness.

A player who understands his place on the court can pass off to the teammate with best chance of scoring, or block a shot he knows is coming.

Understanding perception allows us to create a positive (or negative) image of ourselves, which we send out into the world. We all create a brand whether we like it or not, and understanding how we're perceived allows us a better chance of success in whatever we do. It is a tool to greatness.

CHAPTER TWENTY-EIGHT

"Passion is energy. Feel the power that comes
From focusing on what excites you."
Oprah Winfrey

J OHN BRADY WAS COACHING the Samford Bulldogs of
Homewood, Alabama, that fall, and when they beat LSU, I had
to call and congratulate him.

"At LSU, too, man," I said. "Somebody's gonna take notice,
Coach. Maybe you'll get yourself a big-time job."

He laughed. "If that happens, you're my assistant," he said.

At the end of that year, John Brady was hired as head coach at LSU.

It's hard to describe how I felt when I heard the news. I was
really happy for him, but I have to admit I thought a lot about that
conversation we had had a few months before on the phone. LSU was
my dream. I've enjoyed every place I've coached, but *LSU*.

The phone didn't ring.

I ran into John at the Final Four. "Congratulations, Coach," I
said, smiling.

He went right to it since my smile was probably a little too wide.

"I only had one assistant job open, Butch," he said. He was keeping on a longtime assistant, which I understood, of course. "I hired Kermit."

"Kermit!" I said. "That's great, Coach." Kermit had been my teammate and a graduate assistant at Mississippi State when John was an assistant coach. It made a lot of sense. I was happy where I was, but it was *LSU*. LSU was an elite school, and it was *home*.

I think I didn't hide my disappointment very well, because John reached out and squeezed my shoulder. "Who knows what'll happen, Coach?"

Sure enough, that longtime assistant left soon after, and Coach Brady asked me to come down and see him. I was on the next flight out.

Melvin wasn't very happy. I'd been there only a year, and we'd just had another great recruiting season. We'd just gone to the tournament. I was big part of that success. As I mentioned, it takes a lot of hard work to build a successful program, and when you have a good thing going, you want to keep it going as long as possible. It was not a very pleasant surprise for Coach Watkins.

"Coach, you remember what I told you when you brought me here?"

He shook his head.

"I told you I wouldn't leave," I said.

"Yeah?" he said.

"Unless it was for LSU," I added.

Now he remembered. He shook his head slowly and sighed. "Right," he said.

Actually, I had told him I wouldn't leave unless it was for LSU or another SEC team, but I didn't want to rub it in.

"Let me know how it goes," he said, "and good luck."

"I appreciate that, Coach," I said, and I did. I know he didn't want to lose me.

I went down to see Coach Brady with a list of questions. I'd been to a lot of interviews, both for head coaching positions and assistant coaching positions, and I usually surprised the interviewers by interviewing them, too. It almost always got a positive reaction, but I didn't do it for that reason. I was very thoughtful in my questions, which were tailored for the job. I never wanted to leave an interview without knowing what I was getting into if I took the job.

One of the answers he gave me was a surprise, however. Tim Floyd had recommended he hire me, in pretty strong terms. "You need to hire Butch Pierre," he said, telling me what Tim had told him.

The reason I was surprised was because my last interaction with Tim Floyd had been an argument. I got up in his face, maybe one of those times I could have been a little more diplomatic, but apparently he hadn't held that against me. I was impressed by his referral.

I was even more impressed when Coach Brady hired me, even though others were against it. John believed in me and told him he needed to hire his own staff, and that's what he did.

I thought of how Melvin dealt with his situation at Charlotte, winning over those who were against him, and I vowed to do the same at LSU.

I do have one condition, Coach," I said.

"What's that?" he asked, sounding surprised.

"I want my kids to go to school where yours go," I said.

John smiled.

Langley enrolled in the University Laboratory School right on campus, and Josh and Joe were in a private school for the first year and then transferred into the same school as my daughter.

It really was like a dream come true. I had always wanted to be there. I knew the people and they knew me. When I met with the athletic director, he told me it would be very important to recruit within Louisiana because he would never want to lose a great homegrown player to another school. He threw out the names of various high schools around the state and asked me if I knew the coach at each one by name. I did, of course. Then I named about twenty more. Needless to say, he was very impressed by that. I guess he'd pulled that trick with some other applicants. "None of them knew those names, Coach Pierre," he said.

I just smiled. "I know Louisiana basketball."

In spite of all the good news, the first two years were going to be rough, and everybody knew it. Sanctions for some NCAA recruiting violations were coming, and we only had six scholarship players left. Some players left after the great coach Dale Brown retired, and some may have transferred out because Coach Brady was known to be a very tough, demanding coach.

That was just what the team needed, in my opinion. Brady was tough but fair, and an outstanding coach. And he had to be aggressive right away if we wanted to reestablish ourselves as a force in the SEC. And of course, he was also following in the footsteps of a legend, a man who'd coached there for the previous twenty-five years. We all had a lot to prove, so John put together a close, tight-knit staff, and we went to work.

Seeing the NCAA report on the recruiting violations was an eye opener for me, and one of the best things that could have happened to me at that point in my career. Times were changing, and reading that report showed me what could happen if I wasn't vigilant. I had always been an aggressive recruiter, walking up to the line of what was allowed without crossing it, but reading the report showed me I needed to be even more careful to stay on the right side of NCAA rules. Big-time recruiting is extremely competitive, and the more successful you are, the more scrutiny you receive. Our probation would last for four years, and our scholarships would be limited, so it was important we were very aggressive but imperative we didn't add to our problems.

We signed nine players that first year, and I brought in eight of them. Under the circumstances, it was probably my finest recruiting year ever.

Since Kermit was technically the lead assistant, I held back my opinions a little more than I should have, seeing as we missed out on a couple of excellent players we should have taken. But overall, it was a stellar recruitment class.

John trusted me and always had my back, but he probably micromanaged me a little bit too much, at least in the beginning. He was under a lot of pressure to perform after the sanctions, and let me tell you, the LSU boosters *do not* play around. LSU is known as a football school, but basketball boosters are every bit as passionate about their sport. And they watched us like a hawk, as did the local media.

I think this brought the staff even closer. We were living together in a fishbowl, and there were a lot of cats out there ready to pounce if we made a mistake.

My first official meeting with Coach Brady didn't go as well as I'd hoped.

"Forget about him," John said.

I practically bit my tongue. I took a deep breath and made sure my tone was nice and even, because Coach Brady was dead wrong; I'd never felt more strongly about anything in my life.

"We need him, Coach," I said.

Brady sighed. I'm sure he was biting his tongue a little too. He obviously thought I was out of my mind thinking I could bring the best player in the country to LSU when we'd just been hit with probation. "Coach, he's one of those kids who could go straight into the NBA from high school," Brady said.

"Which is why we need him in our program," I countered.

"We can't get him," John said, exasperated. "How are you gonna convince him to come here when he could go anywhere?"

"My goal is to win a national championship, Coach," I said. "I'll get him."

Brady just looked at me. He couldn't believe I was serious. "Kermit!" he yelled.

We sat looking at each other across his desk. It wasn't a stalemate, exactly, since Coach Brady had all the power. I worked for him, and he could tell me who to go after and who not to go after if he really wanted to.

Kermit walked in. "What's up, Coach?"

Coach Brady told Kermit what I'd said and what I planned to do. Kermit's eyebrows went up, but, to his credit, he just turned to Brady and shrugged. "Just let Butch work, Coach."

Brady nodded and Kermit left the office. "All right, Butch," Brady said. "Go to work."

I stood up, happy to do so. But before I left, I turned back to Coach Brady. "Look, Coach, I'm gonna tell you where I go and who I talk to. You won't have to ask. But you also won't have to tell me who to call, because I know all that."

Brady smiled. "I know you do, Butch."

"I'm gonna sign some of the best players in the country, Coach. If I don't, I don't even need to be here."

I walked out, determined to sign Stromile Swift, the best college basketball player in the country.

It was a big opportunity for me, and I was eager to get to it. I was always an early riser, and that continued. I was up at 5:30 every morning. I took my kids to school, hit the weight room, and was in my office before anyone else. Every morning, I would hear John come in from my office, where I was already hitting the phones. "Anyone you want me to call, Coach?" I'd call out. When he left at 10:00 that night, I'd make sure and stick my head out. "See you tomorrow, Coach!"

After a few days of that, Coach Brady stepped into my office. "I get the point, Coach Pierre," he said. "Just let Butch work."

After that, he didn't do too much micromanaging.

When it was time for our first big home visit to see Stromile, Coach Brady was really nervous. He always gave a good presentation from what I had seen, but he knew we had a lot on the line for this one. He wanted to drive instead of fly, so we could go over things on the way there. It was four hours in the car, but I figured if that's what he thought we needed to do, that's what we'd do.

Every coach has a slightly different presentation for the recruit and their family, but the format is mostly the same. You tell them a little about yourself, the school, academics, and the facility. And of course, the team's past successes on the court. If you've been to the Final Four, that's big. Also how many, how fast, and can you get me to the NBA. Coach Brady gave an energetic presentation, but of course there were drawbacks I knew Stromile's mother would be concerned about the sanctions. His reputation as a disciplinarian. She was a single mother and a very strong woman. She didn't suffer fools, if you know what I mean. The first time I spoke to her on the phone, she came right out and told me she didn't like me.

"What's that?" I asked. I heard what she had said, but I wanted to figure out how to respond. I was playing for time, you might say.

"You heard me," she said. "You talk too fast. Only reason I'm talking to you at all is you're LSU."

Woah. This lady's tough. "That's all right," I said. "You're gonna meet my family, and you'll like me a lot better. My mama's the sweetest woman in the world."

"Mmm-hmm," she said.

I think I impressed her just a little bit by mentioning my mother, but time would tell. Stromile was very devoted to his mother. His sister, too. If he came to LSU, we'd have to get them both on board.

By the time we went to see the family, several other coaches had been there, coaches with national championships. Nobody gave us a chance, so nobody paid us too much attention, even though we were LSU.

But I had done my research. Everybody thought Stromile would probably go to Georgetown or someplace like that, but he was a Louisiana kid who needed to be comfortable. And what makes a kid from Shreveport comfortable is what's familiar. I knew he wasn't just going to go for a name. I knew he wanted to keep wearing Number 4, just like in high school. He was 6'10" but he wanted to be more than just a post player, also like in high school.

And his mother wasn't looking for a father figure for her son like some single mothers might have been. She was strong enough to be the mother and the father to her boy, so appealing to her in that way was the wrong way to go. She didn't need a man to take her place. No man *could* take her place.

That's where my background and life experience paid off. I knew everybody in the area, so I made calls and found out everything I could about him and his family. I felt like I really knew them because I knew so many like them.

On the ride up, after we discussed what we would say, I turned on the radio so John could relax. He knew the words to every song from the 70s and 80s, from Aerosmith to Earth, Wind, and Fire, which you never would have guessed to look at him. He also knew the Bible and could quote scripture for days on end. I used to tell him he had missed his calling, that he should have been a preacher.

"Just talk to them like you're talking to my parents, and you'll be fine," I told him, and he relaxed a little more. My parents just loved him. "Any white man who knows the words to every Temptations song and all that scripture like you do is gonna be just fine." He laughed at that and that relaxed him even more.

I was driving pretty fast through one of these little Bayou towns, and we got pulled over. I got out of the car and gave the officer my license.

"Where you going?" he asked.

"Shreveport," I said.

"Mmm-hmm," the cop said, looking me over.

Just then, John gets out of the car, real impatient. All the relaxation was out the window. "Just write the ticket so we can get out of here," he snapped.

"Get back in the car," the cop told him.

"Yeah, John," I whispered. "Get back in the car."

"Just write the ticket," he said, and got back inside.

"What's his problem?" the cop asked, sounding a little angry.

I decided to diffuse the situation. "He's just nervous cause we're going to see about a basketball player for LSU."

"Basketball player?"

"Yeah," I said. "That's John Brady, the new basketball coach at LSU."

The cop got real friendly after that. "You don't say? What player?" He motioned for his partner to get out of the cruiser, and I told them about Stromile.

To make a long story short, I didn't get a ticket, after all. Those two cops were really excited that they'd pulled over the new head coach at LSU. What's funny is that it took longer for the cop *not* to write the ticket than it would have if John had stayed in the car and just let him write me the ticket in the first place.

When we pulled up to the Swift residence, which wasn't in the best neighborhood, it was like we weren't expected.

Nobody was in the driveway looking for us, nobody was on the porch waiting for us. Usually there was someone to greet us, but this time, nothing.

At least, his sister opened the door when we knocked. She even invited us inside.

I could tell John was a little deflated, but I just said, "Let's get set up," and we put out all our materials on the living room table. His mother and sister sat down, his high school coach sat down, I sat down. John looked up. "Where's Stromile?" he asked.

"Oh, he's sleeping," his mother said. "Go wake up your brother."

That just about killed Brady's morale. "We don't have a chance," he whispered to me while we waited.

"That's just the way he is, Coach," I whispered. "Just remember, like you're talking to my parents."

When Stromile came in, John shook it off and got into the presentation. A key point was how he connected to Stromile's sister, Shalanda. She started calling him JB, which he really liked, and then Stromile's mother Mary would chime in and call him Brady, which was also felt very familiar, which was, of course, what made Stromile comfortable. Family.

After John was through, I spoke about how long I had known him, from the time I was seventeen. How he'd connected to my parents so well and then taken me into his home.

How I drove his car, and how sometimes he drove me, which the other head coaches always laughed about because the assistant coach is supposed to drive the head coach. I loved John like a brother, and I used my feelings about our relationship to maybe soften his reputation as a disciplinarian just a little bit.

"John is like family to me," I said. "And our team will be family to you."

When we were finished, John made one of the all-time greatest recruiting moves I'd ever seen. Stromile's mother had made dinner for everybody, and John just walked in the kitchen and lifted a lid off one of those pots and smelled the food, and then got himself a drink out of the fridge, telling her how hungry he was. He made himself at home because they made him feel like he was at home. That's family, and that's what they were looking for.

Before we ate, John said the blessing, and he sounded like a preacher doing it, which also made an impression on Stromile's mother. The only thing that would have made it better was if he sung a little Al Green at the end.

Coach Brady was a real finicky eater, though, and the only time I was worried was when he looked at one of these little bitty meatballs Mary Swift had made, which had these white specks in them. I saw the look on his face when he cut into one. I could almost hear the words on the tip of his tongue—*What the dog are these white things in this meatball?*

Luckily I caught his eye and gave him a look like—*Don't say a word, just eat the damn thing,* which he did.

We had a great visit, but as soon as we were out of the driveway, he turned to me and asked about those white specks. "What do you suppose they were, Butch?"

"I don't know, Coach, but I'm gonna tell everybody you wanted Stromile Swift so badly, you ate meatballs with termites to sign him."

We laughed about halfway home at that one. It was probably just rice. At least, I hope so.

John was in such a good mood, he decided to drive, and he went even faster than I'd driven on the way up. So, you know what happened. He got pulled over. This time it was one cop, a lot older than the first two, a gray-haired guy with a pot belly.

John got out of the car and gave the cop his license. As soon as he did that, I couldn't resist. I jumped out of the car, just like John had done to me. "Write him a ticket!" I said. "Write him a ticket so we can get out of here!"

John looked at me like I was crazy, but the cop, who was holding John's license in his hand, busted out laughing. John, now thoroughly confused, turned back to the officer. "What on Earth are you laughing about?"

The officer handed back his license. "I'm chief of police," he said. "Two of my patrolmen bragged to me today that they pulled over the new coach at LSU, and now I can tell 'em I did, too!"

Stromile made three or four other official visits, but the next year, we signed him and he came to play for us at LSU. He was a little slow to develop, but once he hit his stride, he did some unbelievable things on the court. He put on 20 pounds to go about 230 between his first and second years and was nearly unstoppable.

His sophomore year we went 28-6, won the SEC championship, and went to the Sweet Sixteen, losing a game to Wisconsin we should have won. Had we done so, I think we would have gone all the way. Stro was SEC Player of the Year, and John was Coach of the Year. We had a lot of talent on that team. The second team I had coached that I really and truly believed had what it took to be national champions.

Besides Stromile Swift, we had Brian Beshara, a transfer from Rice who was what I call a "glue guy," one of those players who, by ability or personality, holds a team together. Lamont Roland, who transitioned from a scorer to a defensive stalker for the good of the team. Ronald Dupree, Jermaine Williams, Collis Temple III, Brad Bridgewater, walk-ons Jack Warner and Brandon Landry, and freshmen sensation Torris Bright. They were all great players, but they also collectively had that intangible quality every championship team needs—chemistry. They played, fought, won and lost together—like a family. When it's a team, you call it chemistry.

But the most transformational player on the team was our big man at center, Jabari Smith. Stro was the dominant talent, but Jabari just had a personality that meshed with Stromile, and they brought out the best in each other. The entire team started hitting on all cylinders after that.

The funny thing was, both Stromile and Jabari, who were with us over two years, were kind of a mess their first year. They both had what I call a transition year. They needed time to come into their own, and I give John a lot of credit for being patient with them, as well as their teammates, who rallied around them when they struggled early.

There's a lot of pressure on someone like Stromile, after being so highly sought after, to live up to all the hype. Jabari was older, a transfer from junior college, and he was under a lot of pressure, too, after a disappointing start. I think the combination of supportive teammates who had their back and a patient coaching staff was what caused our team to explode in their second year. It was my third year, too, and I was learning right alongside them.

Jabari became a real leader and great teammate after that slow start. Both he and Stromile had a rough first season but really came into their own that second year, the year we should have won it all.

Once Jabari actually got between Coach Brady and Brian Beshara after a pretty tense exchange on the sideline, something that didn't happen very often. Jabari calmed them both down immediately, showing a level of maturity and judgment that amazes me to this day. He just seemed to understand all the team's personalities and had a way of smoothing things out.

I also give a lot of credit to Coach Brady for his patience with Stro and Jabari, who developed into great players. When they struggled early on, I think it humbled them, and John was able to use that to help them become better players, and better men.

In the case of Stromile, I also have to credit his mother, Mary. A lot of parents in her situation might have blamed the coaches for his poor first year, possibly even resenting the fact we recruited him at all since Stro could have gone straight into the NBA from high school and gotten a big payday.

Mary Swift would have been in a nice new house out in the country by then, after raising three kids on her own, keeping them safe in a very rough neighborhood. Even though she was dealing with health issues that NBA money would have made a lot easier to handle, she was patient with her son, patient with us, and just grateful that her son was surrounded by teammates and coaches who really cared about him.

In the NBA draft the next year, Stromile was the second pick overall, and Jabari went early in the second round. Stro had a decent career in the NBA, playing for several teams and making a lot of money, and eventually he built that house out in the country for his mother. But he never played for anyone like he played for us that one amazing season.

His mother passed away in 2009 while he was with the New Jersey Nets, and I know it hit him hard. I think the cold business of big-time professional basketball just wasn't the same as the warm, supportive atmosphere we had created for him at LSU. I doubt Stromile ever felt that same family atmosphere playing basketball again.

Hopefully, the other players did at some point, but it's a rare thing, a season like that. So many factors have to come together just right in order to achieve that level of success, on the court or off. It was a special time, and a special team, but there was a lot more to come.

CHAPTER TWENTY-NINE

"R-E-S-P-E-C-T, find out what it means to me."
Aretha Franklin

WHILE THE LSU MEN'S BASKETBALL TEAM was making history in my third season, there was something else going on at LSU that made a little news. Some fella by the name of Nick Saban was hired to coach the football team.

At the beginning of the year, the university had hired a new chancellor, Mark Emmert, and as soon as I met him, I knew he was sharp. It was at an alumni event at a private home, one of those fundraising things coaches are sometimes invited to attend. I find them useful because I like meeting movers and shakers, people with influence who can have a big impact on your team and your career.

The powerful people at these events are not the only influencers, as I've mentioned. Sometimes a custodian or first year instructor can have just as great an impact, depending on the circumstances. But there's no denying that alumni and booster groups have a lot of influence on big-time college athletics, particularly in a small state like Louisiana, where LSU holds such a prominent place in the state's history.

I didn't know anything at all about Chancellor Emmert when Clemmie and I chatted with him at the event about the school, his background, and his past experiences. All I knew was that new and powerful people were coming into my world, and it would be a good idea to introduce myself. It's always a good idea to make a good first impression on the boss and his wife.

Later, I heard him give a speech about the school and the changes that were coming, which only confirmed my instinct that this guy was different. I thought he would be a real hands-on type guy, not a typical chancellor who didn't do a whole lot that was visible. Most chancellors, at least in my experience, kinda took a low profile, but I could tell this mover and shaker was looking to shake things up. Boy, did he.

Nick Saban coming to LSU was big. He wasn't quite the legend back then that he's now become, but anyone could see it was only a matter of time. He was a great football coach, and since we were doing so well, it just felt like LSU athletics had reached a whole new level. And all of this was happening in just my third year.

Saban went to a lot of our games, which was always great because it got the crowd just a little more fired up, like when a celebrity goes to a rock concert. Nick Saban was a bona-fide coaching celebrity, so it also meant he brought in even more recruits and attention to the school.

At the end of the year, I was at a conference in Atlanta when I got a phone call I wasn't expecting.

"Nick Saban, Coach," the voice on the other end of the line said. "I just wanted to call and introduce myself."

I hung up and he immediately call back.

I'm not sure, but I might have actually held the phone out and looked at it like they do in the movies. I thought it was a joke at first, but I didn't want to say that because what if it wasn't?

"Good to meet you, Coach," I said, "at least on the phone."

He chuckled, and that's when I knew it was really Nick Saban. Not that I was familiar with his laugh or anything, but it just sounded like how a famous person like him might respond to the situation.

"That's actually what I wanted to talk to you about, Coach. I'd like to schedule a meeting in person when you're back in town."

He obviously knew my schedule.

"That'd be just fine," I said. "But call me Butch."

"I've heard good things about you, Butch. I'll have my secretary call your office and set something up."

"Sounds good, Coach," I said, and we ended the call. I couldn't quite bring myself to call him Nick. But since I didn't have a secretary, I called John and told him to make sure someone was answering the phone in my office.

"Don't you have an answering machine?" he asked.

"I don't want to miss my meeting with Coach Saban."

There was a pause. "Hold on," he said, and put down the phone. After what seemed like forever, he picked up again. "His secretary said to drop by Coach Saban's office tomorrow at nine," he said.

"What do you think he wants?"

"I don't know, Butch," John answered. "I hear he's looking for a good wideout."

I laughed and kidded him about getting to talk only to Saban's secretary and hung up.

The next morning. I went to meet Nick Saban. I was pretty impressed even before I went into his office, because when I knocked on his door, it slid open like in some James Bond movie. And after the meeting, he pushed a button at his desk to close it behind me. Everything was top of the line when it came to Nick Saban. I'll bet he's got *two* of those doors at Alabama.

It turned out he really *had* been hearing good things about me. On recruiting trips.

There's a lot of overlap among elite athletes, since in high school you can play multiple sports. Michael Clayton was from Baton Rouge and excelled in both basketball and football, and apparently had mentioned my name. *There's that wide receiver,* I thought. Marcus Spears was another Baton Rouge kid he was looking at who played both sports. A Diamond in the rough, longtime New York Giants Cory Webster from my back of the woods. Also Stromile's best friend and high school teammate Ronnie Prude.

I knew them, of course, having recruited them, and knew their parents, too, and told Coach Saban what I thought he could use. Those players were program-changers, and Saban would end up winning a national championship with them and others a few years later.

We discussed some other players and talked for almost an hour. He wanted to build a new academic center, which I thought was a great idea. He wanted me to smooth that over with John. We talked about Louisiana life and culture, and he told me Jimbo Fisher, who was his offensive coordinator at the time, would be calling about Michael and Marcus to see if it was possible for them to play both sports. Neither one ended up playing basketball, but they sure were stars for Saban.

Jimbo, of course, went on to head coach the football team at Florida State and, at the time of this writing, Texas A&M. If you want to be great, surround yourself with greatness.

Coach Saban and I had a great working relationship. I helped with recruiting whenever I could, since I knew everybody in Louisiana athletics, from the high school coaches to the elite athletes. I also worked quite a bit with his recruiting coordinator Derek Dooley, who by now has coached at both the college and professional level.

They got the academic center built, which was a great addition to the school and a real selling point in terms of recruiting. Chancellor Emmert, whose Flagship Agenda had been all about improving academics at LSU, really came through for the university in ways far beyond athletics. He improved nearly every aspect of the school and took us to a whole new level. Hiring Saban was just a part of that. Emmert is now the president of the NCAA.

Later he also built an athletic complex because they had to keep up with the Joneses in the SEC. He didn't like driving to practice, wanted a one-place shop for his players, worked 24/7, and wanted everything housed under one roof. They called it Sabanville, which I heard he hated, but the name stuck, anyway. That's just the way it goes sometimes.

After the LSU Tigers beat the Oklahoma Sooners to win the BCS National Championship in January of 2004, I received a championship ring, which was pure class. I was technically not on his staff, but I'd helped so much with recruiting the players on that team.

"Thanks, Coach," I said." That means a lot to me, but I'd do anything for LSU."

"I know you would," he said, and we both meant what we said.

The year after we went to the Sweet Sixteen, Alabama offered me a position as assistant coach. I was always looking out for a head coaching job, and this was a lateral move, but I seriously considered it. I had to because it was a lot more money.

My kids were young, but that cut both ways. On the one hand, I wanted to put away as much as I could for their education, but on the other, they were kids, and kids need stability.

I knew we were all going to get raises after that incredible season, and when I was called in to see Athletic Director Dean, I knew what it was about.

"I heard about Alabama, Butch," he said.

I just smiled and nodded. It felt good to be pursued, but in contract negotiations, you don't want to give too much away. They assumed I was leaving, which was a distinct possibility at that point.

"I can give you fifteen thousand more," he added, getting right to it.

I was a little surprised. Alabama had offered to almost double my salary. I was almost insulted, but I thought for a moment, and then I definitely offended him by saying, "You know Mr. Dean, I think you should have asked me what it would take to get me to stay."

His face turned bright red, which was how I knew he's been offended. "No disrespect," I added, and it was true. I hadn't meant to insult him, but I knew my value to the team and the university better than he did, apparently, as did Alabama.

"If you need more, you'd better talk to John," he said.

I was really torn. Alabama was sending a private plane down for me, and I knew they weren't planning a sightseeing trip. If I got on that plane, it was to sign my name in Tuscaloosa. I talked to Clemmie and packed an overnight bag.

John called and asked what was up, and I told him about Alabama's offer. He whistled softly and told me he'd call back. I finished packing and got ready to leave. I was at the airport in New Orleans when John called back. John said we can't match that offer, but I will give you all my raise and bonus. Kermit also called and said I could have his 10K. I didn't take Kermit's 10K, but that was nice of him to offer. Everybody wanted me to stay.

I mean, *really* wanted me to stay.

I hung up and looked at Mark Gottfried, Alabama's head coach who'd flown down to take me back with him to Tuscaloosa. He shook his head. He could see it in my face.

"You're not coming, are you?"

I shook my head. "I can't get on that plane, Coach."

He shrugged his shoulders. "Nearly had you, didn't we?"

I nodded and put up my thumb and forefinger. *This close.*

"I already topped out," he said. "Figured we'd need to go big to get you. Shock and awe."

I laughed. We shook hands, and he walked back to the plane. I stood there and watched it take off. I was still a little shocked and awed, myself. After all the machinations that afternoon, LSU had actually come close to Alabama's offer. Did I say I loved LSU?

I went back to work, secure in the knowledge that I was in the right place for myself and my family, in a place that recognized my value to the team.

My family loved LSU as much as I did. We thrived there, as a family and individually. Clemmie was doing great in her new business, the kids loved going to school on campus, and I was feeling fantastic. No matter how late I worked the night before, I was up early for a five-mile run, after which I took my kids to school.

When my daughter kissed my cheek and told me she loved me before getting out of the car every morning, it made my whole day. There's nothing like it. Then I'd lift weights and get to work. The hours were long, but on occasion, I would pick up my kids after school and take them home before going back to work. I could hear about their day and see when they were dragging or excited about something or upset. I got to see all their school plays and other activities.

My daughter was doing especially well. My sons lagged behind a little, probably because they were boys. Being raised by a strong, intelligent mother, flanked by her daughter, and married to my wife, I've always just accepted the fact that women are hard for us men to master But we do our best, and my sons did theirs.

We had a lot of cookouts, sometimes inviting the players to my folks' house just 30 miles down the road, which my parents loved. They took great joy in meeting the new players each year. Our world was centered around LSU, where everybody knew the Pierres. It was one big happy family from the moment I walked on that campus in the morning to the moment I went home that night. Every day was special.

It helped me grow as a coach, too. Being a good family man helps you develop the skills to be a good coach. It makes you observant. Hearing the voice of your child, looking them in the eye, watching them develop, gives you a sixth sense about their emotional well-being. And that sense helps in coaching, too. You get an instinct about trouble before it starts, and you learn to resolve conflicts more easily. You learn to raise those players, in a way, just like your own children. You see them grow and develop, and you become invested in that growth, the same as with your own. And you constantly find opportunities to teach them, even as you're learning.

I remember I had an idea one morning on the way to school. I took a detour and took my kids over to see Stromile, who had an 8:00 class for which he was notoriously late almost every day. A lot of teachers cut the athletes a break, but I think that practice didn't have much value.

I told my sons to pound on his apartment door, which they did, and to yell, "Wake up, Stromile!" which they also did.

He came to the door, still half-asleep, and looked at me and then down at my boys. "Time for school, Stromile!" they screamed.

"Okay, go get in the car, boys," I said.

"Why'd you do that, Coach?" he asked.

"Two reasons," I said. "They need to learn to get their butt up on time, just like you, and you're going to the NBA, son. They'll remember this their whole life."

Stromile yawned and went back inside to get ready for class. At least, I hoped he did.

We did the same thing the next morning. When Stromile opened the door, he nodded. "I got it, Coach," he said, and after that, he was almost always on time for that first class. Almost.

My sons got an education in the locker room, too. They were ball boy for our games, helped the equipment managers, and saw a lot of things only a coach's son would see. Some good, some bad, but everything is an example if you use it as such. For example, they heard a lot of bad language, but, to this day, neither one of my sons curse. They never saw the kind of rough neighborhoods I saw when I was their age, but that's all right. As a parent, you always want your kids to have it better than you did. It was enough that I saw those neighborhoods so I could be a positive example for them.

I began to coach more from the floor and take a more visible role. The Villa 7 Conference for (top assistant basketball coaches in the country) and Clemmie helped me soften some of my rough edges for public speaking. I began to really cultivate my image to show the world who I would be as a head coach once the opportunity came. As a recruiter, I had an image as a gunslinger, an aggressive guy who won more than he lost and would do anything within the rules to sign a player I wanted. Because of my success, there were some who assumed I was dirty, but I had never worried about what other people thought. I just did the job the only way I knew how, balls to the wall. But times change, and so do the rules. Adapt or die, as they say. If a head coach has to be more aware of his image because he's the face of the school, then that's what I'd do.

I always had job interviews at the end of each year, but head coaching jobs were elusive, at least the ones I felt I could take, if offered. I was one of the hottest assistants in the country and also one of the highest paid.

There were plenty of head coaches who made less than I did, so I was in a unique position. I simply couldn't afford to accept a promotion to a lot of the schools that needed my services. I was offered several head coaching jobs that would have required me to take a pay cut, and that's tough thing to do.

Bottom line: my situation at LSU would be pretty hard to give up unless the offer was outstanding. Especially if it was just a lateral move.

After that great season, it was inevitable we'd have rebuilding years. I was at LSU for eleven years. There were good and bad seasons, just like any team. True greatness in sports is often fleeting. You reach the mountaintop and sooner or later you'll slide back down into the valley, because you have to go through the next valley to get to the next mountain. True greatness is not in the championship; it's in the journey. What you do, how you perform, the sacrifices you make. And how you behave once you get there.

If you win with class, you have to lose that way, too. Because eventually, it all falls away. Even the very best will be tested. But if you fought with honor and integrity, you'll still have it when the awards are long forgotten, and that's what matters.

That's what a great head coach understands. And that's the kind of head coach I plan to be.

CHAPTER THIRTY

"The will of God will not take us where
the grace of God cannot sustain us."
Billy Graham

COACH SABAN LEFT to coach the Miami Dolphins in 2005, replaced by Les Miles, another top coach who would lead the team to another BCS Championship in 2007. Life went on. I was still constantly on the lookout for impact players, and I went after every one of them. Some we got and some we didn't, but some of the best were Brandon Bass, Tyrus Thomas, Marcus Thornton, Garrett Temple, Glen "Big Baby" Davis, Chris Johnson, Anthony Randolph, Darrnell Lazare and a special kid by the name of Tasmin Mitchell, who would become like a son to me. Which was why I almost missed him.

His mom called me out of the blue when he was about twelve years old. She was a single mother and sought me out because she wanted a strong male role model in his life. I'd heard the name before, since my own sons were only a couple of years younger and were playing basketball, too. Of course, I saw hundreds of guys his age every year because I got calls to come see so-and-so play, and I always took every call.

Leave no stone unturned was my motto.

But this was the first time I'd gotten a call just to be a role model. That was really all she wanted. Not to see him play, although it was inevitable I would.

No, his mother just wanted him to meet a positive male role model he'd have something in common with, and since the kid loved basketball, she figured I would be a good choice. I'd also met his grandmother way back when I was in high school.

I went out to meet him in Denham Springs where he lived, watched him play, and we kind of took to each other right away. He was a great kid, and I'd talk on the phone with him and answer his questions and just kind of be there for him. He was tall for his age and had quite good skills, so I thought he'd be pretty good one day, but our relationship was mostly a father-son type deal.

His mother Collette even asked me to go with him to some of those parent/teacher nights at his school. I had to ask Clemmie about that one since I'd missed one or two of those with our own kids. I knew that would come up.

"Clemmie, you know his mama works for the sheriff's department. I can't argue with a woman who packs heat, now."

The look on her face told me I didn't want to argue with her, either, but I introduced the two of them and they became good friends. Then it was all good. Our kids spent time with Collette's kid, and they became like part of the family. I even became his godfather, with a church ceremony and everything, which was a very big deal for the family. His father was out of the picture at the time and had been so for a while, so it was pretty emotional for everyone.

So, of course, when Tasmin was named a McDonald's All American, along with too many other honors to name, Coach Brady kept on me to go after him. Everybody assumed he would commit to LSU anyway because of our relationship, but it was because of that that I couldn't pursue him like a typical top recruit. It just didn't feel right.

Besides, I knew he'd been dreaming of Kentucky. He wanted to play for Tubby Smith, a good friend of mine who'd brought a national championship to Kentucky in his very first year as head coach, the first team to do so in twenty years without a first team all-American. Tubby was *my* mentor, and if Tasmin wanted to play for him, I definitely understood. If my godson had his heart set on Kentucky, how could I even think about convincing him otherwise?

Coach Brady insisted we needed to make a presentation, anyway, and I had to agree. I just didn't want to pressure him. To be honest, I was the one getting all the pressure. His mother begged me to sign him. "You can't let my baby leave the state," she said.

So it was rough. Especially since I knew how great he would be at LSU. He wasn't real big, somewhere between a post and a wingman, but he was a gamer. He had a knack for seeing plays before they developed. What he wanted was the three-spot away from the goal, and I knew he could be great at that position. He was a real hard worker.

We made our presentation, and it was a good one. I didn't hold back, but I didn't pressure him, either. He really liked our players, and after that visit, he knew he'd get a shot at that three-spot and be a starter on our team.

His next home visit was Kentucky, and the kid was *really* excited. I knew Tubby and his team, as well as the way he thought. If Tubby answered wrong when Taz asked him the same questions he'd asked Brady and me, or even hesitated, I figured we had a shot.

I guess Tubby answered wrong, or was too slow, because as soon as Tubby left his mother's house, Tasmin called and told me he was coming to LSU. I love that headstrong kid. To this day, I'm not sure Tubby knows he could have signed Tasmin or at least made my job a lot harder if he'd answered those questions differently, but if you're reading this, Tubby, I'm sorry, man. You win some, you lose some.

John was pretty happy, although somebody, whose name will go unmentioned, made a comment to *USA Today* that caused compliance to inquire about me being his godfather. Something about how he guessed you needed to be a godfather to sign players nowadays.

I kind of expected something like that, sour grapes and all, but I had all my ducks in a row, and it didn't amount to anything. Still, it was irritating. Your reputation is important, and I didn't like my integrity being questioned like that.

But in the end, it was all worth it. In four years, Tasmin helped LSU to two SEC championships and a run at the top spot in 2006 when our nineteenth-ranked team beat No. 12 Texas A&M, No. 1 Duke, and No. 9 Texas before losing a heartbreaker to UCLA in the Final Four. He finished as LSU's third leading scorer of all time. First was Pistol Pete Maravich. Pretty good for a kid from Denham Springs.

There were plenty of tough times during my tenure at LSU, though, both personal and professional. I was on a recruiting trip to Atlanta when I got a call from Clemmie telling me to come home right away because our house had burned. That really shook me up, because it was an electrical thing that could have happened anytime. We were lucky because no one was home, but what if Clemmie and the kids had been asleep? What would I do if something happened to my family? Something like that really reminds you what's important in life.

And then there was Katrina. We were at home on hurricane watch, and everybody could see it was gonna be bad. Clemmie and I had been out of town before it hit, and we had a hard time getting back to get to our children. We couldn't get a flight into any city anywhere near home, so we flew into Houston and rented a car, and there weren't many cars left, even in Houston.

I drove 90 miles an hour in the wrong direction to get back to my children. All the traffic was going the other way, so at least I had an open road. By the time we made it back, there was no way we were getting back out, so we pitched in to help on campus, along with the entire basketball team and a whole lot of others.

The storm hit and we rode it out, but afterward, things were as bad as you remember from the news and probably worse. It was like a war zone, with helicopters buzzing overhead and delivering people to campus, which had a hospital and a pharmacy, along with bodies that were stored in our practice facility.

It was a horrible thing to see, but I could not have been prouder of my team. Those young men volunteered to help with all the scared people coming in on buses. They saw things no one should see, especially at that age, but they just kept working through it all.

John and I eventually made everyone go home if they could. More National Guard troops had come in, and we thought it was just too much for them. Some of them wanted to stay, but we made it an order. If they had a safe place to go, we wanted them to be there.

Baton Rouge wasn't New Orleans, but it wasn't far, and it had been hard hit.

Katrina was a bonding experience for everyone, from the players to the coaches. Seeing something like that changes a person. I thought my house on fire and destroyed had changed me, but that was nothing compared to Katrina. Clemmie and I were separated from our children. What if we hadn't made it back? What if they'd gone missing? There were people everywhere who had been displaced. People who had lost family and people who were missing family. I couldn't imagine being in that position.

After things got settled down some, I went back to work. But I'd lost my star recruit.

DJ Augustin was a high school phenom from New Orleans who grew up in the shadow of LSU. I wanted him badly, and I think he was eager to come. But no one had seen him or his family. Nobody knew where he was, and I called everybody. Then I started checking the shelters, and that meant visiting each one. You couldn't just call and ask for someone.

Seeing all those suffering people moved me in a way that's hard to describe. Anyone who was there probably feels the same way. It was just indescribable. I was looking for a basketball player to help my team and other people were looking for their children, their parents, even their pets. It made everything else seem insignificant by comparison.

But my job was to coach and recruit, and so I went back to it. In a way, it helped me deal with everything. Throwing myself in my work was good therapy.

I kept looking. I drove back to Houston and walked through the Astrodome, where lots of Louisianans had been taken. I spent the day there and another day in the city but didn't have any luck.

Two weeks later, I got a call from a family friend I'd left word with, who told me where he was. Back in Houston, where I'd just been. He was safe with his family there. They were even staying with someone I knew personally but hadn't thought to call.

I could feel that something had changed in DJ. Something had changed in all of us, I think, but in him it just felt more profound. His parents were very concerned about coming back to all the devastation, and I couldn't say I blamed them. I reestablished my relationship with DJ, and he came up for a good official visit, but it was never the same. He had strong ties in Texas, and they wanted him, too. I could feel him slipping away, and the thing was, I understood. After what he'd been through, why not just stay where his family felt safe?

He enrolled in high school for his senior year down in Missouri City, Texas, a suburb of Houston, and finished as a McDonald's All American with a whole bunch of other honors and awards. He played for the Hightower Hurricanes.

DJ chose Texas, as I had a feeling he would, and was a stellar point guard for two years with the Longhorns before going to the Charlotte Bobcats as the ninth pick in the 2008 NBA draft.

Around that time, I kind of had a crisis of faith. Both personally and professionally, it was a low point. I'm not sure why, but Katrina and that recruiting season, the loss of DJ and everything else, affected me in ways I hadn't anticipated. It just felt like something was off, and I didn't know what to do about it.

My whole life I had been driven by one thing or another. Driven to make the team, driven to start, driven to get into a great school, driven to score, driven to graduate, driven to go to the NBA, driven to make my parents proud.

Most of that, I accomplished. Now what?

For six months, I asked myself that question in different ways. Things felt soft and directionless. I felt like I had lost touch with who I really was and who I wanted to be. Ego and pride kept me from acknowledging things for a while. As a man, a husband and a father, I had always been taught to hold it together, hold things in, hold my cards close to the vest. But Katrina shook me to my core. Maybe things had been going so well for so long that I didn't know how to respond. When things are bad, we lean on faith to get us through, but when things were good what was I leaning on?

I took a step back and examined my life and rededicated myself to God, my family, and basketball, in that order. I told myself I would do whatever it took to straighten myself out, and in my rededication to my faith, I came through it. I made a promise to God.

I had seen all the terrible things people dealt with after the hurricane, and I told myself that people are strong and they would get through it. I prayed for them and for my family and told myself life would go on, and it did. I began to see my crisis of faith as my own personal hurricane. I thought I had emerged unscathed after Katrina, but it turned out the effects of that storm just took a little longer to manifest themselves in my case.

I'm blessed to have a family who stood by me during that difficult time, especially Clemmie. I don't deserve her and have no idea what I would ever do without her.

Even though it was a terrible time for me, I became a better person as a result. A better husband and father and more disciplined in my faith.

I feel almost embarrassed writing about it because there were so many who lost so much, but it was a real lesson for me about strength and weakness, and my place in the world. I think I became a better coach as a result of my personal crisis, more patient and perceptive. Everything is a learning experience. Everything.

FAMILY

Family is everything and anything.

What I mean by that is that everything we are, everything we do, and everything we become springs forth from family. But nowadays, family isn't always defined quite like it used to be. Family, it seems, is what you make it.

When I coached at LSU and we went to the Sweet Sixteen in 2006, that team was a family. Every team usually gets close during the course of a long season, but we just had a unique group of guys that all complimented each other in positive ways. Everybody knew their role and excelled, making everyone around them better. They fought each other and fought together, but at the end of the day, there was real love and respect, which is what family is all about.

We each have family by blood, and then there are the families we find along the way. The families we create for ourselves out of need, out of convenience, out of love.

Be true to your family, whoever they are, with special attention to the original. Because while you can always join another team, there's no changing that one.

Be good to those that love you. Treat them well, lean on them when necessary, and make your family the center of your world. Friends may come and go, but family is forever. Treat it with the respect it deserves, because family is the origin of you.

A person with family at the center of their life will always be more stable, more loved, and more successful. Life's better with company.

Family is the foundation of greatness, and the cornerstone of success.

CHAPTER THIRTY-ONE

"Wanna fly, you gotta give up the
shit that weighs you down."
Toni Morrison

I T WAS TOUGH ON EVERYBODY when John Brady was fired. We
were 8-13 with a 1-6 record in conference play with ten games
to go, so it was obvious there were a lot of unhappy people at
LSU, but I never expected that, and neither did John.

The 2008 season was winding down, definitely not one of our
best, and that afternoon, John was late for our 2:00 practice. John
was *never* late for practice. I'd been associate head coach since 2002,
and he always ran the practices. By that time, we were a well-oiled
machine. We rarely even had staff meetings because we knew each
other so well.

2:30 p.m., no John.

I started practice at 3:00 and sent one of the assistant coaches to
look for John. I was getting the feeling that maybe John was meeting
with someone at the wrong time. That was the only reason I could
think of for him missing practice like that.

John showed up before the assistant came back. His expression was grim.

"Where you been?" I asked.

He didn't answer. "Come by my house tonight at 11:00 and tell the team I'll see them tomorrow at 2:00." And then he walked out.

Something had happened, that was for sure, but no one seemed to know. John and I talked about everything, but he hadn't said anything to me about whatever he'd been doing all day.

I went to his house that night at 11:00, as requested. He'd gone to see the AD and was told he'd finish out the year, but that was it, and John was too proud to stay, so they fired him. Eleven years at LSU was done.

In our business, you always keep in the back of your mind the reality of things. Coaches are hired to be fired. They are (almost) all expendable. But it's still a shock when it happens to you.

And then he said four words that shocked *me*. *"You're coaching the team."*

I exhaled. I really didn't know what to say or how to respond. John sensed that I was uncomfortable, so he got up, shook my hand, and told me to go talk to Clemmie.

Clemmie! I had to get home and discuss things with Clemmie. I hugged John and left him with his thoughts, which I'm sure were pretty complicated. Sometimes an assistant coach would also leave in such a circumstance, either by choice or fired, but there wasn't another school John was going to, so with me it would be involuntary.

There was no plan. Everything was too sudden for there to be a plan.

Besides, John wouldn't have told me I was coaching the team if he expected anything like that, but who coached the team the rest of the season wasn't up to John, anyway. And I had a family. I couldn't quit unless I had another job to go to, so if LSU decide to keep me, I would probably stay. But it would be tough if they brought in someone else as head coach. It would be an insult to me I might not be able to allow.

I went home to talk to my wife. We never talked about things like that in front of the kids. We never argued in front of them, either. Once I made sure the kids were in bed, I took Clemmie in the bedroom and closed the door, sharing what I knew.

She couldn't believe it, either, but she got right down to it. "We need a plan to tell the kids," she said.

I hadn't thought of that, but it was true. They loved John; he was family. They shouldn't hear about it at school. Plus they loved school, and I knew they would be worried about that. Langley was a junior, and the twins were in the tenth grade. We didn't want to stress them out before we knew what was going to happen.

Langley flat out refused to move. "I'm staying till I graduate," she said.

"Okay," I said. "I guess that's settled." I let it go because there wasn't any point in arguing anything different at the moment.

I went into the office the next morning. The AD came down shortly after I had arrived and told the staff that John had been fired, and he wanted to see me in his office. Once I was there, he asked me to stay on as interim head coach.

"Of course," I said.

Be careful what you wish for. I'd been hoping to get a head coaching job for many years, but it had just come at the expense of one of my best friends.

Of course, that's not really true. John wasn't pushed out because I was hired, it was the other way around. But it still felt strange. I had no idea how to deal with John and our relationship. I didn't ask the AD any questions; I figured John would tell me what had happened. It was a short meeting, to the relief of us both, probably, and I walked back to my office in a daze.

There were only nine games left in the season, but I would be coaching them. We had Tennessee in two days.

I began to think of the logistics and my new responsibilities. I would have to release a statement to the media, of course. I had to talk to the players, who would be confused and angry, most likely. I went back to my office, closed the door, and made a few calls. My attorney, a couple of trusted friends. Mentors. People whose advice I trusted and needed right then.

We were somewhere around ninth place in the conference, but I didn't plan to stay there. I wanted to win every game just as I always did, even more, and I felt like I had something to prove.

Nine games to turn a negative into a positive. Make sure the players make it through a difficult changing time. Prove I'm worthy of the job. I got to it.

"You've all heard it a million times," I told the team. "No distractions." I looked out at their faces. The players looked incredibly young, all of a sudden. They'd been having a tough season, and now it had just gotten even tougher. LSU was in the national spotlight every game, but there would be a lot of extra scrutiny after this. I kept it short.

I tapped my head and then my heart. "Stay focused," I said. "We'll help you. Practice in five. Let's go!"

The team instinctively gathered around me like they did before a game. I put out my hand, and they placed theirs on top. "Break!"

The players, as confused as they were, were the easy part of the equation. Coaching was second nature to me. It was all the administrative duties that fell to the head coach and only the head coach that took so much time and energy. There was the press conference, which would be one of many. There was the weekly call-in radio and TV show, the regular SEC teleconference, the boosters, the alumni groups, the fans, more media, the AD and other school officials, and of course, the actual coaching.

Did I mention we play Tennessee in two days?

I would be asked if I saw myself as a head coach, what I planned to do differently, what would be the same, had I spoken to John, how did it feel to take over, why had he been fired, and on and on and on.

I tried to be clear, concise, and honest, but the one rule that was paramount in my mind was not to say anything that could be perceived as negative about John. He'd hired me against the advice of others and kept me around for eleven years, in good times and bad. I owed him that.

The AD came down to my office again. I didn't need to talk to him again so soon, but I remembered to be patient and diplomatic. "John was a nice guy, I'm sorry it happened the way it did."

I just nodded. "Is what it is," I answered.

"The associate AD will travel with the team. Let him know if you have any problems or give me a call, anytime."

"I appreciate that," I said.

"Probably won't win, anyway," he added. "The line is twenty-four."

That got me a little hot. "Why would you say that?"

He looked surprised. "The line is twenty-four," he repeated.

"So?"

"So, you haven't been winning much, and you're playing one of the best teams in the country."

I stood up and showed him the door. "We'll see," I said.

I had a lot of confidence in our guys. We'd had some injuries and some bad luck, but they were a good team, better than their record.

I decided to change the leadership of the team. We had a guy who was probably taking too many shots, which I thought was a problem. Sometimes a small adjustment like telling a player to pass more often can have a major effect. A game ebbs and flows and finds its own rhythm, and so does a team. An orchestra with one instrument out of tune might sound terrible, but make that adjustment, and it sounds great again. Sometimes that's all it takes. One thing always leads to another. Good play and good players affect those around them in positive ways.

The assistant coaches were all really supportive, which was important. They knew me, but they didn't know me as a head coach, but they adjusted quickly. The players, too. I checked the team into a hotel, even though we were playing in Baton Rouge, just so I could keep them away from the media frenzy.

Before the game, I looked into the eyes of those players. Some of them I'd known since they were twelve years old. I had recruited all of them, and I knew they would play their hearts out for me. I reminded them of the changes I wanted to see in our game plan, and then I told them this: "I love this game. Loved it my whole life. All I ever wanted to do was play basketball on TV so my mama could watch."

There were some chuckles, but their faces remained serious. Their game faces. I looked at Tasmin, who was injured but still dressed for games at my insistence.

"I want you to know there's no team on Earth you can't beat tonight. None. Believe that."

I scanned their faces and saw fire in every eye.

"You're gonna remember this game for the rest of your lives, so go out there and play. I already know you're gonna play for me. So play for your teammates. Play for your school. Play for yourselves."

They were nodding. Intense and focused.

"I love you guys," I said. "You make me proud."

It was an amazing crowd in Baton Rouge. Packed more than usual and electricity in the air. I don't know whether everyone was there out of support or curiosity; probably both, but it made no difference to me. I was in a zone and so was the team.

We led early, but they were up by three at the half. We kept things fairly close, but they led by as many as 12 points in the second half.

We tied it up with a buck fifteen to go.

Anthony Randolph got a defensive rebound with forty seconds left.

Timeout.

I brought them in. "Get it to Anthony," I said.

They did, he made the shot but was waved off and was called for a charging foul. We had another opportunity, but the ball didn't bounce our way. One of their players got the ball and threw it down the court to JaJuan Smith for an easy layup.

Tennessee by two.

The opposing coach, Bruce Pearl, was very complimentary of our performance. He knew he'd dodged a bullet. There was a lot of cheering as we left the floor. We'd been so close to beating one of the best teams in the country; it was almost surreal.

The next day, the question I was asked was whether I was going to apply for the job permanently. I gave the same answer I'd given to the AD when he told me we'd lose. "We'll see." Also I'm not auditioning for the job.

As the games wore on, the most nervous I ever got was during the pregame press conference. National TV took some getting used to unless I was on a basketball court. Once the game started, all of those distractions melted away. It was the most amazing high I'd ever experienced.

We beat Florida at Florida, which was pretty great, and then lost two in a row, close at home to Kentucky and a beating in Arkansas. And every Monday, I put on my coat and tie and sat in on that SEC conference call, waiting patiently for my turn, and then answering questions for fifteen minutes.

I don't know what the future holds, I'm just glad to be here. The players are doing well. We've had a lot of setbacks this year, but they're fine. Character through adversity. Morale is good. Spirits are high. Great attitude. No excuses.

Etc. Etc.

I was beginning to understand the pressures of a head coach. It wasn't the games or game planning; the games and preparation were my escape. All the media activity and administrative duties were what wore you down.

Be careful what you wish for.

Even so, I loved it. It was what I'd always wanted.

Then we went on a tear, winning four in a row against Mississippi, South Carolina, Georgia, and Alabama. We lost our final regular season game at my alma mater, Mississippi State, going 5-4 with me as head coach. Then we lost to South Carolina in the first round of the conference tournament, a team we'd beaten less than a month before. It was one hell of a ride.

At one point during that time, the new chancellor congratulated me on beating Florida and his guy Billy Donovon but told me we still weren't very good. I was with Clemmie, and we both just looked at him in shock. He tried to play it off, but I was pretty upset. I sent him a handwritten note thanking him for the compliment about Florida and predicting we'd prove him wrong about the rest.

I posted it on the bulletin board just before we went on that four-game winning streak. Everything is a lesson, and everything is motivation.

After the season was over, the AD and the president told me that I was being considered for the job, which was disappointing. I figured it was a courtesy interview, but I was more than prepared. I kept a positive attitude, as I'd done the last several weeks, but I was hoping after our performance that I'd be offered the job outright.

They had interviewed several candidates and finally settled on Trent Johnson from Stanford, who was the first African American head coach in the history of LSU, if you don't count the *interim* head coaches.

He kept me on at my old position, but there was really no way to go back once I'd been in charge, and I left LSU for Oklahoma State under head coach Travis Ford, who'd been one of the candidates for the job at LSU. We got along great, and I stayed in Stillwater for eight years.

During my tenure as associate head coach at OSU, I coached two more teams that I truly believed could have gone all the way. Both made it to the tournament but lost in the early rounds. Those teams reminded me how tough it is to reach the top spot. So many teams fall short even when they have everything it takes to win it all. Sixty-eight teams are invited to the tournament, but only one comes out on top. There can only be one champion.

Those two teams had some truly great players, including guards Marcus Smart for his freshman and sophomore seasons, L.B Nash and Markel Brown for his junior and senior seasons, all whom I recruited. Marcus and Markel both play in the NBA today, and, like so many other players over the years, too many to name, I consider it an honor to have coached them. I've probably learned just as much from the young men I've coached as I hope they did from me.

After leaving OSU, I moved on to a brief stay at North Carolina State, and then Memphis, where I took on an administrative position as director of player personnel for my old friend, Tubby Smith. But when Tubby left, I left, too. Which gave me a little time to finish this book.

The lessons I learned as a player and a coach are the same lessons I learned as a husband and a father, and if this book makes a difference to even one young man or woman, one husband or wife, one parent or child, one businessman or woman, one mentor or mentee, then it will have all been worth it.

But the truth is, it's already worth it to me. Success lies not in the ending or the beginning, but what falls in between.

COACH PIERRE'S 10 STEPS TO SUCCESS FINDING BALANCE IN YOUR LIFE AND WORK

Relationships – Family, friends, co-workers, superiors, subordinates, loyalty

Core Beliefs – Defining yourself and living your faith, character building

Attitude – Creating a winning attitude, understanding how to win and how to lose

Adversity – Dealing with adversity, turning negatives to positives

Organization – Goals, details, and routines

Mentors – Finding one, being one

Discipline – Personal and professional

Perception – Understanding it, positive vs negative images, creating your brand

Working Smart – Dealing with success and failure, the business of you

Family – Where it all begins and ends

Career   **Family**

BUTCH PIERRE

Louisiana Oak

COACHING TREE

Eugene Witek - Elementary School (first grade - seventh grade)

This was the first white man that the community embraced to the point that everyone trusted him. From the students, teacher, staff administration to the parents, and community leaders, they understood his value to the people and kids. He was a mild-mannered person that loved our community. He made it a point to understand a student's strengths and weaknesses in the classroom and as individuals. He also challenged us as an athlete in fitness activities. One memory that will always stand out to me was the Limbo Rock Champion of the elementary school. Also, he demanded and suggested that I would always have a leading role in the school plays. When he introduced the Boy Scouts of America to our community and elementary school, this form of bonding was so valuable to all of us. The campouts and sleeping for two days in a camp with all of the other boys was the greatest experience at an early age that I ever encountered. When he was a member/teammate of our Negro League baseball team, he made all of us understand that we could communicate, trust, depend, and have friendships with a white person. Everyone thought he was so cool, and they trusted him. He was my first coach away from home, community, and family. He taught me certain things that I couldn't have learned from being around black people all the time. I would ask him all kinds of questions and topics, and he would give me his honest straight up opinion. What was really important to me, as he was white, was that he had the same value system as my father: Sit up in your chair; don't be late for class or the bell; be courteous and kind to grown-ups, teachers, and girls; respect school rules and tough love in athletics, just to name a few. And he was a white man.

Mr. Bartley knew exactly what he was doing when he hired him as a teacher. Mr. Bartley was the principal but also a leader, coach, mentor, father, political figure, community organizer, and counselor, and would do anything to prepare his students for life in the real world. When I left for college in 1980, I never saw or talked to Mr. Witek. I never understood why he never kept in touch with all of us. I guess he moved on to his next venture of being a coach/teacher. Sometimes I wonder why he chose Marchand Elementary School in a small black community and embraced it as if he was one of us. We need many more coaches and teachers with the same motive as what they say of making America the best country in the world. Thank you, Mr. Witek, for having a great foundation for young black boys' first encounter with day-to-day teachers/coaches that was positive for the rest of his life.

Richard Brown - Junior High (eighth grade)

Coach Brown was my eighth grade assistant football and head basketball coach. I remember when I first met him. He was single, owned a Volkswagen beetle with mag wheels. He was well dressed, articulate, and well spoken, respected, and educated. He was also a college graduate and in great shape. Everybody—students, teachers, administrators, and parents—loved him. He was smart and a great communicator. I wanted to be just like him. He just passed away in 2016, and I was able to talk to him a few days earlier.

After football season, we had junior high tryouts. For once, I thought I would not make the team. They had a lot of students to choose from, and I was far from the best player at the time. After tryouts, I would stop by his office every day and ask him, "Did I make the team?" He would never tell me yes or respond to my question. I feared that every day, my name wouldn't show up on the door after practice. Finally, I made the fifteen-man eighth grade roster, and that was the last tryout I encountered to this day. Until the day he passed, I always remembered the reason he gave for not telling me I had made the roster. He said every day is so easy for you, but if you want to be great, not just good, prepare, work hard, and next time, fear and doubt will not be a factor. He introduced me to basketball shooting and ball-handling drills. He also introduced me to what was big at that time—the weight room.

I wasn't the best player on the team. Let's just say, the fifth best. But I was the starting point guard. One of my fondest memories of him was when he didn't play me enough minutes in a game, and we lost. My mother waited for him outside of the locker room after the game. She lit into him like a firecracker. Almost to where I could see tears in his eyes. She can do that when she gets mad and thinks something is not right. But she was not only speaking up for me but for all of the players. Some things she said were right and sometimes wrong. The next school day, I went to his office. I was expecting him to say something bad about my mother. He turned to me and said, "You should always listen to a parent. Most of the time, they are concerned about their child. Not saying everything she said is right, but maybe one suggestion that she said out of many, I might use to make him a better player or a better person. What made me think and feel bad was that she spoke up not only about you, but the rest of the players." I learned something from that situation. Most head coaches have a hard time dealing with parents. Sometimes I thought that parents behaved worse than the players. What Coach Brown taught me was how to communicate during adverse situations with parents for the good of the player, coach, and most important, the team! Coach Brown was the best coach and teammate to this day.

Glenn Bourgeois - Junior High (ninth grade)

Between my eighth and ninth grade years that summer, my life changed. I dedicated every single day to practice, shooting, and ball-handling, weightlifting, conditioning, and running the Mississippi River levee. I also played pickup games with older guys and my cousin Clay who was on the varsity team at East Ascension High School. The first day of tryouts, I was choosing who was going to be on the team. Coach Bourgeois was hard core and demanded high level practices and workouts for his players and team. I thought I wasn't his leader or favorite player, but it didn't matter, I was the best player by far. As a matter of fact, the best player in the area. My fondest memory was the first game we played that year at Port Allen High School. I scored 27 points by halftime and broke the school record. He played me only one minute in the second half and said it was because I would put the record out of reach for years to come. To this day, I never understood that logic. It could have had a negative effect on me as a coach. I worked hard that summer to become an outstanding player, and now he was holding me back, as they say. The game was a blow out! In the back of my mind, I was thinking "racist," but he wasn't that type of person. It was the first time as a player that I had an opinion of how I needed to be treated! I immediately didn't make it a conversation but said that I would never put a player in that situation if I knew he was working hard to accomplish a goal. If so, I would explain to him in detail why I had made that decision. His coaching style was different because it was more about what he thought than the players. He was a very good coach and won most of his games. Sometimes when you win most of your games, I guess that happens. What he taught me was dealing with an authority figure as a coach makes a player feel mostly angry and mad; however, it does teach a player how to be sensitive and aware of their defense mechanisms. It was his personality as a coach, but it was very effective. Some guys didn't understand or respond, but for the most part, we won. What was hard for me was that I understood my dad being that way but not my coach. We are friends until this day, and I thank him for being demanding, hardnosed, and detailed. I remember being in the ninth grade, and things were changing physically and mentally. Sometimes it is important for you as a parent or coach to meet the ninth-grade coach.

Ron Huey - Senior High (tenth grade)

Coach Huey was as laid back as they come. He understood how talented I was from day one. As a ninth grader, I played and practiced at times with his team. He was a smooth talker and could convince anyone, players of all races that he was fair, honest, sincere, and always telling the truth. It seems that he never got rattled about anything. I always thought that he would have made a great politician or poker player. One thing that I learned from him was to try always to keep an even keel, control your emotions, and stay humble. Later in his life, he became a State Farm agent and a politician. Every once and a while, I would hunt him down, and he never changed his approach in communicating with me. He started off by saying how proud that he was of me, how is your mom and dad, your kids, you've grown, and how long have you been married. He said that every single time. Then he started talking about basketball. Just the other day, I checked my messages, and one was from him. He said that he saw my sister, and she had given him my new Memphis phone number. Guys like him stay connected with people that touch his life. This reminded me of the book by Bob Beaudine titled *The Power of Who.*

Lee Janis - Played Varsity (tenth grade)

Now this was a rude awakening for me as a player. My first real X and O organized, detailed, defensive-minded, offensive guru, and disciplined coach. He was tough on me from day one. I remember as a tenth grader, dressing out with the varsity team. We were doing strength and conditioning drills. This came easily to me because I was squatting 275 pounds a number of reps and bench pressing 225! We were doing an exercise, and as we finished, I said, "That was easy." And he said, "Do it again." In my mind, I never had anyone other than my father challenge me like that and press my defensive adversity button (defensive mechanism enzyme in your brain). When I finished the second set, he said, "Give me fifteen more reps." All of the upperclassman, my teammates, and my cousin Clay were looking at the time. I was exhausted, fatigued, and wanted to quit. I remember that feeling to this day. I reached down deep and somehow took it to another level. The team clapped and cheered for me when I finished. My respect level rose to another level, and Coach Janis made me mentally and physically tough in times of crisis. The streets and my parents were the only things that could get me to respond under those conditions. Sometimes when I have this same scenario or a similar situation out of players or recruits today, I see a different response such as: quit, curse out the coach, say "this is not fair," "the coach is picking on me," accompanied with a weak mentality and possibly quitting on their teammates and storming to the locker room. That's why when recruiting or hiring an employee, I think that it's important to talk to teachers, custodians, administrators, bus drivers, and the neighborhood leader. When hiring an employee who is going to give you a bad reference, talk to the unknown!

Coach Janis watched most of my games and talks to me to this very day. He is very critical as usual, but it is the truth. He says things such as: "Your coach can't coach. Players don't play hard. You all weren't prepared. You need to execute better on offense. Your players are selfish. You need to defend screening action better." Sometimes he even writes me letters with drills, practice plans and every other idea that comes to his mind. The good thing is, most of the time, he is right.

When I look at him, I always say in my mind, he is a national championship coach. In hindsight, he was one of those coaches that always told it like he saw it, and sometimes from an administrative standpoint (or playing for him), people could misunderstand his motive or objective. Very few great coaches sometimes have a tough time advancing in the coaching profession or keeping their jobs. But somehow if they piss off the wrong person no matter what, it costs them their job and future. I don't know if this happened to Coach Janis, but I tell you this, I could play for him and work for him, and he is one of my closet friends for life. At least you know what you are dealing with: an honest man that tells you like it is.

Tommy Wall – High School (eleventh grade and twelfth grade) (The Man - Love Him)

Here is a guy who never coached black kids and embraced me and us from the very first day. It is amazing how everyone loved, trusted, and remained loyal to him. When he saw me in the gym for the first time, or may I say the first INTERVIEW, I was sold. Coach Wall was not an X and O coach. He wanted all of his players to have fun and play up to their potential. We didn't spend a lot of time playing defense in practice, drills, and wasting time. Everything was offense, fast break, quick hitters, full court pressing, and man & zone defense. We played a 1-3-1 zone defense and man defense when we played weak teams. We had five starters that could dunk the ball, and we were an exciting team to watch. In those days, a starting five that could all dunk was unheard of in high school. Our team and coaches were so close and had a great relationship. The staff was also very loyal and trustworthy to each other. What I learned from him was how he could get everyone—teachers, administrators, janitors, students, and just about anyone—to like him and trust him. When Hot Rod Williams, my teammate, was going to court about a point-shaving scandal at Tulane, he was with him every single day. He stayed close to all of his players and valued these relationships after they graduated from high school. We would always get his opinion in life situations. This coach not only coached us but made a difference in the community, the school, social changes, and race, and he changed people's lives. I never heard one person say a negative thing about Coach Wall. That is a leader!

Jim Hatfield-Mississippi State (freshman year) Recruited me

Coach Hatfield was the first salesman that I met that made me feel like I was family. The reason that I liked him was because he was somewhat like Coach Wall. He was an easy-going guy that was great to play for, and he had his players' best interest at heart. It wasn't all about him as a coach. He was a player's coach. What I learned from him is that sometimes you must be careful who you recruit because if hard discipline is what you needed, you'd better have a staff member that can identify that and help you. He was a coach that had a personality that was all about you being family, happy, and working together. My freshman year at Mississippi State, we were very talented and in a tough conference of the Southeast Conference, with NBA players on every team. Whenever there are guys on a team that are from different places with different attitudes, motives, goals, and personalities, the head coach must wear different hats. He had a good staff. But when pressured to win games and face adversity, that is when you know what kind of staff you have. There always comes a time at the highest level in coaching when the staff and the head coach are in the hot seat. The question is: Can you survive or do something special to not get fired? The previous year, before I was recruited, I didn't realize that Mississippi State lost at home to Alcorn State in an NIT game. That game might have started the pressure to win. Later on in my career, when this same scenario comes up, I've always pushed a little harder to survive the situation.

My relationship with Coach Hatfield today is the best. He has been in my life and involved with my family, wife, and kids, and really, we have created a long-lasting relationship. What I learned from him is that you can't be positive all of the time and in every situation. I also learned that not all players on your team will buy in to positive enforcement. Coach Hatfield was a great mentor because he could recruit anybody, anywhere, and under any circumstances.

Dave Farrar - Assistant Coach, Mississippi State, Recruited me

Coach Farrar was the first coach that was straightforward, no nonsense, never lied, played no games, and had a dry personality. My mother loved him because he was honest and disciplined while also being a man of his word. Every time a coach came in our home (home visit), she would usually say things like a coach was: slick, lies, can't be trusted, too soft, cares about himself, doesn't take care of his players, your relationship won't last forever, and things of that nature. But when it came to Coach Farrar, she would always say that in the long haul, he would not tell you what you want to hear, but he will tell you the right and honest things. She was right! That was the best fit for me and my personality. She knew that I was very sensitive. If it was the truth and I didn't like it, I would be fine. But if it was manipulation or a lie, then my relationship with my coach was destroyed. I am still like that to this day. My wife is also like that—straightforward—and she speaks her mind, no matter if it hurts. Boy, I do not like it, but I am all about principles and have learned to deal with it.

Coach Farrar was all about principles. He was a guy that I knew was the last person on Earth to buy a color TV. He would say, "Why get a colored TV when you can watch the same thing in black and white?" That's the truth, a black and white TV. I signed to play at Mississippi State for Coach Hatfield and Coach Farrar.

Bob Boyd - Mississippi State – (sophomore, junior, senior years)

Great coach - detailed, disciplinarian, and authoritative, Graduate Assistant, two years

Things happen that you can't control. Here comes a coach that had nothing to do with my decision about choosing or playing for Mississippi State my sophomore year. He replaced Coach Hatfield. He was tough, a disciplinarian, authoritative, and hard to play for, but a great coach. He was well known throughout the country as one of the best collegiate basketball coaches of all time and couldn't beat John Wooden. At least that was what he said to me all of the time because back then they only took 32 teams to the tournament.

Man, to this day, I say that if I would have played at Southwest Louisiana (University of Louisiana at Lafayette), I would be in the NBA. I had NBA talent. Playing for him, I never showed it because of his coaching style. But as I look back, God had another plan for me. Coach Boyd molded me to be tough, focused, detailed about everything, and competitive from a team and individual standpoint, as well as a molding me into a man. I learned how to teach and gain a competitive advantage about everything. He challenged me and my teammates in every way possible on and off the floor and in the classroom. He was such a strong leader that he controlled everything and everyone around him. But one thing stands out and that is that he made everybody better. He also made all of the Mississippi State assistants very successful head coaches. All of them that came into Mississippi State in his five years became head coaches, except for one—me. I feel that to this day, that I have always had the best feel for winning at the highest level and was the best out of the bunch

(Terry Truax, Ron Brown, Dave Farrar, Richard Williams, John Brady, Larry Eustachy, Kermit Davis).

I can remember everything and every detail about my experience as a player and as a graduate assistant. The good and the bad. I even wore a coat and tie to work as a graduate assistant, which is unheard of today. As I look back, these were all life experiences that I use today—the good and the bad. Because of the difficult times that I had as a player, it prepared me for the coach, teacher, father, person, and mentor that I am today.

Lastly, Mississippi State was the perfect school for me. People say a lot of things about Mississippi. But I learned a lot of positives things while living in the state. Sometimes you just have to look at things in different ways. It would definitely make you understand life in different situations and under adverse conditions. There isn't a week that goes by that I don't think about something that I have learned or experienced from my years with Coach Bob Boyd. He was the national championship coach to me!

Paul Peck - First College Job - Kentucky State

Coach Farrar got me my first coaching job. He knew Coach Peck, made a phone call, and Peck hired me. It was the most demanding job that a young guy could ever have at an early age. I was teaching college classes, coaching, serving as an academic advisor, mentoring, attending faculty meetings, and doing everything full time while only making $17,442 a year. But I was excited. It prepared me for the hard grind and long hours that come so easily for me now. What I remembered most about Coach Peck was that he was the best at communicating with administrators (presidents, VPs, the AD, teachers, faculty, alumni, and boosters). At a Division II school, I thought that we had everything that we needed to win at a high level. He believed in me. He gave me so many duties in every aspect of the program, and I learned so much. I did everything from sweeping the gym floor to handling the budget like a head coach. Boy, he was great at understanding power brokers within the university and the basketball program. We had a great relationship. He gave me confidence in every way, every day. What was most unique about my experiences is that he was a white coach and was doing all of this at an historically black university, and I learned from that.

Marty Fletcher - Second Job (eight years – USL - now ULL)

This was my first Division I job. I never met a man with such enthusiasm, energy, and a positive personality, and players loved playing for him. This was the perfect job for me. I loved being in Louisiana. It was a basketball school that was filled with tradition. I have always believed, to this day, that you could compete for a national championship at this school. Coach Fletcher was one of the greatest salesman that I ever encountered. During in home visits with a prospect, he had an unbelievable formula. In thirty minutes, those parents trusted him, believed in him, and were ready to sign on the dotted line. His attitude carried over to the team in game situations. What's amazing is that he never raised his voice or cursed at a player at practice or a game. Never. Once I understood and realized what he was all about, I recruited through his personality. He coached only by using positive reinforcement. He never, I mean never, used negative reinforcement. It was unbelievable that he could even make non-shooters make jump shots. They played with so much confidence that they overachieved as players. Players were also positive with each other and that was really amazing. He was definitely a player's coach. Because of my past of using negative enforcement, I learned from him that you can use more positive enforcement to achieve things at a higher level.

Melvin Watkins - Third Job, UNCC (one year)

From the very first time that we met as assistant coaches, we were like brothers. We are still that way until this day. After seventeen years as an assistant coach at Charlotte, he was hired as the head coach, and I was his first phone call. I made the decision to go with him, even though ULL was my future and becoming the head coach. He gave me the opportunity to coach and do things that I wouldn't have done at this early stage in my career. It is not often that you can be the best of friends and be able to work hard at a higher level (while still staying close). We won games right away and had an outstanding staff. Coach Watkins had a knack for letting each coach on the staff coach and contribute in all phases of the game and to their own strengths. His leadership skills were the same when he was a player. For example, he was not the best player on his team but the most valuable player on the team that made a Final Four appearance. As a player and a coach, he made people perform outside of their comfort zone as both individuals and as a team. He was a true leader. For us, he was the heart and soul of his coaching staff for the one season that I worked there. What I learned from him was that it takes a strong staff to survive.

Coach John Brady - Fourth Job - LSU (eleven years)

From the day that I met Coach Brady my sophomore year at Mississippi State (and when our high school teams played against one another and he was the head coach of Crowley High School), I have been helping him recruit. As a player at Mississippi State, I helped him recruit the top two players from his high school team. Coincidentally, he came along as an assistant coach in this same deal.

While he was the assistant coach, the next three years we bonded and became close. Every drill that he oversaw, I was always on time, and I never took plays off. I also hosted every player that he recruited on their official visit. Coach Brady always had my back when I was a player and supported me.

When I became a graduate assistant, I went on scouting trips with him, was always in his office, and assisted him in every way possible. On every trip that we took, I drove the car, and we even slept in the same hotel room (I was always his roommate). We became brothers, friends, and family throughout my career as a player and later in my coaching profession. When he got the job at LSU, he was determined to hire me, no matter what. Coach Tim Floyd even told Coach Brady that I was one of the best in the business in the South and ESPECIALLY in Louisiana, which reinforced the fact that Brady was making a great decision in hiring me at LSU. I never forgot our first commitment, Jabari Smith, who was a 6'11", 230-pound big-time player from Atlanta. I thought that Jabari was a pro and later he was. When Coach Brady saw him, he immediately said that we couldn't get Jabari. After recruiting him for many years and building our relationship, we got a commitment on the in-home visit. Next up was the number one high school player in America, Stromile

Swift. The first thing that Coach Brady said when we recruited Stromile was that the college coaches that are recruiting him are all Final Four coaches at schools that have won national championships and coach NBA players (John Thompson from Georgetown, Nolan Richardson from Arkansas, and Tubby Smith from Kentucky). He said, "I have never won a national championship and coached NBA guys—we have no chance." In my mind, I knew that I had the right relationship with his coaches, family, and everyone surrounded by him to get him to commit to LSU. I knew everything about him and I knew that he wouldn't leave Louisiana and his mother. The recruiting got so intense that Brady even offered me an extra $10,000 on my salary to sign Stromile. The bad thing is that he said this in front of my wife, Clemmie. Coach Brady did end up paying the day of the commitment.

He was always a man of his word, and credibility meant everything to him. If he said to a player that he would play him thirty minutes a game, then he did. If he said in the process of recruiting a player that you would start, then from day one, that player would be a starter. He was a man of his word with his players and coaches, and anything that he said, he would do. The thing that he stood for was family when it came to me. He never missed anything that involved my kids Langley, Joseph, and Josh and their birthdays, Christmas plays, church events, family get-togethers or social gatherings at my home. That was truly him, but if you didn't know him, he was misunderstood and called an asshole by many. When you won like we did and produced NBA players as well as graduating them and molding them into men under pressure and adversity at such a high level, you know that he was not only a good person but a real coach.

He was coach, father, mentor, leader, and teacher, and he always made a difference. As I said before, what I learned from him was that the word credibility with your players means everything. If you are going to make a player uncomfortable in a teaching-coaching situation, you better care about them, be truthful with them, and never manipulate or lie to them. That was what I learned in the eleven years at coaching at the same school at the highest level.

Travis Ford - Fifth Job - Oklahoma State (eight years)

I always tell my sons that everything is an interview when you meet someone that you have never met before. The way that Travis and I met was when he was asking me about other assistant coaches that he was looking to hire at Oklahoma State. This happened at a recruiting trip at the Real Deal on the Hill AAU tournament. One week later, coincidentally, a person that we had in common (our stockbroker) called me and said, "Travis really liked you, and would you consider working with him at Oklahoma State?" That was it. Later, Billy Donovan also told Coach Ford that it was a no brainer to hire me, which really pushed him to take the final step (which included a "thumbs up" by Coach Pitino, too). Coach Donovan and I knew each other a long time in the coaching profession. Coach Ford and I were a perfect match for each other at the time. Me being a veteran guy and him getting a high-level basketball job that was used to winning big-time games. Man, we made a great team and believe me, I learned a lot of things from him, even though he would say that he learned a lot of things from me. I never met a guy who was so driven about the game of basketball in my life. It was a twenty-four-hour situation in his livelihood. He was as self-made player and coach. He was absolutely obsessed, which included strategizing for long hours, practicing hard, developing players while constantly watching tape and drawing plays. He never missed the opportunity to become better as a coach and to expand player development (as well as team chemistry). If I hadn't had twenty years coaching experience at the highest level, then I wouldn't have been prepared for such a challenge. He couldn't believe that I worked longer hours than he did and had such a great work ethic. I could match his intensity, work habits, and I also understood his spontaneous actions and demanding personality. I loved the emotion and drive that he had for winning, which was his greatest strength and sometimes his greatest weakness. Not all players throughout the years understood Coach Ford's personality, but the team that included Marcus Smart, Markel Brown, LeBryan Nash, Phil Forte, Michael Cobbins, and the walk-ons understood him to a T. We did some special things at Oklahoma State.

I have always said throughout my career that I was associated with only five teams with the ingredients that could have won or competed for a national championship: one at USL (now ULL), two teams at LSU, and two teams at Oklahoma State. As coaches know at the highest level, trying to win a national championship involves a lot of variables. This includes match ups in the NCAA tournament, teams peaking at the right time, players playing at a high level, playmakers making plays at the last two minutes of a game, sometimes injuries, and having the moment on your side.

Mark Gottfried - NC State (one basketball season)

Here is a guy that was entering his sixth season with a very talented basketball team. Sometimes when changes are made, good and bad things happen. I never took a job with a staff and coach that had been in place for a number of years. I have always been in a situation where I was instrumental in building or fixing a program. Sometimes when a head coach has been at a school for many years, you have to do something special because one cannot survive on past success. When I was at LSU and our backs were against the wall, we shocked everyone by making it to the Final Four. I thought that I could help Coach Gottfried win immediately, but as it turns out, I didn't have enough time. I wasn't there long enough to impact the program. That always created a bad feeling for me, especially because I came from many successful programs in the past where we had achieved (and surpassed) high expectations. As I look back, I have always turned a negative into a positive. I did, however, accomplish my goal of coaching and competing in one of the best conferences in the country—the ACC. It had some of the best venues and many Hall of Fame coaches. What I did learn from Coach Gottfried and admired about him was how he could command a room and how his Southern background made everyone feel at ease and believe that he was the best.

Tubby Smith – One basketball season - University of Memphis

I have been a personal friend of his for twenty-seven years, which includes his wife, Donna. We have always talked about working together since his University of Kentucky days. It couldn't have come at a better time in my career to work for and with a legend and, someday soon, Hall of Fame coach. He is a great coach, outstanding human being with great values, a winner, and someone who is admired worldwide. His deep family connections and Christian faith, along with other qualities, make him not only a good basketball coach; he could even run for president! I've made a few mistakes along the way (never in coaching), but choosing a friend, mentor, and brother in my next career venture was an effortless choice. I was on his staff in a player development role, and he asked for my opinions. When I was at the University of Memphis, I needed his opinion, too. Sometimes when things happen in your life, you say, "Only God could have done this." If you have God in your life and faith in good and bad times, He will guide you on the right path.

YOUR RELATIONSHIP WITH YOUR SUPERVISOR

Checkpoints

- ✓ First and foremost, think like a head coach but act like an assistant.

- ✓ Understand good cop/bad cop.

- ✓ You have to develop <u>trust</u>, <u>loyalty</u>, and <u>dependability</u>.

- ✓ You have to establish the word <u>credibility</u>.

- ✓ You need to establish a belief system between you and the head coach/boss.

- ✓ When adversity strikes, what happens?
  - How do you respond, and how does it affect reliability?
  - Does it make the relationship stronger?
  - You must move on quickly with no carry-over.
  - Did you develop a personality conflict? How did you resolve the conflict?

- ✓ Do both of you do things to make the relationship better away from basketball/work?

- ✓ Are your family values similar?
  - If values are different, can you adjust without affecting the relationships?

- ✓ Does the head coach/boss listen to your suggestions?

- ✓ Do you listen to the head coach/boss suggestions?

- ✓ Does the head coach/boss understand your ego?

- ✓ Do you understand the head coach/boss's ego?

- ✓ Do both of you know what makes each other <u>tick</u>?

- ✓ Does the head coach/boss keep tabs on you?

- ✓ What are your bad habits, the head coach/boss's bad habits?

- ✓ Can you as an assistant take his or her negative and turn it into a positive?

- ✓ Can you sell the head coach/boss to your mother/father?

- ✓ How much confidence does the head coach/boss have in you?

- ✓ How much confidence you have in the head coach/boss?

- ✓ How do you handle it when assistants, fans, boosters, co-workers, and administrators say negative things to you about the head coach/boss?

- ✓ <u>How would you measure your relationship from 1-10?</u>

- ✓ Will/does the head coach encourage you to become a head coach, get a raise, promotion, praise you publicly? Does he or she give you any credit or hold you back because you are too valuable to the program/business?

✓ Deep down, do you love, like, hate, respect, look up to him or her, aspire to be like him or her? Are you jealous of him or her, and do you believe that he or she can make it happen beyond expectations?

✓ You need to believe in the culture, be committed to the culture, and promote the culture.

ABOUT THE AUTHOR

Joseph U. "Butch" Pierre Jr. was a prep All-American at St. Amant High School in Louisiana and a four-year starting point guard at Mississippi State University where he stayed on as a graduate assistant, thus beginning his journey as one of the most successful assistant basketball coaches in the country.

After attaining a master's degree in education from his alma mater, Butch coached at Kentucky State University, the University of Louisiana at Lafayette, the University of North Carolina at Charlotte, North Carolina State University, the University of Memphis, Louisiana State University, and Oklahoma State University. As associate head coach at both LSU and OSU, his teams went to the NCAA tournament, advancing to the Final Four and the second round, respectively. He also served as interim head coach at LSU, only the 19th man to hold that position in a hundred years.

Butch has coached Division I & II basketball in the Sun Belt Conference, Conference USA, the ACC, the SEC, and the Big 12. His coaching journey from the lower levels to the Power 5 conferences prepared him with the insights he shares in this book. Known as one of the most successful recruiters in the country, Butch excelled in rebuilding, with an eye for talent and a knack for turning losing programs into winners: 15 post-season appearances and many conference championships.

Throughout his career, Butch has advised and mentored student-athletes to achieve greatness in both the classroom and on the court, emphasizing education and a college degree while still helping many of his players reach their goal of playing in the NBA. Whether naturally gifted or in need of nurture and development, Coach Pierre did whatever it took to set his players on the right path.

Butch recruited and coached five NBA lottery picks who became instant millionaires, as well as many others who went on to play professionally. His proudest accomplishment as a coach is the great number of former players who went on to coach high school, college, and professional basketball, as well as those who have excelled in business, education, and as entrepreneurs. And of course, those who achieved greatness in the most important positions of all: husbands and fathers.

CPSIA information can be obtained
at www.ICGtesting.com
Printed in the USA
LVHW030239071118
596099LV00003B/256/P